West Academic Publishing's Law School Advisory Board

Evidence

Sydney A. Beckman
Professor of Law

A SHORT & HAPPY GUIDE® SERIES

WEST
ACADEMIC
PUBLISHING

a short & happy guide series is a trademark registered in the U.S. Patent and Trademark Office.

© 2018 LEG, Inc. d/b/a West Academic

444 Cedar Street, Suite 700
St. Paul, MN 55101
1-877-888-1330

Printed in the United States of America

ISBN: 978-1-68328-937-1

Acknowledgments

I have had the pleasure of working with a number of individuals at West Academic for more than a decade. I want to thank all of them and specifically thank Louis Higgins and Staci Herr for all of their assistance over the years with my various projects and listening to my crazy (I mean brilliant) ideas.

Many people helped make this book happen. I owe a special thanks to Sergeant James Marple, United States Marine Corp., Macey Woldt, and Tori Smith, my research assistants; Julie Matthews (a/k/a Genie) and April Hurley, my faculty assistants; and Allyson Beckman for their proofing and suggestions.

I also want to thank my family—Allyson, my wife of over 15 years, and my two "rug rats" Brayden and Madisyn. My family is my inspiration and my drive. Finally, I must thank my students—those in the past, those in the present, and those yet to come. It is the love of teaching, and watching them learn, that led me down this career path. To you I owe the greatest debt.

Syd Beckman
Professor of Law
Knoxville, Tennessee

December 2017

Copyright Attributions

Unless otherwise noted, all icons used herein are Copyright, and used courtesy of, Freepik from www.flaticon.com.

Other icons, unless noted, used under paid license. All graphics are either original or used under paid license.

Table of Contents

Prologue

I love evidence. To me it is logical and useful. As a law student, being a trial lawyer was not my desire. Nevertheless, I became one; and what I found was that those lawyers who knew the rules—*really* knew the rules and how to use them—always had a distinct advantage even when the facts were not in their favor. Textbooks are designed with a particular purpose. Usually, that purpose is to teach with the aid of an instructor. This book, on the other hand, is not designed for that purpose. This book is designed to make you understand evidence—for your exams, for the bar examination, and for trial.

A note with regard to citations: Throughout this book you will find citations to cases and rules. However, the vast majority of the references to cases have been omitted. The reason for these omissions is that few students would have the need to look up the actual case. The additional case references would clutter the book, increase its length, and have a negative impact on the aesthetics; therefore, the decision was made to omit, rather than include, the references.

If you love the book, like the book, have thoughts, suggestions, or questions, please drop me a line at HappyEvidence@gmail.com.

Before you begin your studies, here are a couple of quotes that you should always keep in mind:

"We must remember always that accusation is not proof and that conviction depends upon evidence and due process of law."

— Edward R. Murrow

"[I]f I can't introduce something in court, it doesn't exist, legally . . . "

— Ted Crawford
Played by Anthony Hopkins in
the motion picture,
"Fracture."

A Short & Happy Guide to Evidence

CHAPTER I

Introduction

A. The Study of Evidence

The study of evidence is a challenging one. This book is designed to assist you in your understanding of this difficult subject. The book is—relatively—short. Its tone is light and occasionally funny; at least I think so, but then—I wrote it. There is only one way to learn evidence. Work very hard. That's it. That's the secret. So, let's get started.

I come from the generation that grew up with board games and learned to play *Dungeons and Dragons*.[1] So, forgive the following analogy. Let's suppose you are trying to go from point A (the entrance of a dungeon) to point B (the exit). If you do not like dungeons, pretend it is a forest path. The analogy still works. Look at the following map (Figure 1):

---

[1] In the event you are unfamiliar with the game *Dungeons and Dragons*, here is an abbreviated version of the Wikipedia description: "Dungeons & Dragons (abbreviated as D&D) is a fantasy tabletop role-playing game (RPG). . . . It was derived from miniature wargames with a variation of the Chainmail game serving as the initial rule system. D&D's publication is commonly recognized as the beginning of modern role-playing games and the role-playing game industry." https://en.wikipedia.org/wiki/Dungeons_%26_Dragons.

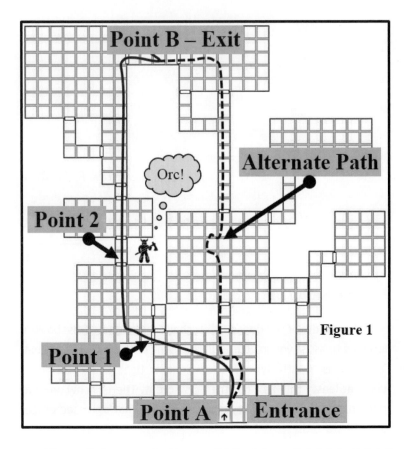

Figure 1

The path (represented by a solid line) from Point A to Point B might appear quite straight forward. But look at Point 1. There is a door there. That door stands between you and your next step on the path. How can you get through the door?

Evidence may be thought of in much the same way. You begin at Point A. That is, a particular piece of evidence is not admitted. You want to get to point B. Point B represents that the piece of evidence IS admitted. How do you get there? All of the barriers must be overcome. This book illustrates what these various barriers are and how, if possible, to overcome them. Points 1 and 2 represent the barriers. Assuming you have effectively overcome the first barrier (Point 1), you might encounter a second obstacle. This obstacle may vary depending upon the type of evidence you are trying to offer. Think of Point 2 as a terrifying Orc.[2] If you are also an Orc, he might leave you alone. But if you are a Wizard, he might not want you to pass. *Important note: If you ever actually encounter an Orc, you will likely face some horrible death.*

The study of Evidence intends to equip you with the right weapons (see what I did there?) to help you navigate the evidentiary path. The other critical lesson in Evidence is that there may be more than one path to admission. Look at the dotted line on the dungeon path. This is an alternate path with the same outcome.

With this book supplementing your Evidence class, you will learn how to interpret and apply the rules, and also *when* to apply the rules. In class, you will review relevant cases and other authority to evaluate evidentiary issues. This is the "hard work" I discussed on the first page. This book will help with your understanding of the rules of evidence and their application. But no book will take the place of doing the work. Now, let's get into the substance of the rules. Oh, and don't forget to carry a broadsword—in case you run into an Orc.

---

[2] For the uninitiated, "an orc . . . is a fictional humanoid creature that is part of a fantasy race akin to goblins. While the overall concept of orcs draws on a variety of pre-existing mythology, the main conception of the creatures stems from the fantasy writings of J. R. R. Tolkien, in particular *The Lord of the Rings*. In Tolkien's works, orcs are a brutish, aggressive, repulsive and generally malevolent species, existing in stark contrast with the benevolent Elvish race and generally pressed into the service of an evil power." Thank you again Wikipedia. https://en.wikipedia.org/wiki/Orc. For the record, I'm not a fan of Wikipedia, but there are no formal legal references for definitions of mythical characters.

B. Features of This Guide

There are three primary features of this book that should aid your studies. First, the book offers examples to aid you in your understanding of the application of the rules. Second, the book is littered with flowcharts at strategic points to provide a visual aid as you learn how to apply the rules. Third, there are various text boxes used in the book. These boxes should *not* be overlooked, as they offer integral pieces of information relevant to the material. The types of text boxes used are as follows:

Reality Check

There is, at times, a disconnect between what is taught in the classroom and the way matters are actually handled in a courtroom. Because we are preparing you to be lawyers, these boxes are designed, in part, to bridge the gap between the academic learning and the reality of practice.

What Does This Mean?

These boxes are used to explain the meaning of a phrase or term that might not be obvious or might vary from a layman's understanding of the phrase or term.

I'm Confused

Occasionally, an explanation might seem contradictory or require another perspective to assist in your understanding. These boxes are designed to provide that additional perspective.

Common Sense

These boxes are designed to provide some common-sense advice with regard to the application or understanding of a rule.

Attention!

These boxes are designed to highlight a point or bring your attention to a particularly important point.

CHAPTER II

The Study of Evidence

A. Overview

At its core, evidence refers to the "stuff" that a judge or jury may consider when making a decision. There are many kinds of evidence; that is, there are many types of *things* that are subject to consideration. Oral testimony (testimony from the lips of a witness), recordings (audio recordings, video recordings, etc.), pictures (digital or print), email messages, text messages, written correspondence, and printouts from websites (such as Facebook) are all examples of this "stuff."

The study of evidence involves a number of steps but only has one goal: to readily determine what evidence will or will not be admitted into evidence.

With regard to any particular piece of evidence, you (as an advocate) will take one of three

> **What Does This Mean?**
>
> Throughout this book you will see the term "fact-finder." In this context, fact-finder refers to the person or persons who make a determination of what is, and is not, a fact in the case. The fact-finder will be either a judge or jury. So when you see "fact-finder" think "judge or jury."

positions: you want it admitted; you want it excluded; or you don't care either way. To be able to effectively seek admission or exclusion, you must be competent with the rules.

So, what *is* admission? Generally speaking, one may think of the admission of a particular piece of evidence in the same way we think of a light switch. Many years ago, you learned how to turn on a light switch and turn it off. You also became aware of the consequences of turning it on or off. The study of evidence is quite similar. Much like a light switch being "on" or "off," a piece of evidence is either "in" (*admitted*) or "out" (*excluded*).

The rules are designed to help determine what pieces of evidence should be considered by the fact-finder. Only evidence which has been admitted may be considered by the fact-finder. The rules are the "mechanisms" we use to determine whether evidence is admitted or excluded. Do not misunderstand me; the judge is the only one who determines whether evidence is admitted or excluded. We use the rules to argue for the admission or exclusion of evidence.

B. Where Do the "Rules" Come From?

Where do these rules of evidence come from? The majority of the rules of evidence are codified at the federal level. Although a state's rules may differ, most states have codified the evidentiary rules, and have likely modeled their rules after the Federal Rules. Of course, these rules are subject to case law, which interprets the rules, and also the interplay of other laws, rules, and the Constitution. This book will focus on the rules and other relevant authority that you, as a student, are most likely to see in the classroom.

C. The Basic Flowchart

Examine the following flowchart. The steps outlined below provide a basic visual overview of the steps you will undertake in any evidentiary analysis. Note: Some steps are left out of this flowchart, for now.

Basic Evidentiary Flowchart

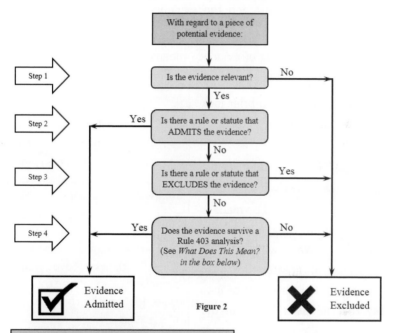

Figure 2

What Does This Mean?

What in the world is a Rule 403 analysis? At this point, do not concern yourself with this rule. Be aware of it and take note that in virtually all cases (*with two exceptions that we will discuss later*) any evidentiary analysis must undertake a 403 analysis. When we cover Rule 403, it will make much more sense!

To begin, look at the end. *(This isn't a fiction novel, looking at the end isn't cheating.)* Your goal is to analyze whether a particular piece of evidence will be admitted or excluded. Place yourself in the position of being an advocate. You have a particular piece of evidence, let's say a photograph, and you want the judge (or jury) to consider it. If the photograph is admitted, it can be considered by the judge. On the other hand, suppose you are on the other side of the case, and you do not want the photograph to be admitted. If you meet your objective, then you have prevented your opponent from reaching her goal; you have, effectively, made it to the "X" mark in the flowchart and the evidence will be excluded from consideration.

An understanding of evidence means that you understand the necessary steps to take to have the evidence admitted or excluded.

Now, let's take a brief look at the steps in the flowchart above.

Step 1: Again, let's use a photograph as the example. The first determination to be made is whether or not the photograph is relevant. We will discuss relevance in greater detail in Chapter III. For now, suffice it to say that it has a "role" in the case. If it does not, then it is

> **Common Sense**
>
> In a trial or hearing, just because a piece of evidence is objectionable, it does not mean you should object. If, relatively speaking, the evidence doesn't really "hurt" your case, then let it in. Do not waste time arguing against the "little" things. Save your arguments, and the court's time, for the important pieces of evidence.

"irrelevant." Under the Federal Rules of Evidence (and all state rules for that matter), if a piece of evidence is irrelevant, then it will not be admitted (*but see the Reality Check below*). If a piece of evidence is irrelevant, the analysis ends. There is no reason to continue because irrelevant evidence will not be admitted. How do we know this? We have a specific rule of evidence that tells us. Rule 402 states, in part, that "[i]rrelevant evidence is not admissible." That's it. No exceptions. End of Story. Stick a fork in it—you're done.

But if the photograph is relevant, we have more to do. Now we go to Step 2.

Reality Check

So you have learned that irrelevant evidence is not admissible. Does that mean irrelevant evidence is not considered by the fact-finder? It's considered all of the time. Confused? Don't be. For any piece of evidence that is offered—to be excluded—someone must object. Judges can do this, but they rarely do. Review the *Common Sense* box above. Frequently, if a piece of evidence is truly irrelevant, it will not have any impact on the case and, therefore, no one will waste time objecting to its admission.

Step 2: We have determined that this photograph is relevant. Is there a rule that automatically admits it? There are not a lot of those rules, and I will make this one easy. No, there is not a rule that automatically admits a photograph. Now we move on to Step 3.

Step 3: Generally, relevant evidence is admitted. That is, a judge or jury will consider all relevant evidence unless—it's the "unless" that is tricky here—"unless" there is a rule that *keeps it out*. With evidence, this is the hard part. As a lawyer (or a law student), you need to think of every possible rule that might keep out a piece of evidence, and how that rule applies. For example, Rule 406 governs evidence of a person's habit. Let's assume that this photograph is of a furry little bunny. That bunny has nothing to do with a person's habit. Rule 406, therefore, has no application to the photograph. You would not do any kind of analysis with regard to Rule 406 and the photograph. But, you have to at least think about Rule 406 and decide that it has nothing to do with that piece of evidence.

The bad news (not really that bad) is that there are quite a few rules to think about. We generally "clump" these rules together, which makes it much easier to think about. In the chapters that follow, you will see how these rules are analyzed and how they interplay together.

Step 4: This last step (almost always) applies. At this stage, it can be confusing. We will examine this in greater depth later. For now, just remember a 403 analysis must be done.

You're finished. That's it. Easy, right? After going through all the steps, you can make a decision as to whether or not a particular piece of evidence is going to be admitted or excluded.

Recap: So, we have a photograph of a furry little bunny. It's relevant (Step 1), no rule automatically admits it (Step 2), no rule keeps it out (Step 3), and it survives a 403 analysis (Step 4). The judge gets to see the photograph of the furry little bunny. Woo-hoo! Now, for those die-hard evidence gurus out there, I left one step out: authentication. But let's save that for a little later. Just enjoy the moment.

D. The Interplay of the Rules

Recall the discussion in the Introduction that many pieces of evidence may have multiple rules that apply. For example, suppose that you are seeking to admit a police report in a particular trial. A police report may need to be authenticated (which implicates rules discussed in Chapter IX) and might need to overcome the hearsay rules (which are discussed in Chapter VI), and the police report may also include evidence relating to the character of a party (which would be governed by the rules discussed in Chapter V). The point is that a single piece of evidence often implicates many rules. A thorough understanding of Evidence will require the familiarity of the rules and an understanding of which rules are implicated by any particular piece of evidence.

E. Where the Rules Are Applied

There are three different settings and different approaches with regard to how the rules are applied: the courtroom, the classroom, and the bar examination. We will briefly look at all three.

1. The Courtroom

You go to law school to be a lawyer, right? One of the places a lawyer applies her trade is the courtroom. The courtroom is to a lawyer, like a canvas is to an artist. Okay, that may be going overboard, but you get the drift. In a court of law, you, as an advocate, must always plan for the worst and hope for the best. You must be prepared to defend each and every piece of evidence that you intend to offer, and you must be prepared to attack each and every piece of evidence offered by your opponent. Now here's the important part—*don't*. Do not *attack* every piece of evidence offered by your opponent and (trust me here) she will not attack every piece you offer. There is not enough time, and to do so is just plain silly. Remember when I said:

> *"With regard to any particular piece of evidence, you (as an advocate) will take one of three positions: you want it admitted; you want it excluded; or you don't care either way. To be able to effectively seek admission or exclusion, you must be competent with the rules."*

A common position will be that you do not want the evidence in, but you know there is no realistic way to keep it out. Another common position will be that you really don't care whether it comes in or not. Remember the story about the boy who cried "wolf"? If you object to evidence that you don't really care about or evidence that you know is going to be admitted, when you finally make a strong objection to evidence that should *not* be admitted, your objection may fall on deaf ears. Don't make that mistake. Object when it *is* important. Argue for the admission of evidence when that evidence is important to your case; otherwise, keep a lid on it.

This book is not intended to teach you trial strategy or help you understand when to, and when not to, address evidence in the courtroom. This means that the little paragraph above is about all the trial strategy you will get from me. Suffice it to say that strategy is important and, as a trial lawyer, you will learn to effectively strategize with regard to the admission and exclusion of evidence.

2. *The Classroom*

In practice, the most common objection to evidence is usually made as follows: "Objection." That's it. Period. Just "Objection." Now, nowhere in the Federal Rules of Evidence or (to this author's knowledge) any state rules is the word "Objection," by itself, sufficient in a court of law to properly object to a piece of evidence, or to preserve an objection. Nevertheless, you will hear it—and often; not just in the movies. In the courtroom, it often works. The reason it works is that contextually, everyone knows the basis for the objection. But in the classroom, simply saying "objection" will not cut it, nor will you find it has any benefit on an examination. You might as well speak or write the word "Snoopy." It will have the same effect. A classroom setting and an examination require a thorough and thoughtful analysis of evidentiary issues.

This book will help you. Now let me be clear. This book is akin to "CliffsNotes®."[1] It will help you with your understanding of the material, but it is neither intended to be a substitute for those incredibly interesting reading assignments assigned by your Professor nor does it take the place of the deep and stimulating

---

[1] CliffsNotes is a Registered Trademark of Houghton Mifflin Harcourt. See what this profession has turned me into?

classroom discussions. So, go to class; read the assignments; and then read this book for additional help.

This text will help you in two ways. First, it provides a condensed version of an Evidence class. It teaches the rules in smaller bites, easier to digest than a full-length class on Evidence. Second, it provides a different way of looking at the rules. Instead of the traditional form of cases, rules, and lectures, this book attempts to teach the rules through visual representations and anecdotes that convey the rules in a manner that should prove easier than trying to distill them through the traditional process.

If you expect this book to be an effective substitute for assigned reading—let me put that idea to rest. It's not.

3. *The Bar Examination*

A thorough understanding of the rules will help you with the bar examination. Although bar examinations do not test to the depth of a traditional law school course, they frequently test the rules of evidence with a significant breadth. The examples and illustrations found within these pages should provide a valuable resource when studying for the bar.

F. Rules, Rules, and More Rules

There are a ton of Rules of Evidence. Yes, "ton" is a legal term—at least in my world. Okay, not really a ton—but there are 68 separate rules. Not a particularly big deal until you realize there are a ton of subparts. There I go again. Depending upon how you count them, there are 382 rules, including the subparts. Actually, that's how I counted them. That's a lot of rules. There is not a law school in the country that can teach every rule and every subpart in a single class. There just is not enough time. So, how do we pick what rules to teach? I have used three criteria to select which rules to discuss in this book. One, rules which are commonly used in the courtroom; two, rules which are particularly challenging; and three, rules which are, I believe, frequently tested on the bar examination. If a rule falls into one of these categories, it has been included and is often taught in most Evidence classes.

Here's a specific example. When you study hearsay, you will study exceptions to the hearsay rule. Don't worry about what those are right now, but one of the hearsay rules contains 23 exceptions. That rule (Rule 803) along with Rules 804 and 807 contain a total of 29 exceptions. You may find that your textbook covers many, but not all, of the exceptions or that some of the exceptions covered in this text are not covered in your book. Do not be concerned. If it is not covered in your class, you can certainly skip it in this book— although I wouldn't.

G. Admissibility

As mentioned earlier, with regard to evidence, your goal is to keep something *out* ("excluded") or get something *in* ("admitted"). But the concept of admissibility is not quite that simple. Evidence may be admitted for "any purpose," which means what it says: anything and everything. Unless a judge, or rule, specifically provides otherwise, all evidence is admitted for any purpose. But, evidence may also be admitted for a "limited purpose." That is, the evidence may *only* be considered for that purpose specified by the judge. This is called "limited admissibility," and there are two types of limited admissibility: 1) evidence which is admissible for one purpose but not another; and 2) evidence which is admissible against one party but not another.

1. Admissible for One Purpose but Not Another

On occasion, evidence may be considered for one purpose but not another. Many rules expressly permit (or require) this condition.

The Character Evidence rules are a prime example. You will study these in Chapter V. For example, Rule 404(b)(1) prohibits the admission of evidence of a prior crime to show that a person committed the crime for which he is currently charged. Don't you think that it would be relevant? Sure! If Johnny has previously robbed thirteen liquor stores, and you are on the jury when he is being tried for his fourteenth liquor store hold-up, you would want to know about the other thirteen, right? Those thirteen previous robberies are relevant! But, the rules prohibit their admission to prove number fourteen.

Why? Because the rule-makers believe that you (okay, not you but *somebody*) might find Johnny guilty of robbery number fourteen because he had committed a similar crime thirteen times before.

Before we continue the example, think about how these previous crimes might be analyzed in the flowchart we previously examined:

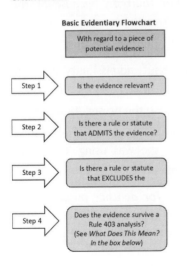
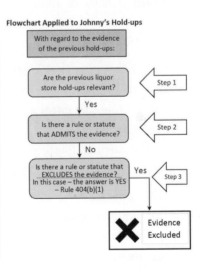

You will note that the analysis never reached *Step 4*. By following the flowchart, you can observe how the evidence was excluded under the rules before *Step 4* was reached.

Based on what you have learned so far, evidence of the previous hold-ups would not be permitted to show that Johnny committed number fourteen and would be excluded under FRE 404(b)(1). Rule 404(b)(1) provides the following:

> *Evidence of a crime, wrong, or other act is not admissible to prove a person's character in order to show that on a particular occasion the person acted in accordance with the character.*

In this example, evidence of Johnny's previous hold-ups is not admissible to prove that, as to hold-up number fourteen, Johnny acted in accordance with the character—of being a guy that commits hold-ups. Get it? So, it's inadmissible because we don't want a jury to convict Johnny of robbery number fourteen *because* of the previous thirteen. Rather, evidence specifically linking number fourteen to Johnny should be all that is admitted to find him guilty.

But remember, I am talking about admissibility for one purpose, but not another. There are a few rules in play here. There is ANOTHER rule that *might* apply. Suppose the prosecution was not using evidence of the previous hold-ups to demonstrate that Johnny committed number fourteen; instead, she was using it to show something else. Rule 404(b)(2) provides the following:

> *This evidence may be admissible for another purpose, such as proving motive, opportunity, intent, preparation, plan, knowledge, identity, absence of mistake, or lack of accident. . . .*

I will cover the specifics of this rule later. But for now, let's just look at one example. Suppose that in the thirteen previous hold-ups for which Johnny was convicted, he used a rubber bunny mask and a pink gun. Coincidentally, let's assume that the robber in number fourteen used a rubber bunny mask and a pink gun. The prosecution might be able to have the previous hold-ups admitted to prove Johnny's method of operation ("MO"). It might seem like splitting hares (okay, it's actually hairs), but it's not.

So, in this example, evidence of Johnny's previous hold-up convictions could be admitted for "one purpose" (the MO), but not another (that he must have committed number fourteen because he committed thirteen before).

Although we will examine character evidence in greater detail later, simply remember this example as an illustration of evidence that is admissible for one purpose but not another.

2. *Admissible Against One Party but Not Another*

The second type of limited admissibility is similar to the above concept. Evidence may be admissible against one party but not another party. Many cases have multiple parties. One example might involve a person's statement. The rules against the use of hearsay may keep such statements out of evidence as against one party but not another.

Suppose that the state has filed armed robbery charges against Abby and Bruce, and they are being tried together in criminal court. The state has a statement that Abby made, which implicated both she and Bruce in the robbery. For sake of argument, let's assume that the rules exclude the statement if used against Bruce but permit the statement if used against Abby. See the problem? They are being tried in the same courtroom in front of the same jury.

FRE 105 addresses this situation. The rule provides that:

If the court admits evidence that is admissible against a party or for a purpose—but not against another party or for another purpose—the court, on timely request, must

restrict the evidence to its proper scope and instruct the
jury accordingly.

As you can see, under Rule 105, the court could permit the admission of the statement as against Abby but not permit the same statement to be considered in the prosecution of Bruce. Got it? Good, let's keep going.

Recap of Admissibility

Evidence may be:

1) Inadmissible (excluded);

2) Admissible for all purposes;

3) Admissible for one purpose but not another; and

4) Admissible against one party but not another.

---

3. *Jury Instructions*

Recall that the fact-finder in a given case might be a judge or a jury. When evidence is admitted either for a limited purpose, or against one party but not another, a jury must be properly instructed as to how to use this evidence. With a judge, no instruction is necessary. We presume that a judge can consider evidence for purposes permitted by the rules.

The rules specifically provide for this instruction, which is called a "limiting instruction." Under these circumstances, Rule 105 requires the judge to "instruct the jury accordingly." This is the method by which the rules regarding limited admissibility are applied. Although we presume that a judge can consider evidence for purposes permitted by the rules—we also presume that juries can accomplish the same task—with proper instructions.

H. Classifications

Evidence may have different classifications. These classifications are found in two primary areas: 1) direct or circumstantial evidence, and 2) testimonial, documentary, or real evidence. To fully understand the rules, you must have a basic understanding of the type of classifications.

1. *Direct or Circumstantial Evidence*

You may have heard the phrase "circumstantial evidence." People frequently believe that circumstantial evidence is less persuasive than "direct evidence." On the contrary, circumstantial evidence can be significantly more persuasive than direct evidence. Let's examine the two types.

"Direct Evidence" is evidence which does not require an inference to answer the issue in question. For example, if the Defendant is on trial for assault, and the Witness saw the Defendant punch the Victim, then the Witness can testify as to what she saw. The direct evidence is her observation of the attack.

"Circumstantial Evidence" is evidence which requires an inference to resolve the issue. Suppose, instead of witnessing the attack, that immediately after the attack Witness saw Victim on the ground and Defendant running away. After approaching the Victim, Witness sees the Victim has blood coming from his nose and mouth. There is no direct evidence of Defendant's actions. A fact-finder would have to make the "logical leap" that Defendant's running from the scene and Victim's physical condition was because Defendant just attacked Victim. But there is no direct evidence. In fact, Defendant could have been running to get help for Victim. A logical leap—or an inference—is required to link the Defendant to the allegation of assault.

Again, you might think direct evidence is always stronger than circumstantial, and you might also think that circumstantial evidence requires pretty significant inferences. Let's look at another example:

The Case of the Missing Chocolate Cake

Direct Evidence

Suppose you come home one day to find that the chocolate cake you made that morning was missing a piece. (I realize you might be saying that you don't ever bake, but this is a hypothetical, so work with me here). So back to the cake. That cake is missing. There are three primary suspects. Suspect one, your spouse; suspect two, your eight-year-old daughter; and suspect three, your five-year-old son. So, you interrogate each suspect in turn. Each suspect (maybe we should call them persons of interest) is questioned. Each suspect categorically denies any chocolate cake thievery. Nonetheless, no one else had access to the cake. The doors were locked, you had no visitors, and these three nefarious persons all had access to the cake.

Let's recap your *direct* evidence. You know there was a whole cake. You know that the cake is missing a piece. You know that *you* didn't eat it (assuming dementia is not an issue) and you know that your spouse, son, and daughter each had access to the cake. Each suspect has denied any involvement in the missing cake. All of this is direct evidence, and it proves very little—other than that there is a missing piece of cake.

Circumstantial Evidence

Assume all of the facts above. But now let's add some circumstantial evidence. Suppose when you observe the cake with the missing piece, you see tiny little chocolate fingerprints around the cake pan. Also, assume that there are cake crumbs scattered about on the path from the cake pan to your five-year-old son's bedroom. Suppose when you question your son, he is sitting on his bed and has a little bit of chocolate icing on his face.

Do these additional facts establish with absolute certainty that he ate the missing cake? No. This is circumstantial evidence. However, evidence such as this may persuade a fact-finder that the young man did, indeed, consume the missing piece of cake. I mean, you think he did it, don't you?

As you can see, circumstantial evidence can be quite powerful and, in turn, quite persuasive. The concept that circumstantial evidence cannot win a case is a myth. More often than not, all we have is circumstantial evidence.

2. *Testimonial, Documentary, Demonstrative, or Real*

In addition to the classification of direct or circumstantial, evidence may also be classified as testimonial, documentary, or real. Each type of evidence has pros and cons, but more importantly, each has specific rules that will impact its admission or exclusion. The following paragraphs provide general descriptions, and these types of evidence are discussed in greater detail later in this book.

Testimonial

"Testimonial Evidence" is what it appears to be: evidence derived from the lips of a witness. Although much testimonial evidence is admitted through oral communication from the witness stand, other types certainly exist. Depositions, recordings, and transcripts from previous hearings are common types of testimonial evidence that are frequently encountered.

With testimonial evidence, you must concern yourself with a number of factors including: competency, the form the evidence takes, whether the evidence is an opinion or a fact, the credibility with regard to such testimony, and what you may do (under the Federal Rules of Evidence) with regard to the testimonial evidence.

<u>Documentary</u>

"Documentary Evidence" is usually evidence offered in the form of a document, such as a report, a diary, a written statement, a print out, a text message, a photograph, an email message, etc. We used to talk in terms of "writing," but few people actually write anything anymore. With documents, we must concern ourselves with concepts such as authentication (is the document actually what it purports to be), originals (versus a copy or duplicate original), and parol evidence (what the document means).

<u>Demonstrative</u>

"Demonstrative Evidence" can take a number of forms. These forms may include: in-court demonstrations, digital animations, charts, graphs, models, etc. They are used to help clarify facts for the judge or jury in a way that other more traditional types of evidence may not suffice. Remember the phrase, "a picture is worth a thousand words?" Demonstrative evidence exemplifies that statement.

<u>Real</u>

"Real Evidence" is generally tangible evidence. Consider a physical object such as a gun; if the gun used in a robbery was admitted into evidence, then that gun would be "real" evidence. On the other hand, if a similar gun was used in an effort to show the jury the type, size, and shape of the gun used in a robbery, then the similar gun would not be "real" evidence but, instead, would be demonstrative evidence.

3. *Examples*

Consider the following example and what classification that the particular kind would fall into:

1.	A photograph of the gun used in a robbery:	[Direct]	[Documentary]
2.	The actual gun used in a robbery:	[Direct]	[Real]
3.	A description of the gun used in a robbery from an eyewitness:	[Direct]	[Testimonial]
4.	A photograph of bruises on a victim:	[Direct]	[Documentary]
5.	A description from a Doctor of the bruises on a victim:	[Direct]	[Testimonial]
6.	Testimony of a witness that the Defendant walked into the liquor store five minutes before the actual robbery:	[Circumstantial]	[Testimonial]
7.	An audio recording of a 911 call by the victim of a car wreck who saw the car coming:	[Direct]	[Testimonial]
8.	A medical report from the Doctor:	[Direct]	[Documentary]
9.	Testimony of a man who witnessed a car running through a red light:	[Direct]	[Testimonial]
10.	A voice-mail recording of Defendant threatening a Victim:	[Direct]	[Documentary]

These are just a few of many examples.

4.   *Revisiting the Flowchart*

Examine the basic flowchart again. Now observe how the concepts related to various types of evidence might flow.

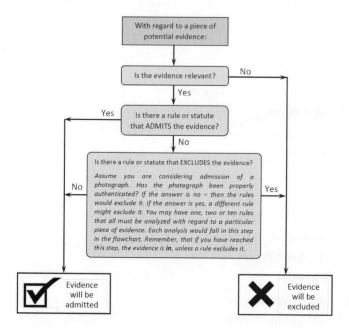

I.   Categories of Evidence

It is often easier to think about the Rules of Evidence in "clumps" or categories. Within each of these "clumps" or categories are a number of rules. The details of the rules are covered in greater detail in subsequent chapters. These categories include: relevance, witnesses, character evidence, hearsay, documentary evidence, privileges, and judicial notice. Although not all of the categories fit neatly within the flowchart, most do. Let's look at a portion of the flowchart again, but this time, let's focus on the first question only: "Is the evidence relevant?" This also leads us neatly into the next chapter.

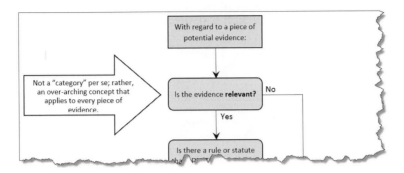

CHAPTER III

Relevance

A. Overview

It might help to think of relevance as the door to wherever you are going. If the door is not open, you cannot get through the door. If the evidence is irrelevant, (and assuming a proper objection is lodged) then the evidence cannot get through the door. A common objection heard in the courtroom is "Objection, relevance." Translation: *"Your honor, I object. The evidence offered is not relevant to any issue before the court"* or language to that effect. But what does that "mean"? Believe it or not, the concept of relevance can be tricky. The best place to begin a discussion of relevance is the rule.

In the Federal Rules of Evidence, Article IV governs relevance. Although Article IV has fifteen rules in it, there are two primary rules with which we will begin. The first, the most basic, and yet most important rules are 401 and 402. Rule 401 is, aptly titled, the "Test for Relevant Evidence." But, why do we care? Why do we care whether or not a particular piece of evidence is relevant? The answer lies in Rule 402. Rule 402 provides, in part, that "[i]rrelevant evidence is not admissible." That's why we care. If a piece of evidence is not relevant, then it is not admissible. Therefore, the initial inquiry (remember the flowchart from Chapter I) is that a piece of evidence must be relevant to be admitted. That, of course, does not mean that all relevant evidence is admitted. To the contrary, much relevant evidence is not admitted. That is the

> **Reality Check**
>
> Although Rule 402 provides that irrelevant evidence is not admissible, in reality a great deal of irrelevant evidence is admitted. The reason is that no one (neither attorney) objects to its admission. Why would an attorney permit irrelevant evidence in? Because sometimes such evidence will have no bearing on the outcome of the case, and objecting to it will waste more time than permitting it.

primary reason the Federal Rules of Evidence exist; they provide a framework for the exclusion of otherwise relevant evidence.

There are a variety of reasons for the exclusion of relevant evidence. Although the details behind the "why" are better suited for an Evidence class, some of the rules that follow dive into the reasons behind the rules. So, back to the rules themselves.

B. Determining Relevance

Rule 401 defines relevant evidence as that which "(a) has any tendency to make a fact more or less probable than it would be without the evidence; and (b) the fact is of consequence in determining the action." As held by the Supreme Court, "[r]elevance . . . under [Rule] 401 [is] determined in the context of

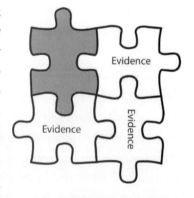

the facts and arguments in a particular case, and thus are generally not amenable to broad *per se* rules [that would exclude the evidence].[1]

1. *Generally*

One way of looking at evidence is to think about it like a puzzle. One piece of the puzzle doesn't "make" the picture, but each piece is helpful in seeing the overall picture. Similarly, an entire puzzle that is missing one piece is not likely to prevent you from figuring out what the picture is supposed to be.

Rule 401 has two very distinct possibilities, which make evidence relevant. The first is that the evidence has "any tendency to make a fact *more* . . . probable than it would be without the evidence." Let's assume that your case involves an automobile wreck. One question is whether the defendant drove through a red light or a green light. The defendant offers a witness that alleges defendant drove through the intersection and the light was green. This evidence (the testimony regarding the color of the light) would tend to make a fact (defendant's claim that he had the right of way) more probable. Under Rule 401, the testimony of the witness would be relevant.

But, what about the second part of Rule 401? The rule also provides that evidence will be relevant if it

I'm Confused

Recognizing that the two witnesses in the example are offering evidence which is completely contradictory to each other, you may wonder how that impacts your relevance analysis. It does not! The issue of whether or not the witnesses' testimony is accurate, and therefore admissible or not is left to other rules, which we will examine later. It does not impact whether or not the testimony is relevant. Of course, if admitted, a fact-finder may still find that a witness's testimony is inaccurate.

---

[1] *Sprint/United Mgmt. v. Mendelsohn*, 552 U.S. 379, 387 (2008).

has any tendency to make a fact . . . *less* probable than it would be without the evidence. Using the same example, suppose the Plaintiff offers the testimony of a witness who also claims that she saw the color of the light when the defendant drove through the intersection. Suppose her testimony would be that the light was red, not green, at the time. This evidence (the testimony regarding the color of the light) would tend to make a fact (defendant's claim that he had the right of way) less probable. Again, under Rule 401, the testimony of *this* witness would be relevant.

2. *Logical Relevance*

How does one determine whether a piece of evidence meets the requirements of Rule 401? Generally, when a piece of evidence relates to an issue with regard to time, an event or a person related to the lawsuit, then it is likely relevant. This is often called "logical relevance." Suppose you offer the testimony of a witness that offered an identification of the defendant. Would the time of the identification matter? It might. What if the identification happened at midnight with very little light? What if it happened in mid-day? The time of day certainly does not "prove" that the defendant is guilty of the crime charged; however, evidence of time of day may support (or refute) other evidence. In the words of the 6th Circuit, "[t]he purpose of an item of evidence cannot be determined solely by reference to its *content*. That's because [r]elevancy is not an inherent characteristic of any item of evidence, but exists only as a relation between an item of evidence and a matter properly provable in the case. Frequently, evidence will be logically relevant in more than one way."[2]

We are not yet finished with the first two rules. Remember, Rule 401 simply defines relevance. Also, remember that a piece of

---

[2]   *U.S. v. Parkes*, 668 F.3d 295. 304 (6th Cir. 2012).

evidence must be relevant to be admissible because 402 commands that "[i]rrelevant evidence is not admissible."

However, 402 also provides something else. Rule 402 provides that "[r]elevant evidence is admissible unless any of the following provides otherwise: the United States Constitution; a federal statute; these rules; or other rules prescribed by the Supreme Court." The reference to "these rules" means the Federal Rules of Evidence. So, any other rule might exclude a piece of evidence that is otherwise relevant.

> **Example of Logical Relevance.** Suppose there is a robbery and the robbery suspect's fingerprints are found at the scene. The presence of the fingerprints does not *prove* the suspect committed the robbery, but the fingerprints make his involvement more probable than without the evidence. The presence of his fingerprints is a fact in determining who committed the robbery. The fingerprints have logical relevance to the primary issue in the case.

3. *Illogical Relevance (Exceptions)*

Okay, so I made up that term—*illogical relevance*. Others (and likely even your textbook) might refer to these as *exceptions* to logical relevance. Exceptions to logical relevance means that certain evidence might be "relevant," even though the direct connection (logical relevance) does not actually exist. The best way to demonstrate this concept is by way of example.

i. **Causation**

Ever heard of the Black Widow? Not the spider—the killer. The Black Widow was a woman who would marry men, kill them, and then inherit their money. Suppose she was on trial for the murder of husband number four. Evidence that the woman caused the death of husband number two may not have "logical relevance" in the strictest sense. However, such evidence might lead to an inference that she caused the death of husband number four.

> **Caution.** Even though evidence such as the Black Widow's previous murder might be relevant, that does not mean it is admissible. Remember that all applicable rules play a part, and although Rules 401 and 402 might not keep the evidence out, another rule might require its exclusion.

ii.   Prior False Claims or Same Bodily Injuries

I am sure you will find this odd—but occasionally people lie. Certain people will occasionally file false claims, or file multiple claims, alleging the same or similar injuries. Amazingly, (note the sarcasm here), the defending party would like evidence of these prior incidents admitted. It is quite likely they will not be admitted. The reason—however—is not that they are irrelevant. They will be excluded based on another rule. We will cover this rule later, but in this example, the reason would be that the evidence of the prior claims might result in a decision being made "on an improper basis [such as] an emotional one."[3]

iii.   Similar Accidents or Injuries—Not for Proving Intent

Suppose John Smith is suing Walmart for a slip and fall accident. Evidence of an incident where Nancy Doe slipped and fell in that same Walmart does not directly relate to John Smith's lawsuit. However, Nancy Doe's incident might be relevant to prove that:

a.   A defect or *dangerous condition* existed (slippery aisles);

---

[3]   *U.S. v. Blackstone*, 56 F.3d 1143, 1146 (9th Cir. 1995).

b.   The defendant (Walmart) had *knowledge* of the defect or dangerous condition; and

c.   The defect or dangerous condition was the *cause* of the injury in the present lawsuit.

The reverse may also be true. That is, a defendant might try to prove the absence of similar accidents or injuries. Courts may admit evidence of a lack of previous injuries to controvert allegations of prior knowledge of the defect or dangerous condition.

iv.   Similar Acts—To Prove Intent

Suppose John Smith (yup, same John Smith above) is suing Walmart for a slip and fall accident. Now—unlike above, Walmart wants to use evidence of John's previous slip and fall to show his motive or *intent* in this slip and fall case. In other words, it was not really an accident. It certainly would be relevant; however, evidence of the previous slip and fall might be excluded under Rule 403 which will be discussed later.

v.   Rebutting a Claim of Impossibility

Given the appropriate circumstances, prior acts may be relevant to rebut a claim of impossibility. The relevance is that the evidence is used to impeach a witness or claim. Suppose in a Worker's Compensation Claim, a worker from Target (see? I don't pick only on Walmart), alleges that his injuries prevent him from lifting more than 50 pounds. But—you have evidence that just last weekend (after the alleged injury), the worker was helping his sister move her apartment full of furniture. Do you know what those solid-wood beds weigh? More than 50 pounds—trust me. This evidence would be relevant to show he can lift more than 50 pounds.

vi. Sales of Similar Property

Suppose you are trying to prove the value of a pocket watch. Why? It does not matter—focus, please! You are trying to prove the value of the pocket watch; how do you do this? Traditionally, experts were employed. You know, someone who knew more about pocket watches than any normal person would ever care to know—and he would testify that this particular watch was worth $1,500—or some such value. But now? Now, we have eBay. Well—we actually have all sorts of things—like eBay. You can use evidence of sales of similar property as evidence of value.

vii. Habit

Finally, another example might be a person's habit. You will review this in more detail when we cover Rule 406. But, let's say you are trying to prove that Sally Smith locked the door to her home before she left. There may be no direct evidence that she locked the door on a particular occasion. However, you might be able to prove that Sally has a habit of locking her door when she leaves her home. A fact-finder might make an inference that since Sally has such a habit, that on the occasion in question she did, in fact, lock her door.

In the chapters that follow, you will find a number of these exceptions. Although the facts may not have a direct logical relationship to the issue or issues, these facts may have an indirect logical relationship.

C. Discretionary Exclusion of Relevant Evidence [403]

Rule 403 is an important rule that provides as follows:

> **Rule 403. Excluding Relevant Evidence for Prejudice, Confusion, Waste of Time, or Other Reasons**
>
> The court may exclude relevant evidence if its probative value is substantially outweighed by a danger of one or more of the following: unfair prejudice, confusing the issues, misleading the jury, undue delay, wasting time, or needlessly presenting cumulative evidence.

This rule permits the judge to exclude—otherwise relevant evidence—if the probative value of the evidence is *substantially outweighed* by the risk of one (or more) of the following:

1. Unfair prejudice;
2. Confusing the issues;
3. Misleading the jury;
4. Undue delay;
5. Wasting time; or
6. Needlessly presenting cumulative evidence.

Application of this rule is seen as a balancing test—weighing the value of the evidence against the factors on the list. If one or more of the factors substantially outweigh the value of the evidence, then the evidence may be excluded. A couple of important points to note

> **Reality Check**
>
> Some states include "unfair surprise" among the list of risk factors. The federal courts chose not to include this factor based on the fact that adequate discovery should eliminate any unfair surprise.

here. First, the test is not to "outweigh" but is to "substantially outweigh." Never—ever—put "outweigh" in your analysis. Second, the rule is discretionary. That is, even if the judge believes that the probative value is substantially outweighed by, for example, unfair prejudice, she is not required to exclude the evidence. This rule is discussed in greater detail at the end of this chapter.

D. Exclusion of Relevant Evidence Based on Policy

The Rules exclude certain types of evidence based upon public policy. The following five rules contain circumstances in which evidence, which would otherwise be admissible, must be excluded. Many of these have little nuances that make their application tricky at times. (Primarily on law school exams). Review them carefully.

1. Insurance

i. When Inadmissible

Rule 411 governs liability insurance and prohibits its use to prove that a person acted "negligently or otherwise wrongfully." The concern—and the reason for the prohibition—is that a jury might decide a case on improper grounds, such as "the insurance company can afford it."

ii. When Admissible

Like all of the rules based on public policy, there are exceptions to the rule of exclusion. If the evidence of insurance is relevant for another purpose, then it would be admissible for that purpose. Although the rule does not provide an exclusive list of permissible purposes, it does provide examples such as "proving a witness's bias or prejudice or proving agency, ownership, or control."

a. To Prove a Witness's Bias or Prejudice

One permissible use is to show bias or prejudice. Showing the bias or prejudice of a witness is almost always permissible (I cannot actually think of an instance when it is not). Suppose that an expert testifies on behalf of the defendant, an insurance company, *and* that expert works for the insurance company. He might be a *little* biased—don't you think? Using evidence of insurance—and the expert's employment would be an example of a permitted use.[4]

b. To Prove Ownership or Control

Another example of a permissible purpose is to prove ownership or control. As an example, suppose that there is an issue of ownership of a vehicle that was involved in an accident. As evidence of ownership, insurance may be used; however, the evidence will be limited to that purpose only.

2. *Subsequent Remedial Measures*

A subsequent remedial measure is a "fix." In other words, after something happens, the "thing" that caused the injury is fixed. For example, suppose that Polly Plaintiff is walking through the ballroom in a Hilton hotel. While strolling through the ballroom, she trips and falls, breaking her wrist. As it turns out, she tripped on a strip of carpet that had come loose. Public policy would prefer that the Hilton fix the carpet in order to prevent additional injuries to other patrons. That "fix" is a subsequent remedial measure. That leads us to Rule 407. The rule is designed to encourage those "fixes" by preventing evidence of the fix (the remedial measure) from being admitted into evidence to prove the various things listed in the rule.

---

[4] See *Conde v. Starlight I, Inc.*, 103 F.3d 210, 214 (1st Cir. 1997) as an example of showing bias or prejudice.

In our example, suppose that Polly Plaintiff wants to show that the hotel was negligent by permitting that carpet to remain loose. To help her support her case, she wants to offer evidence that the hotel fixed the carpet. Rule 407 prohibits the admission of this evidence. Now, let's look at the rule in greater detail.

i. When Inadmissible

Rule 407 prohibits the admission of measures that would make an injury or harm appear to have been less likely to occur—if the evidence is intended to prove:

1) Negligence;

2) Culpable conduct;

3) A defect in a product or its design; or

4) A need for a warning or instruction.

In other words, the rules do not permit the fact that something *was* "fixed" to be admitted into evidence to show that it *should* have been fixed. Think about it. Suppose that the defendant has some broken steps in front of his building. The Plaintiff is injured, and subsequently sues. Public policy certainly wants the defendant to fix the steps, right? Sure. If not, more people might get hurt. This rule is designed for exactly that. If it's broken—fix it.

ii. When Admissible

Are there exceptions? Of course. Evidence of these subsequent measures is admissible for any other purpose; that is, any purpose not specifically prohibited. Again, the rule provides some examples.

a. To Impeach a Witness

Evidence used to impeach a witness is permissible under the rule. However, the rule must be "read narrowly . . . . Consequently, the impeachment exception has been confined to evidence of subsequent remedial measures that is necessary to prevent the jury from being misled."[5] "Evidence offered for impeachment must contradict [the] witness's testimony directly."[6]

b. To Prove Ownership or Control—If Disputed

If disputed, evidence that subsequent repairs (remedial measures) were made by the defendant may be introduced to prove ownership or control. Why? Because who would make repairs other than someone who owned the property?

c. To Prove Feasibility—If Disputed

If disputed, feasibility is a concept that students often find troubling. "Feasibility" means—in effect—a possibility. But it *also* means more than just possible—it means possible *and* effective.

d. Post-Design and Pre-Accident

When measures were "taken *after* the design of a product but *before* the accident," then such measures do not fall within the prohibition of Rule 407.[7]

e. When Used Against Someone Other than the Defendant

When the subsequent remedial measures are offered against someone other than the defendant, the rule does not prohibit their admission.[8]

---

[5] *Minter v. Prime Equip. Co.*, 451 F.3d 1196, 1212-13 (10th Cir. 2006).
[6] *In re Consolidation Coal Co.*, 123 F.3d 126, 136 (3d Cir. 1997).
[7] *Moulton v. Rival Co.*, 116 F.3d 22, 26 n.4 (1st Cir. 1997).
[8] *TLT-Babock, Inc. v. Emerson Elec. Co.*, 33 F.3d 397, 400 (4th Cir. 1994).

3. Settlement Offers

i. When Inadmissible

Rule 408 prohibits evidence of compromise, offers, and negotiations. This rule is longer than most and has quite a few parts. Let's look at each by first looking at the rule.

Rule 408. Compromise Offers & Negotiations

(a) **Prohibited Uses.** Evidence of the following is not admissible—on behalf of any party—either to prove or disprove the validity or amount of a disputed claim or to impeach by a prior inconsistent statement or a contradiction:

    (1) furnishing, promising, or offering—or accepting, promising to accept, or offering to accept—a valuable consideration in compromising or attempting to compromise the claim; and

    (2) conduct or a statement made during compromise negotiations about the claim—except when offered in a criminal case and when the negotiations related to a claim by a public office in the exercise of its regulatory, investigative, or enforcement authority.

(b) **Exceptions.** The court may admit this evidence for another purpose, such as proving a witness's bias or prejudice, negating a contention of undue delay, or proving an effort to obstruct a criminal investigation or prosecution.

This rule is designed to promote effective settlement through negotiation. The reasoning behind this rule is that without the protections it provides, parties would not disclose information which might otherwise work against them in a trial. The rule provides an absolute prohibition against the admissibility of the evidence set out in Rule 408(a)(1) and (2). It is critical, however, to recognize that the prohibition is limited to these purposes:

1) To prove or disprove the validity of a disputed claim;

2) To prove or disprove the amount of a disputed claim;

3) To impeach by a prior inconsistent statement; or

4) To impeach by a contradiction.

> **Common Sense**
>
> The rule does not permit 'sneakiness.' In other words, one cannot disclose information as part of a settlement negotiation with the intent of preventing its later admission because of the rule. Information that is obtained through other means, or that was disclosed outside of the negotiation process, is not protected by the rule.

a. The Claim Requirement

The rule requires there to be a "disputed claim." This does not mean that a lawsuit must have been filed. Rather, it means that a disputed claim must exist. As you might imagine, people may "settle" cases long before a lawsuit is filed. On the other hand, people may "try," but fail, to settle cases before a lawsuit is filed.

As to what constitutes a "claim," courts are not in complete agreement. Borrowing from the 5th and 8th Circuits, it's safe to say that a claim is "fact-specific, and tethered to the rationales underlying the rule,"[9] "when there is [an] actual dispute or difference of opinion about the party's liability for or amount of claim."[10]

This rule excludes virtually anything that is said or disclosed during a negotiation. This may occur in an informal setting, through

---

[9] *Lyondell Chem. Co. v. Occidental Chem. Corp.*, 608 F.3d 284, 296–98 (5th Cir. 2010).

[10] *Weems v. Tyson Foods, Inc.*, 665 F.3d 958, 965 (8th Cir. 2011).

a formal mediation or settlement negotiation, or even through correspondence via email or letter.

b.   The Dispute Requirement

The rule also requires that the claim include a dispute as to either liability or amount. If there is no disagreement as to liability— then the rule would not apply—to liability. If there is no disagreement as to amount—then the rule would not apply—to the amount.

ii.   When Admissible

When does the rule permit this kind of evidence? As with many rules, the list of exceptions is not exclusive and is only a list of examples of permissible uses.

a.   To Prove Bias or Prejudice

"If a witness harbors sentiments which would naturally tend to bias or prejudice his statements and point of view the jury should know such facts for the purpose of weighing his credibility, and, hence, the cross-examiner should be entitled to assure such knowledge on the part of the jury by inquiring as to such facts or sentiments."[11]

b.   To Negate a Contention of Undue Delay

In many cases, one party may argue that an opposing party has intentionally taken actions to delay the proceeding. Under the appropriate circumstances, this rule will permit evidence of compromise offers and negotiations to controvert (negate) a contention that one party has attempted to delay the proceeding.

---

[11]   161 A.L.R. 395 (1945).

c. To Prove an Effort to Obstruct a Criminal Investigation or Prosecution

Much like with the issue of proving undue delay, above, the prohibited evidence may be permissible if offered to prove something other than one of the prohibited purposes. This is another example, "to prove an effort to obstruct a criminal investigation or prosecution."

d. To Interpret a Settlement Agreement

This last permissible use does not come from the rule (again, the list in the rule represents examples only). It does, however, come from a case.[12] If required to interpret a settlement agreement, evidence of the negotiation may be admitted.

4. *Payment of Medical Expenses*

i. When Inadmissible

Rule 409 governs the admissibility of offers to pay medical and similar expenses.

> **Rule 409. Offers to Pay Medical and Similar Expenses**
>
> Evidence of furnishing, promising to pay, or offering to pay medical, hospital, or similar expenses resulting from an injury is not admissible to prove liability for the injury.

ii. When Admissible

The question as to when this type of evidence is admissible is pretty straightforward. Assuming it is relevant (and you should understand by now that evidence must always be relevant), then

---

[12] *In re MSTG, Inc.*, 675 F.3d 1337, 1345-46 (Fed. Cir. 2012).

such evidence will be admitted when it is offered to prove something *other than* "liability for the injury."

iii. Similar Expenses

Students struggle, at times, with the phrase "similar expenses." The phrase was inserted into the rule in an effort to prevent a court from reading the rule too narrowly. Nevertheless, the phrase "similar expenses" does not mean "related expenses." Here is what I mean. Suppose that Victim is injured in a car accident. defendant, believing that the accident is his fault, offers to pay all of Victim's medical bills and the damage to her car. Although the damage to her car is "related" in the sense that the same event caused both her medical bills and her property damage, the two things are not similar. Rule 409 does not govern the offer to pay the damage to the car.

5. *Plea Agreements*

Plea agreements are another area for which the rules of evidence provide some protection. This rule is a bit more complex than the rules we have just covered. Rule 410 governs plea agreements.

i.   When Inadmissible

> **(a) Prohibited Uses.** In a civil or criminal case, evidence of the following is not admissible against the defendant who made the plea or participated in the plea discussions:
>
> (1) a guilty plea that was later withdrawn;
>
> (2) a nolo contendere plea;
>
> (3) a statement made during a proceeding on either of those pleas under Federal Rule of Criminal Procedure 11 or a comparable state procedure; or

> (4) a statement made during plea discussions with an attorney for the prosecuting authority if the discussions did not result in a guilty plea or they resulted in a later-withdrawn guilty plea.

Plea agreements are encouraged for a variety of reasons, not the least of which is the fact that if every criminal case went to trial, the court system would be backed up for decades and would absolutely fall apart. The rule is designed to encourage plea agreements and discussions relating to plea agreements. If a defendant ran the risk of statements made during plea agreements being used against her, then she would likely say little, if anything. This rule permits a free discussion (in theory), thereby helping to facilitate plea discussions which (hopefully) result in plea agreements.

These discussions, however, do not always result in plea agreements and are occasionally withdrawn for one reason or another. In those cases, the rule provides a modicum of protection for those defendants:

1) When the defendant enters into a plea agreement but withdraws that agreement at a later time—that "guilty" plea cannot be admitted and therefore used against him;

2) When the defendant enters a plea of nolo contendere (no contest) that plea will not be admitted;

3) Any statements the defendant makes while participating in a proceeding with regard to a guilty plea (later withdrawn) or a nolo contendere plea under Federal Rule of Criminal Procedure 11 ("Pleas") or a comparable state procedure; or

4) Any statement made during plea discussions with an attorney for the prosecuting authority (i.e., the Assistant United States Attorney) if the discussions did ***not*** result in a guilty plea or they resulted in a later-withdrawn guilty plea.

ii.   **When Admissible**

First things first: a guilty plea that was later withdrawn (410(a)(1)) and a nolo contendere plea (410(a)(2)) are *never* admissible. The exceptions (spelled out in 410(b)) only apply to 410(a)(3) and (4). It is important to note that the exceptions are "may" exceptions, not "must" exceptions. This means that even if the evidence is offered for a permissible purpose, the court *is not required* to admit the evidence.

E. **Rule 403**

In addition to the concept of the path in a dungeon or a forest, another way to think of evidence, and how to analyze evidentiary issues, is like a sandwich. (You can certainly use similar food such as a hamburger but, be careful, a hotdog doesn't really fit). If you consider a sandwich, the issue of whether or not something is relevant (always your first analysis) is the top slice of bread. All of the other rules that may exclude evidence are the "ingredients" that make it a sandwich. Rule 403 is considered the bottom slice of bread. With very few exceptions (discussed later in the book) every piece of evidence must undergo an analysis under Rule 403.

Here is a visual:

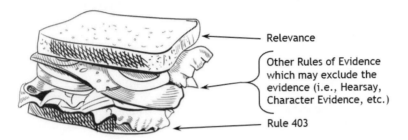

Let's be clear—the sandwich does not represent Rule 403— although it has made me a little hungry. Rather, the sandwich represents where 403 falls in your analysis. Thinking back to Chapter I, it is kind of like the final Orc you must slay before reaching your destination.

Now let's look at the rule itself:

> **Rule 403. Excluding Relevant Evidence for Prejudice, Confusion, Waste of Time, or Other Reasons**
>
> Evidence of furnishing, promising to pay, or offering to pay medical, hospital, or similar expenses resulting from an injury is not admissible to prove liability for the injury.

To understand the rule, we need to look at two things. First, why does this rule exist? Second, what are the elements of the rule?

1. Purpose and Elements

The purpose of the rule is to permit the court to exclude otherwise relevant evidence because the value of that evidence, with regard to the current trial, would be substantially outweighed by one of the factors in the rule. This will make a little more sense when we break the rule down.

i. *The evidence in question must be relevant.* Remember that relevance is the first step in analyzing any piece of evidence. Per Rule 402, "Irrelevant evidence is not admissible." That means that you would *never* be conducting a Rule 403 analysis on evidence that is irrelevant.

ii. *The evidence must be evaluated against each of the 403 dangers:*

   a. Unfair prejudice;

   b. Confusing the issues;

   c. Misleading the jury;

   d. Undue delay;

   e. Wasting time; and

   f. Needlessly presenting cumulative evidence.

Each of these dangers (we often call them "counterweights") could, potentially, cause a judge to exclude otherwise relevant evidence.

iii. *The evidence may be excluded if the probative value is substantially outweighed by one of the dangers above.* The key to this part of the rule is the phrase "substantially outweighed." As previously mentioned, a common error that students make is that they discuss the rule in terms of whether or not the probative value of the evidence is outweighed by one of the dangers. Such an analysis is wrong because the rule does not use the term "outweighed" by itself; rather, the rule uses the phrase "substantially outweighed." That word— "substantially"—makes all the difference in the world.

2. Example

Let's look at an example. Danny Defendant is accused of armed robbery. Suppose there is a question as to whether Danny was actually armed. Assume "possession of a weapon" is an element of the charge. The prosecution possesses evidence that Danny owns over a dozen guns. Assume for purposes of this example that his ownership of the guns is relevant. Would evidence of his ownership potentially be prejudicial? Yes, it would. Would evidence of ownership be unfairly prejudicial? Possibly. However, none of these facts would permit the evidence—under Rule 403—to be excluded. The question that must then be answered in the affirmative is that the probative value of the evidence (gun ownership) would *substantially outweigh* the risk of unfair prejudice.

> If the answer is no, then Rule 403 does not permit the judge to exclude the evidence.

> If the answer is yes, then Rule 403 permits—but does not require—the judge to exclude the evidence.

3. More than One "Danger" May Apply

You should also recognize that more than one of the dangers (counterweights) listed in Rule 403 may apply to a particular piece of evidence; for example, a piece of evidence could be *unfairly prejudicial* as well as *misleading to the jury*. Any single danger that substantially outweighs the probative value of the evidence would permit (but not require) a judge to exclude the evidence.

CHAPTER IV

Witnesses and Testimonial Evidence

A. Overview

One of the primary sources of evidence comes from live witnesses. Live witnesses can be categorized into two primary areas: lay witnesses and expert witnesses.

1. The Rule

Articles VI and VII govern witnesses. Although lay witnesses are generally required to base their testimony on personal knowledge (per Rule 602), lay witnesses may also express opinions if done so in accordance with Rule 701. Experts, on the other hand, have rules that govern their opinions, which are different from lay witnesses. To make things more complicated, a witness could testify as both a lay witness and an expert witness.

We will try to navigate these waters in this chapter. Regardless of whether a witness is testifying as an expert or lay witness, he or she must be competent; and competency is where we begin our discussion.

B. Competency

Documentary evidence must be authenticated. Unlike documents, people have no requirement of authentication. Rather, we want to make sure that witnesses are competent to say whatever drivel they are spouting from the witness stand.

> **Attention!**
> Do not confuse competency with admissibility. That is, "[a] witness may be competent but be unable to testify as to anything [admissible]. Thus, for example, a witness might satisfy [a requirement with regard to being able to testify as to medical matters] but her testimony would be inadmissible if, under Rule 702 (see Section D.2.) it is not based on sufficient facts or data." *Liebsack v. U.S.*, 731 F.3d 850, 856 n6 (9th Cir. 2013).

1. Who Is Competent to Testify?

Who is competent to testify? Anyone. Well, that is not completely true. However, that *is* the starting point. This means that witnesses are presumed to be competent. How do we know? A rule tells us. Rule 601 provides that:

> "Every person is competent to be a witness unless these rules provide otherwise. But in a civil case, state law governs the witness's competency regarding a claim or defense for which state law supplies the rule decision."

This means what it says. Witnesses are generally competent. For a witness to be incompetent—a federal rule must provide otherwise, unless the claim or defense is based on state law.

2. Children

A common misconception is that children are not competent to testify. Children can, and do, regularly testify. As the 10th Circuit held, "There is no rule which excludes . . . a child of any specified age, from testifying, but in each case the traditional test is whether the witness has intelligence enough to make it worthwhile to hear him at all and whether he feels the duty to tell the truth."[1] Courts have also required that a child be of sufficient age to understand the difference between telling a lie and telling the truth. Sufficient age is not specific but determined by the maturity of the child.

3. *Insane Persons*

Much like children, insane persons may be competent to testify. There is "no rule which excludes an insane person [from testifying and she may testify if] the witness has intelligence enough to make it worthwhile to hear him at all and whether he feels the duty to tell the truth."[2]

4. *Dead Man's Statute*

The "Dead Man's Statute" comes from state-based rules—not the Federal Rules of Evidence. There is no rule at the federal level that reflects the same prohibition. Nevertheless, the state rules will often prohibit certain types of testimony in federal cases where the state law provides the rule of decision (usually in cases based on diversity jurisdiction).

i. **The Prohibition**

Although the specifics of the Dead Man's Statutes vary from state to state, the general prohibition is the same; they generally prohibit testimony from an interested party about communications or transactions with a deceased person (the dead man) when such testimony is offered against representatives or successors in interest of the deceased.

> **Reality Check**
> Dead Man's Statutes may come under other names such as the "Dead Man Act" or "Dead Man's Rule."

---

[1] *U.S. v. Bedonie*, 913 F.2d 782, 799 (10th Cir. 1990).
[2] *U.S. v. Bedonie*, 913 F.2d 782, 799 (10th Cir. 1990).

ii.   The Rationale

These statutes are intended to protect estates from claims of perjury. The assumption (rightly or not) is that the surviving claimant may lie (imagine that)—since the deceased cannot respond.

iii.   Common Elements

As mentioned above, each statute is state-specific. Nevertheless, it is worth reviewing the elements that are fairly common to the prohibition across states.

> **Reality Check**
> Many states have not adopted a Dead Man's Statute. Make sure to check to see if your jurisdiction has adopted one.

a.   Application Only in Civil Cases

The nature of this prohibition is one that only applies to civil cases.

b.   Protected Parties

This rule protects those who claim directly under the decedent. These parties usually include an executor (or executrix), an administrator, an heir, a legatee, and a devisee. If a protected party is on either side of the lawsuit, then the rule prevents an interested party from testifying as to what the "dead man" said. Sometimes, it is best to consider this concept by way of example:

Examples:

1) Plaintiff sues the executrix of an estate for a debt. Let's say the decedent bought a boat and has not paid the full balance. The executrix is a protected party. This means that under the dead man's statute the Plaintiff would be prohibited from testifying as to what the decedent said.

You might be wondering how one would prove the debt under these circumstances? In this case, the Plaintiff would have to rely upon written documents or other proof of the debt, the terms, etc., without testifying as to those matters.

2) Plaintiff sues the executor of an estate contesting the decedent's will. Here, because the Plaintiff is an interested party (he thinks he should inherit under the will), the act will apply. The Plaintiff could not testify as to the decedent's wishes. In this case, the will would have to speak for itself (so to speak).

c. Interested Party

What constitutes whether or not a person is an "interested party?" An "interested party" is one that would be directly impacted by the court's judgment.

iv. Exception and Waiver

In certain circumstances, the prohibition may have an exception or, alternatively, may be waived. In the event an exception applies, or there is waiver, then the interested party is not prohibited from testifying.

a. Exception

To be fair, this isn't really an exception, but it seems easier to remember it as one. The rule does not prevent an interested party from testifying as to a fact which occurred after the death of the deceased. After all, this evidence is not what the rule is intended to protect.

b. Waiver

What about waiver? Can a deceased individual waive anything? No, of course not. But representatives of an estate, and those claiming under the decedent, may waive the protections of the Dead Man's Statute. This might occur under these circumstances:

(1)   Waiver Based on Failure to Object

This is always the case, isn't it? If one who opposes evidence fails to make a timely objection, then the admission of that evidence will almost always be proper. This holds true with the Dead Man's Statute.

(2)   Waiver Based on Previous Testimony

This one can be a little tricky. If evidence from a former trial or deposition is admitted, then the interested person may explain all matters for which he is examined. This is akin to "opening the door." Once it's opened, the interested party can walk right through. However, do not be misled. The door is not "opened" until the testimony from the former trial or the deposition is admitted. It's the admission of that former testimony that constitutes the waiver.

(3)   Waiver by Protected Party Asking Questions

This form of waiver is pretty straightforward. If the protected party asks the interested party a question which would otherwise be prohibited by the statute, then the protected party cannot later object, based on the statute. Nope—he cannot have it both ways!

(4)   Waiver Based on Protected Party's Testimony

If the protected party testifies as to a transaction with an interested person then that, too, would be considered "opening the door." Once opened, then the interested person would not be barred by the Dead Man's Statute.

C. Examination of Witnesses

There are a number of rules that apply to the examination of witnesses. The beginning point, however, is to know which "side" is questioning which, and under what circumstances.

When considering witness examination, it is important to know whether you are asking questions in the context of "direct" examination or "cross" examination. To begin with, let's look at a diagram:

Setting: A Courtroom

Witness: Wendy
(Assume Wendy is a witness for the criminal defendant)

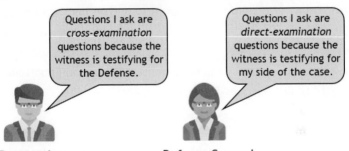

Prosecution   Defense Counsel

It is important to know whether questions are asked on direct examination, or on cross-examination, because we have different rules—depending upon whether questions are asked on direct or cross-examination.

1. *Direct Examination*

We know that when a lawyer is asking questions to witnesses on his or her side of the case, then those questions are "direct examination" questions.

2. *Cross-Examination*

"Cross-examination" refers to questions asked of a witness that is opposed to the questioning lawyer's side of the case. In the diagram above, the witness on the stand is a witness for the defense; therefore, when

> **Attention!**
> You will note that with regard to direct examination that the questions are asked to witnesses that are "for" that side of the case. In other words, a lawyer could call a witness during her case-in-chief that is "for" the other side of the case. Under that circumstance, the questions would be considered cross-examination questions against an adverse witness. The pivotal question is not which side called the witness, but rather *for which side* the witness is testifying.

the prosecution asks her questions, she is *opposed* to the prosecution. Questions asked to her by the prosecution are via cross-examination. Whether or not questions are being asked on direct examination or cross-examination is particularly important with regard to leading questions.

i.   Scope of Cross-Examination

The federal rules have a provision that is only occasionally found at the state level. The federal rules provide that cross-examination is limited to the "subject matter of the direct examination and matters affecting the witness's credibility." [FRE 611(b)]. This rule—although sometimes found in state rules—is primarily one limited to the federal courts. Check your particular jurisdiction to determine whether or not your state has the same limitation.

You might be wondering how you can ask about matters that are beyond the scope of direct when Rule 611(b) limits the scope of cross-examination. Although the court may permit the questions to go beyond the scope of direct, it is not wise to rely on the necessity of permission from the court. So, again, how do you do it? The answer is to call that particular witness on direct. On direct examination, you are only limited by relevance (and other applicable rules). Otherwise, there is no limitation on the subject matter.

3. *Leading Questions*

i. What Is a Leading Question?

"Leading questions" are questions which suggest the answer. For example, the question "Did you run the red light?" does not suggest—one way or the other—whether the witness ran the red light. On the other hand, the question "You ran the red light, didn't you?" suggests the answer. Often—but not always—questions that are framed as requiring only a "yes" or "no" answer are leading questions.

ii. Why Do We Care?

We care what is, or is not, a leading question because as a general rule, leading questions are not permitted on direct examination. That is, they are only permitted on cross-examination. Actually, that's not completely accurate; they are **usually** permitted only on cross-examination. Let's look at the rule:

Rule 611(c) is straightforward:

Leading questions should not be used on direct examination except as necessary to develop the witness's testimony. Ordinarily, the court should allow leading questions:

(1)   on cross-examination; and

(2)   .when a party calls a hostile witness an adverse party, or a witness identified with an adverse party.

You will notice the rule provides that leading questions *should* not be used on direct examination. In practice, courts generally treat this as a firm prohibition. Although they will permit leading questions (on direct)—permission is somewhat rare and usually granted only for a specific purpose. When a witness is called and acts hostile, adverse, or identifies with an adverse party, then courts will permit leading questions because the witness is acting as though he supports the other side of the case.

4.   *Examination by the Court*

We usually think of questions, in a trial, as being asked by the lawyers (or in cases without lawyers, by the parties). But what about the judges? Can they ask questions? Yes. Believe it or not, there is a rule that addresses this very issue, Rule 614:

(a)   **Calling.** The court may call a witness on its own or at a party's request. Each party is entitled to cross-examine the witness.

(b)   **Examining.** The court may examine a witness regardless of who calls the witness.

(c)   **Objections.** A party may object to the court's calling or examining a witness either at that time or at the next opportunity when the jury is not present.

You can see that Rule 614(b) permits a court to examine witnesses regardless of which side called the witness.

D. Types of Witnesses and Testimony

Now, let's get back to the two types of witnesses: lay and expert. Generally, lay witnesses testify as to facts and experts are frequently used to offer opinions. As we examine witnesses, we will break down the discussion into three parts: lay (fact) witnesses; lay opinions; and expert opinions.

1. Lay (Fact) Witnesses

The best place to begin this discussion is Rule 602:

> A witness may testify to a matter only if evidence is introduced sufficient to support a finding that the witness has personal knowledge of the matter. Evidence to prove personal knowledge may consist of the witness's own testimony. This rule does not apply to a witness's expert testimony under Rule 703.

As you can see by the rule, witnesses (this means lay witnesses) must base their testimony on personal knowledge. What is lay testimony? Lay testimony is any testimony that is not expert testimony. Easy right? Let's move on. Just kidding.

Lay testimony is testimony that reflects personal observations or experiences. For example, "I saw the Honda Civic run the red light." This testimony is based on the personal observation of the witness. How do we know? Because she testified that she *saw* the car run the red light. What if the testimony was, "Jenny told me she ran the red light?" That is still personal knowledge and, therefore, still appropriate under Rule 602. It's a fact that was relayed by Jenny to the witness, not an opinion. You might be thinking that the statement "Jenny told me. . . " creates a problem. You would be right. The statement triggers other potential rules. In this case, hearsay is the obvious one. But we are not yet concerned with hearsay. All that matters at this point is that you understand the statement "Jenny told me she ran the red light" would qualify as personal knowledge and, therefore, under Rule 602 be appropriate.

Put another way, if a witness has knowledge not based on speculation or opinion, then the testimony is appropriate under Rule 602. The 9th Circuit put it best:

> "Rule 602 requires any witness to have sufficient memory of the events such that she is not forced to fill in the gaps. . . . Witnesses are not permitted to speculate, guess, or voice suspicions."[3]

Lay witnesses often testify as to facts of which they have personal knowledge and offer opinions. If you only read Rule 602, you might think that a witness's opinions are always objectionable. However, Rule 701 (below) does permit lay opinions in certain circumstances and, as the 9th Circuit articulated, "personal knowledge includes opinions and inferences grounded in observations and experience."[4]

2. *Lay Opinions*

Lay opinions are permitted under Rule 701:

Rule 701. Opinion Testimony by Lay Witnesses

If a witness is not testifying as an expert, testimony in the form of an opinion is limited to one that is:

(a) rationally based on the witness's perception;

(b) helpful to clearly understanding the witness's testimony or to determining a fact in issue; and

---

[3] *U.S. v. Whittemore*, 776 F.3d 1074, 1082 (9th Cir. 2015).
[4] *Id.*

> (c) not based on scientific, technical, or other specialized knowledge within the scope of Rule 702.

i. The Prohibition

As you can see from the rule, there are three requirements. Let's begin with a discussion of the third requirement, 701(c), that the opinion not be "based on scientific, technical, or other specialized knowledge within the scope of Rule 702."

The reason for this requirement—which is really a prohibition—is to clearly distinguish between the kinds of opinions offered by experts which require specialized knowledge, skill, experience, training or education from lay opinions which have a much more lax standard. The reason for the prohibition is the belief that fact-finders will give more weight to an opinion from an expert.

ii. Rationally Based on the Witness's Perception

This requirement is significantly different from the requirements put on the testimony of experts. The rule is intended to permit lay witnesses to give opinions which are logical based on their perception.

Let's look at some examples:

1) Values

A lay witness could give her opinion as to the value of her residence. Why? Because courts believe that, as an owner, she would be able to ascertain a value based on her "perception." Might her value be wrong? Sure. An appraiser is likely to give a much more accurate value. Nevertheless, the rules do not require the testimony to be accurate.

What about the value of someone else's residence? Could this same lay witness use the same kinds of factors that she used in valuing her own residence on someone else's home? Yes, however, a court would not allow it. She would have to be qualified as an expert.

She could also value her car (but not someone else's), value her jewelry, and even value her antiques.

2) Causes

A lay witness could testify as to why something happened as it relates to themselves personally. For example, she could give her opinion as to why she collided with another vehicle if her opinion is rationally based on her perceptions.

3) A Large Variety of Opinions

The rules do not limit the kinds of things for which a lay witness may offer an opinion. As the 7th Circuit put it, "[t]he [FREs] limit—but do not bar—lay witnesses' ability to testify as to their opinions. . . ."[5] And the 6th Circuit:

> "In distinguishing proper lay testimony from expert testimony . . . lay testimony results from a process of reasoning familiar in everyday life, whereas an expert's testimony results from a process of reasoning which can be mastered only be specialists in the field. Thus, a lay witness may testify, for example, that a footprint in snow looked like someone slipped, or that a substance appeared to be blood, but cannot testify that skull trauma caused bruises on the victim's face."[6]

Courts have been fairly liberal in permitting lay opinion testimony if the testimony is "well founded on personal knowledge and subject to cross-examination."[7]

---

[5]   *U.S. v. Locke*, 643 F.3d 235, 239-40 (7th Cir. 2011).

[6]   *Harris v. J.B. Robinson Jewelers*, 627 F.3d 235, 240 (6th Cir. 2010).

[7]   *Id.*

iii. Helpful to Understand Testimony

Assuming the lay opinion is not prohibited by 701(c) and meets the requirements of 701(a), then the testimony must also be "helpful to clearly understanding the witness's testimony or to determining a fact in issue" under 701(b). The 1st Circuit describes this portion of the rule as follows:

> "Lay opinion testimony will not be helpful to the jury when the jury can readily determine the necessary inferences and conclusions with the aid of the opinion. The nub of this helpfulness requirement is to exclude testimony where the witness is no better suited than the jury to make the judgment at issue, providing assurance against the admission of opinions which would merely tell the jury what result to reach."[8]

As you have seen, lay witnesses may testify as to their opinions—as long as their opinions do not cross the 'imaginary line in the sand' established by the rule. However, experts are permitted more leeway.

3. Expert Opinions

Experts have their very own rules: 702-705. Fundamentally, an expert's testimony must satisfy three requirements:

1) The expert must be qualified;

2) The testimony must help the trier of fact; and

3) The expert's testimony must have a proper basis.

---

[8]   *U.S. v. Diaz-Arias*, 717 F.3d 1, 12 (1st Cir. 2013).

i. The Expert Must Be Qualified

Rule 702 provides five different bases, each of which (or any combination) may qualify the expert:

1) Knowledge; 2) Skill; 3) Experience; 4) Training; or
5) Education.

Any of these may qualify an expert. All too often, students (and lay people) believe that to be an expert, one must have a formal (usually advanced) degree related to the subject. For example, you wouldn't ask an automobile mechanic with no medical training to testify as to the medical cause of death, would you? No, but a farmer, with no formal education, who has spent forty years raising cattle, might be able to tell you with great accuracy what caused a cow to die. Would he be less qualified than a person with four years of vet school who has studied a cow but never looked one in the eye? The answer is no, the farmer would be appropriately qualified— maybe more so than the vet.

ii. The Testimony Must Help the Trier of Fact

One concern that the rule-makers had was that when an expert testifies, a fact-finder (especially a jury) would simply accept an expert's opinion without using his or her opinion to help them with their decision. Rule 702(a) seeks to minimize this concern by permitting an expert to testify only when his or her testimony will "help the trier of fact to understand the evidence or to determine a fact in issue." [Rule 703(a)]

iii. The Expert's Testimony Must Have a Proper Basis

The next requirement is encompassed in the last three parts of the rule. The Rule requires that the expert's testimony be:

1)   Based on sufficient facts or data [702(b)];

2) The product of reliable principles and methods [702(c)]; and

3) Based on principles and methods that the expert reliably applied to the facts of the case [702(d)].

a. Sufficient Facts or Data [702(b)]

Unlike a lay witness (who must have personal knowledge), an expert may gain facts from multiple sources. These include:

1) Facts the expert personally observed [703]

If the expert has conducted a test, or observed the scene and came to a conclusion, or any circumstance where the expert has personally observed the facts, then the expert may testify accordingly.

2) Facts obtained outside of court if (and only if) such facts are the kinds of facts which are reasonably relied upon by experts in his or her particular field [703]

The expert may obtain facts outside of the courtroom from virtually any source. This may include reviewing documents, interviewing witnesses or other people with knowledge. If you are thinking "Hey, does that mean the expert could hear hearsay?" or "Hey, doesn't that mean the expert might review inadmissible evidence?" The answer is yes, absolutely—positively—yes; and Rule 703 permits it. The only "catch" is that the facts must be "the kinds of facts which are reasonably relied upon by experts in his or her particular field."

3) Facts learned at trial

Facts learned at trial can come from the expert merely sitting in the courtroom and listening to, and observing, the evidence. It could also come from the expert sitting on the stand and being fed additional facts either directly or, if appropriate, in the form of an opinion.

b.   **Reliable Principles and Methods [702(c)]**

This one can be tricky. After all, what's "reliable"? What is, or is not, reliable is, in truth, up to the judge. In one, now infamous, case the court set out factors for establishing reliability:

> "*Daubert* set forth a non-exclusive checklist for trial courts to use in assessing the reliability of scientific expert testimony. The specific factors explicated by the *Daubert* Court are (1) whether the expert's technique or theory can be or has been tested—that is, whether the expert's theory can be challenged in some objective sense, or whether it is instead simply a subjective, conclusory approach that cannot reasonably be assessed for reliability; (2) whether the technique or theory has been subject to peer review and publication; (3) the known or potential rate of error of the technique or theory when applied; (4) the existence and maintenance of standards and controls; and (5) whether the technique or theory has been generally accepted in the scientific community. The Court in *Kumho* held that these factors might also be applicable in assessing the reliability of non-scientific expert testimony, depending upon "the particular circumstances of the particular case at issue."[9]

The factors, unfortunately, resulted from scientific testimony which, when it comes to expert witnesses, can be fairly narrow. After all, how would these standards apply to "soft sciences" like

---

[9]   FED. R. EVID. 702 cmt. *citing Daubert v. Merrell Dow Pharms.*, 509 U.S. 579, 592-93 (1993) and *Kumho Tire Co. v. Carmichael*, 526 U.S. 137, 141 (1999).

Psychology or Sociology? The short answer is that courts have permitted expert testimony with regard to soft sciences. The Supreme Court has held that "the test of reliability is flexible and *Daubert's* list of specific factors neither necessarily nor exclusively applies to all experts or in every case."[10]

c.   Reliably Applied to the Facts of the Case [702(d)]

The Advisory Committee note concerning the Rule expounds on this requirement:

> " . . . [W]hen an expert purports to apply principles and methods in accordance with professional standards, and yet reaches a conclusion that other experts in the field would not reach, the trial court may fairly suspect that the principles and methods have not been faithfully applied. . . . [T]he trial court must scrutinize not only the principles and methods used by the expert, but also whether those principles and methods have been properly applied to the facts of the case. [A]ny step that renders the analysis unreliable . . . renders the expert's testimony inadmissible. This is true whether the step completely changes a reliable methodology or merely misapplies that methodology.

> If the expert purports to apply principles and methods to the facts of the case, it is important that this application be conducted reliably. Yet it might also be important in some cases for an expert to educate the factfinder about general principles, without ever attempting to apply these principles to the specific facts of the case. For example, experts might instruct the factfinder on the principles of thermodynamics, or bloodclotting [sic], or on how financial markets respond

---

[10] *Kuhmo Tire Co. v. Carmichael*, 526 U.S. 137, 141 (1999).

to corporate reports, without ever knowing about or trying to tie their testimony into the facts of the case."[11]

d.   Disclosure of the Underlying Data

Remember when I said (okay, wrote) that the experts may rely on evidence which is not admissible? Well, there is a small catch. If the expert relies on inadmissible evidence, then the expert may not disclose the inadmissible evidence to the jury unless its "probative value in helping the jury evaluate the opinion substantially outweighs their prejudicial effect." [Rule 703]

E.   Credibility and Impeachment

Now that we know what kinds of witnesses might testify, how do we impeach them? "Impeachment" means showing that the witness is lying. Well, not necessarily lying. She *could* be lying but, in reality, impeachment is merely putting her testimony in question. The inaccurate testimony could come from dishonesty, but it could also come: poor memory, poor perception, inaccurate portrayal of the facts, etc. Anything that casts doubt on the accuracy of the testimony is impeachment.

1.   *Who May Impeach?*

As was discussed before, any party may impeach a witness, even his or her own witness. [Rule 607]

2.   *Bolstering*

While impeachment refers to challenging the credibility of a witness, bolstering is the opposite. Unlike impeachment, however, a party may not bolster her witness until the witness has first been impeached.

---

[11]   FED. R. EVID. 702 cmt notes.

For a detailed discussion of permissible and impermissible bolstering, see the discussion in the next chapter: *Character Evidence*.

3. *Methods of Impeachment*

There are many methods by which a witness can be impeached. The methods include:

(1) Prior Inconsistent Statements;

(2) Bias or Interest;

(3) Conviction of a Crime;

(4) Specific Instances of Misconduct;

(5) Proof of Reputation or Opinion; or

(6) Sensory Deficiencies.

> **What Does This Mean?**
> "Sensory deficiencies" would include poor: perception, memory, mental ability or the inability to narrate the facts accurately. Each of these is discussed in greater detail in the *Impeachment* section below.

i. **Prior Inconsistent Statement**

Do not confuse this discussion with the discussion of Prior Inconsistent Statements under the *Hearsay* chapter. As used here, Prior Inconsistent Statements are used as a mechanism to *impeach* a witness. Rule 613 governs this method of impeachment.

The rule has four requirements:[12]

(1) The statements must be inconsistent; (hopefully this requirement is obvious)

(2) The inconsistency must be relevant to the case at hand; (also should be obvious but just in case, the 8th Circuit thinks it is important)

---

[12] *U.S. v. Larry Reed & Sons Prtshp.*, 280 F.3d 1212, 1215 (8th Cir. 2002).

(3) The inconsistent statement must, on request, be disclosed to opposing counsel, the witness allowed to explain the inconsistency, and opposing counsel allowed to question the witness; [Rule 613(a)] and

(4) The district court should instruct the jury about the limited purpose of the earlier statement.

ii.   Bias or Interest

If a witness is biased and/or has an interest in the outcome of the case, then that witness has a motive to be less than truthful. Evidence that the witness is biased or has an interest in the case may be shown by virtually any means. Because of this, the evidence which shows the bias or interest, is not admitted for substantive purposes. That is, the evidence is not use to support or controvert an issue in the case. Rather, the evidence is only admitted to impeach the witness.

a.   Examples

There are as many examples of bias as there are people in the world. Because a list of examples would take an additional volume, I thought I would just share two:

(1) Jailhouse Snitch

You've seen them in the movies, right? A con sharing the same cell with the defendant testifies about what the defendant told him one night? Sure! Of course, in exchange for his testimony, he gets a reduced sentence or some such benefit. Is he biased? Certainly. Evidence of this agreement could be admitted to illustrate how the witness is biased.

(2) Scorned Spouse

This doesn't really come up at the federal level, but it is such a great illustration, I couldn't pass it up. Oh, and you *will* see it at the state level with great frequency. Frequently, one spouse has been *wronged*. It could have been as a result of many things, such as infidelity, mismanagement of money—you name it. In a divorce, for example, the "wronged" spouse may have a reason to "twist" his or her testimony.

iii. Conviction of a Crime

This is a fairly strong method of impeachment—whether warranted or not. It's the "once a bad guy, always a bad guy" mentality that many people possess. For a thorough discussion of Rule 609, see the next chapter on Character Evidence.

iv. Specific Instances of Misconduct

The thought that once a person does something wrong, he or she will tend to do that again goes far beyond requiring that someone be convicted of a crime. Therefore, Rule 608(a) addresses the limited circumstances when a witness's character for truthfulness may be attacked. For a thorough discussion of Rule 608(a), see the next chapter on Character Evidence.

v. Proof of Reputation or Opinion

Evidence of this kind is also contained in Rule 608; however, the second part of the Rule, 608(b) addresses specific instances of conduct. Yes—you guessed it—I talk about it in the next chapter on Character Evidence.

vi. Sensory Deficiencies

Did you ever see the movie, "My Cousin Vinny?" If you didn't, go rent it. No, seriously, go rent it. There is a scene in the movie when the criminal defense lawyer, played by Joe Pesci, is cross-examining an eyewitness. He asks her how far she was from the defendants when she saw them leaving a store where they allegedly robbed and subsequently shot the clerk. She said about

"50 feet away." Pesci then asks the witness to hold the end of a tape measure, and he walks all the way back to the entrance to the courtroom. He tells her that he is less than 50 feet away from her. When he holds up three fingers on his hand and asks her how many fingers he is holding up, she can't tell him accurately.

Pesci uses the demonstration to illustrate for the jury that her vision was bad. Put another way, he challenged her capacity to perceive the scene. It was a very effective demonstration. Challenging a witness's capacity is an acceptable way to impeach a witness. There are four areas in which capacity may be challenged: Perception, Memory, Narration, and Mental Ability.

a.   Challenges to Capacity

(1)   Poor Perception

As illustrated above, sometimes a witness has poor perception of the scene about which she testifies. It could be as a result of poor vision, poor location, bad lighting, physical impairment though drugs or alcohol, lack of sleep, or any other factor which impacts a witness's ability to accurately perceive an event.

(2)   Memory Failure

As I have gotten older, I have had this particular issue impact me personally, more and more. Sometimes, we just cannot remember events, or cannot remember the little details about the events, or we remember events inaccurately. Has this ever happened to you? You know it has. Showing that a witness has misremembered one event can, if presented properly, cast doubt on other events she narrates for the case.

(3)   Narration

Speaking of narration, sometimes we tell the story wrong. It is not necessarily from lying—by the way. Remember the telephone game? Everyone sits in a circle. Someone writes down a phrase. This phrase is whispered to one person who, in turn whispers it to the next, and this continues all the way until the last person is reached. Upon reaching the last person, after it is whispered to her, she then repeats the phrase out loud for all to hear. Then the phrase is read out loud from the paper. It will almost never match the phrase recited by the last person. Is this because she lied? No—stories told over time across many people change. This is also one of the reasons we have rules regarding hearsay to try to eliminate these changes in story.

(4) Mental Ability

It is important to remember that a lack of mental capacity does not, in and of itself, prevent a witness from being competent to testify. On the contrary, a mentally incompetent person can testify if a judge believes that she has the ability to recall and narrate events accurately, and understands the difference between telling the truth and a lie. Nevertheless, courts have permitted evidence of a mental diagnosis for consideration of a witness's credibility.

b. Lack of Personal or Appropriate Knowledge

(1) Experts

Recall that experts need not have personal knowledge. Nevertheless, they must have appropriate knowledge to testify with regard to a particular field. For example, a psychologist who obtained his Ph.D. by mailing the required amount of funds to a mail-order "university" probably does not have the requisite knowledge to offer a valid diagnosis. Although that scenario is somewhat unlikely, here is one that is more likely: An expert goes beyond her expertise and testifies to matters that are outside of her knowledge, training, etc. It happens somewhat frequently.

(2) Lay

Remember that lay persons must have personal knowledge with the caveat that certain opinions are permissible. For an in-depth discussion of Lay Witnesses, see the section under Character Evidence.

4. *Collateral Matters*

Witnesses may be impeached with regard to matters that are at issue in the case, but not on matters collateral to the case. Does that sound confusing? Yes—until you look at an example. This example should remove the fogginess. Suppose that the case involves negligence and the issue is who had the right of way at an intersection. Wendy the Witness testifies that on her way home from her pedicure, she saw Danny Defendant run a red light. Suppose that you have information that Wendy was not coming home from a pedicure but, rather, she was coming home from her rendezvous with her lover (not her husband) at the time. Could you impeach Wendy with evidence that she was not coming home from a pedicure? No! That is because it is a collateral matter that has nothing to do with what is in issue the case. You are 'stuck' with her story.

5. *Hearsay Declarant*

First things first, let's look at a rule we have not seen yet, Rule 806:

> ### Rule 806. Attacking & Supporting the Declarant's Credibility
> When a hearsay statement—or a statement described in Rule 801(d)(2)(C), (D), or (E)—has been admitted in evidence, the declarant's credibility may be attacked, and then supported, by any evidence that would be admissible for those purposes if the

declarant had testified as a witness. The court may admit evidence of the declarant's inconsistent statement or conduct, regardless of when it occurred or whether the declarant had an opportunity to explain or deny it. If the party against whom the statement was admitted calls the declarant as a witness, the party may examine the declarant on the statement as if on cross-examination.

The significance of this rule is that even when the declarant does not testify, evidence may be admitted which contradicts (or impeaches) the declarant. If you have not yet learned what a declarant is, do not worry. Simply come back to this rule after you study declarants in the Hearsay chapter.

6. *Rehabilitation*

The other side of impeachment—is rehabilitation. While one side wants to show a witness is *not* to be believed, the other side wants the fact-finder to believe the witness. There are a number of ways to rehabilitate a witness:

i. Redirect Examination

The most obvious (and common) method to rehabilitate a witness is for the proponent of the witness to ask questions on redirect which would rehabilitate the witness. This permits the witness to explain or expound on the prior testimony.

ii. Reputation for Truthfulness

Under Rule 608, once a witness's credibility for truthfulness has been attacked, then evidence of truthful character is admissible.

iii. Prior Consistent Statements

a. Prohibition

Generally, a party may not rehabilitate a witness by offering a prior statement that is consistent with her testimony.

b. Exceptions

Guess what? There are exceptions. Imagine that!

(1) To Rebut a Charge of Recent Fabrication

Peter alleges—"Hey, Mary just made that up!" But she didn't. In fact, she said the same thing to Nancy a month ago. That former statement that she made to Nancy may be admitted. Why? To rebut a charge of recent fabrication or a motive to lie.

Of course, the statement had to have occurred before the alleged recent fabrication, or motive, occurred.

(2) When the Witness Has Been Impeached on Other Non-Character Grounds

If a witness has been impeached on a ground other than recent fabrication or motive then, if appropriate, a court may allow testimony that controverts the impeachment (i.e., rehabilitates the witness).

> **Attention!**
>
> Note: Evidence of a prior consistent statement is not permitted to rehabilitate a witness whose *general character* for truthfulness has been attacked (i.e., criminal convictions, reputation, or opinion testimony.

How about an example? Suppose that Officer O'Reilly recognized Danny Defendant based on his tattoo (demonstrating that Danny was a member of the Sons of Anarchy Motorcycle Club). On cross-examination, opposing counsel tried to effectively impeach Officer O'Reilly with evidence of O'Reilly's report that did not mention Danny's tattoo. In order to rehabilitate Officer O'Reilly, the prosecutor may offer evidence that he had previously mentioned the tattoo to another officer.

F. Common Objections, Exceptions, and Offers of Proof

Objections (effective objections) are a necessary part of the trial process. In practice, lawyers will frequently offer evidence which would violate the rules. As a general rule, in the absence of a proper objection, evidence will be admitted regardless of whether the evidence complies with the rules. For example, suppose one side offers evidence that is, without question, irrelevant. Unless the opposing

> **Reality Check**
>
> Judges do not actually say things like "objection." After all, they *rule* on objections. But a judge can effectively "object" by refusing to let testimony in. The judge might say things like "that's irrelevant—move along" or some such verbiage.

party objects, the evidence will be admitted. Why? Because (again, generally, but not always) a judge will not object *sua sponte*. Without an objection, there is nothing for a judge to rule on.

Objections must be based on the proper rule—and valid. Even then, judges will many times overrule objections improperly. Nevertheless, those are issues for appeal. We are just focused on trial-level evidence at this stage.

1. Where Objections Are Made

Objections are typically made in one of three scenarios: at trial, at a hearing, or at a deposition.

i. Trials and Hearings

Although the rules with regard to objections made at a trial and at a hearing are the same, in practice, judges tend to be more lenient in hearings because there is no jury present. Judges are presumed to be able to sift through permissible and impermissible evidence and make decisions based only on permissible evidence.

Regardless of the setting, trial or hearing, timing is critical. Generally, objections must be made at the first available time. In other words, as soon as an objectionable question is asked or an objectionable answer is anticipated, an objection must be made; that is, before the answer is given (if possible). If not possible, as soon as the answer is given. If properly made after an answer is given, and sustained (granted) by the judge, then the objecting party must make an oral motion to strike the answer.

Failure to object timely will mean that a judge may properly overrule the objection.

ii.　Depositions

Depositions, being a form of discovery, are governed by the Rules of Civil Procedure. [FRCP 30] In depositions, objections to the form of the question must be made at the time of the deposition or they will be waived. An objection to the form of the question would be, for example, "overly broad;" or that the question calls for "hearsay." Additionally, an objection based on privilege must also be made at the deposition or it will be deemed waived. Federal Rule of Civil Procedure 30(c)(2) governs objections during a deposition.

2.　How Are Objections Made?

There are two types of objections: general and specific.

i.　General Objections

General objections are vague and overbroad (i.e., "I object" or words to that effect). General objections do not preserve error (although you hear them used in movies all of the time). That is, if a general objection is made and overruled (denied), then the objection will be deemed meaningless on appeal and insufficient to preserve appeal. An appellate court cannot review it. On the other hand, if a general objection is made and sustained (granted), then the objection will be upheld on appeal. That is, an appellate court will presume that the objection was made on the proper grounds.

> **Attention!**
> Some errors do not require an objection to preserve them. In those cases, no objection is necessary for them to be reviewed on appeal.

ii. Specific Objections

If a specific objection is made and sustained, then the objection will be upheld on appeal if the objection was made on proper grounds. For example, "Objection, Hearsay," if sustained, will be upheld if the question asked for inadmissible hearsay.

3. Bases

Objections may be made on a number of different bases. The list of possible bases is extremely long. While most objections are tied to specific rules of evidence by name, many objections do not tie—readily—to specific rules. Objections that readily tie to specific rules would include ones such as "Objection, Hearsay;" "Objection, Leading;" etc. Objections that are not as easily connected include: "Misleading;" "Compound;" "Argumentative;" "Conclusory;" "Assuming Facts Not In Evidence;" "Cumulative;" "Harassing or Embarrassing;" "Calls for a Narrative Answer;" "Calls for Speculation;" "Lack of Proper Foundation;" and "Nonresponsive Answer." Make no mistake, each of these objections does tie to specific rules of evidence; it is simply that they are not as obvious as objections that refer to the rules by name. For example, the objection that a question "Calls for Speculation" refers to the rule which requires personal knowledge. [Rule 602] As you can see, the term "speculation" is not found anywhere in the text of the Rule.

It's not necessary at this stage in your education to make all of the connections. Just be aware that they *are* there.

4. Exceptions

In the movies, and on television, you might have heard lawyers say "exception" when a judge rules against him or her. In the "old" days, this device was a means to preserve error such that an appellate court could review the trial court's ruling. No more, at least not at the federal level. Most state courts have abolished the use of this term as well.

5. Offers of Proof

An offer of proof is a method of preserving a specific kind of error. When a court has excluded evidence, the offer of proof is a means by which the excluded evidence is inserted into the appellate record for the higher court to review. For example, let's suppose that the trial court excludes the testimony of an expert witness because the court found he was not qualified. There are three basic ways to make offers of proof:

i. Oral Testimony

An offer of proof may be made by oral testimony from a live witness. In this circumstance, the jury is not present. In a bench trial, the judge need not be present. The only critical person is the court reporter who will take down the testimony which will go into the record for appellate court review.

> *Example:* The expert witness would testify from the witness stand by responding to questions from the attorney proffering the evidence.

ii. Offer by Counsel

A lawyer may read into evidence, in narrative form, what the testimony would be had the witness been able to testify.

Example: Instead of the expert testifying from the witness stand, the attorney would read into the record what the expert would have said.

iii. Documentary Offer

In this case, an exhibit that has been properly marked (numbered) and authenticated, if necessary, is admitted as an offer of proof.

Example: If the expert had prepared a report, the report could be tendered as documentary evidence of her findings.

(b) Offer by Conduct

(c) Death, etc.

CHAPTER V

Character Evidence

A. Overview

What is Character Evidence? Character Evidence is defined as "evidence regarding someone's general personality traits or propensities, of a praiseworthy or blameworthy nature; evidence of a person's moral standing in a

> **Attention!**
> Character Evidence is one of the most difficult areas of the law to understand—second only to hearsay. It is also frequently tested on the bar examination.

community."[1] Put in lay terms, character evidence is often expressed in terms such as: "she's a liar; he's a thief; she's always angry; he's a killer; she's forgetful; he's violent;" etc. So, why do we care about character evidence? We care because of the concern that evidence of a person's character might be used to persuade a fact-finder that a person did something, or acted in some way, because of their "character."

For example, suppose that Judy had been convicted of stealing diamonds on four prior occasions. Currently, Judy is on trial for

---

[1] Black's Law Dictionary (10th ed. 2014).

theft—of diamonds (imagine that). As a prosecutor, you would certainly want the jury to hear about the prior convictions, right? Sure! The thought being, that if she committed four previous diamond thefts she, more likely than not, committed this one. A prosecutor would try to use those *prior convictions* to aid in obtaining *this* conviction.

The rules of character evidence attempt to protect the defendant in circumstances such as these. After all, those prior convictions do not mean that Judy committed this particular crime, do they?

There are a number of rules that qualify as governing character evidence:

Rule 404. Character Evidence; Crimes or Other Acts

Rule 405. Methods of Proving Character

Rule 412. Sex-Offense Cases: The Victim's Sexual Behavior or Predisposition

Rule 413. Similar Crimes in Sexual-Assault Cases

Rule 414. Similar Crimes in Child-Molestation Cases

Rule 415. Similar Acts in Civil Cases Involving Sexual Assault or Child Molestation

Rule 607. Who May Impeach

Rule 608. A Witness's Character for Truthfulness or Untruthfulness

Rule 609. Impeachment by Evidence of a Criminal Conviction

Character Evidence is impacted by three different things: 1) the purpose for which the character evidence is offered; 2) the method used to prove the character evidence; and 3) whether the case is a criminal case or a civil case.

B. The Character Evidence Prohibition

Rule 404(a)(1) sets out the initial prohibition: "Evidence of a person's character or character trait is not admissible to prove that on a particular occasion the person acted in accordance with the character or trait." That's the starting point. Now let's look at it visually.

C. A Visual Overview

The following is a visual overview of Rule 404(a) and its related rules. Do *not* skip over this chart. Seriously—do *not* skip it. Review it. Follow the paths to see how the rules work and interplay with each other.

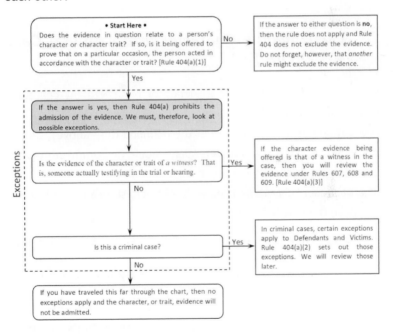

At this point, you have determined whether character or trait evidence will, or will not, be admitted. If it is inadmissible, your analysis is complete. If it is admissible, then you must turn to Rule

405. Rule 405 sets forth the methods by which one may prove character evidence. There is never a reason to look to Rule 405, unless you have determined that character evidence is admissible under 404.

Now, let's get back to determining whether or not an exception applies.

D. Exceptions in Criminal Cases

The first exceptions listed under the Rule [404(a)(2)(A), (B), and (C)] apply—potentially—to defendants and victims in criminal cases only. Do not forget that you will *not* be looking at these exceptions, unless you are attempting to admit evidence under 404(a)(1).

1. A Defendant's Character in a Criminal Case [404(a)(2)(A)]

A defendant may offer evidence of her pertinent character trait. Think about it—if you consider the policy behind the prohibition (consider the story of the diamond thief above), then it makes sense that a criminal defendant should be permitted to offer evidence of her own character. If the diamond thief thinks evidence of a particular character trait will help her, she can take the risk and have the evidence admitted.

Once admitted—the prosecutor may offer evidence to rebut it.

2. A Victim's Character Offered by a Defendant in a Criminal Case [404(a)(2)(B)]

Defendants may offer evidence of the victim's pertinent character trait. However, the admission of this evidence is subject to the limitations in Rule 412 (discussed in Section I, infra).

Just as with the defendant's character, once admitted—the prosecution may offer evidence to rebut it; and, the prosecution may offer evidence of the defendant's same character trait.

3. *A Victim's Trait of Peacefulness in a Homicide Case [404(a)(2)(C)]*

In homicide cases (and only in homicide cases—don't forget this), the prosecutor may offer evidence of the alleged victim's trait of peacefulness to rebut evidence that the victim was the first aggressor.

Example: Doug is on trial for the murder of Val. Doug's defense is that he was attacked by Val, and so he shot Val in self-defense. The prosecutor may put on evidence that Val was known throughout the community as a mild-mannered, peaceful individual that never raised his hand or his voice.

Go back and review the flowchart above. It should make more sense now.

E. Methods of Proving Character

Rule 405(a) does not govern *when* character evidence is admissible, only *how*—in what form—the evidence will be admitted.

1. *By Reputation or Opinion*

Under Rule 405(a), Character Evidence may be proved by testimony about 1) the person's reputation or, 2) an opinion about the person's character. The rule only permits reputation or opinion testimony, not specific examples. However, if that opinion or reputation testimony is admitted, then the court may (*not must*) permit questions about specific instances of relevant conduct.

What does this mean? Let's say that character evidence is permitted as to John Doe. Wally the Witness testifies that, in his opinion, John is a dishonest person (opinion testimony). On cross-examination, Wally could be asked about the time that John found a wallet on the street with $500 in cash and turned it into the police station (a specific instance of conduct).

2.   *By Specific Instances of Conduct*

Rule 405(b) permits specific instances of a person's conduct when a person's character or character trait is an essential element of a charge, claim, or defense. What in the world does that mean? Well, fortunately you (and I) aren't the only ones that find that language a bit confusing. The 9th Circuit gave us some guidance:

> "The relevant question [under Rule 405] should be: would proof, or failure of proof, of the character trait by itself actually satisfy an element of the charge, claim, or defense? If not, then character is not essential and evidence should be limited to opinion or reputation."[2]

F.   **Exceptions for Witnesses**

The exceptions for witnesses permitted by Rule 404(a)(3) apply to both civil and criminal cases. Rule 404(a)(3) provides that "[e]vidence of a witness's character may be admitted under Rules 607, 608 and 609." We will look at each of these, in turn:

1.   *Rule 607: Who May Impeach a Witness*

This rule permits anyone to impeach a witness—even the party that called the witness. This was promulgated because in the "old days" the party who called a witness also "vouched" for them. This prevented a party from attacking his or her own witness. The problem with the old rule was that sometimes a party wanted to call a witness that was not aligned with the party; a "bad guy" so

---

[2]   *U.S. v. Keiser*, 57 F.3d 847, 856 (9th Cir. 1995).

to speak. The old rule prevented that. Now, under Rule 607 a party may call, and impeach, a "bad guy."

2. Rule 608: A Witness's Character for Truthfulness or Untruthfulness

Always keep track of what gets you to this point. To be reviewing evidence under this rule, you have already determined that you are offering evidence which would be impermissible under 404(a)(1) and does not meet an

> **Attention!**
>
> Impeachment can take many forms. It can be that the witness is dishonest/untruthful, biased, or has contradicted himself. Although, for purposes of this discussion, we are only concerned with Character Evidence, Rule 607 is much broader, and is not limited to character evidence.

exception under 404(a)(2). Rule 404(a)(3), however, sets forth exceptions for witnesses under Rules 607 (discussed above), 608 and 609. Let's turn our attention to Rule 608.

Rule 608 is divided into two areas: a) reputation or opinion evidence, and b) specific instances of conduct.

Rule 608(a) provides that:

> **(a) Reputation or Opinion Evidence.** A witness's credibility may be attacked or supported by testimony about the witness's reputation for having a character for truthfulness or untruthfulness, or by testimony in the form of an opinion about that character. But evidence of truthful character is admissible only after the witness's character for truthfulness has been attacked.

Suppose you have a witness and you want to offer evidence with regard to her truthfulness or untruthfulness. Rule 404(a)(3), which led us to Rule 608, permits evidence in both civil and criminal cases. Rule 608(a) identifies *what*, *when*, and *how* it is permitted.

What:	1)	The witness's reputation for truthfulness.
	2)	The witness's reputation for untruthfulness.

When:	1)	Evidence as to untruthfulness may be *attacked* at any time.
	2)	Evidence as to truthfulness *may only be offered* after the witness's character for truthfulness has been attacked.

How:	1)	Testimony about that witness's reputation.
	2)	Testimony in the form of an opinion about that witness's character.

Do not forget that Rule 609 applies to all witnesses, whether they are the defendant or the victim.

3. *Rule 609: Impeachment by Evidence of a Criminal Conviction*

i.   The Exceptions

The last exception for witnesses applies when a witness's character is being attacked by evidence of a prior criminal conviction. This is a fairly long rule. We will examine it in pieces.

> **Rule 609.**
>
> (a) **In General.** The following rules apply to attacking a witness's character for truthfulness by evidence of a criminal conviction:

(1) for a crime that, in the convicting jurisdiction, was punishable by death or by imprisonment for more than one year, the evidence:

    (A) must be admitted, subject to Rule 403, in a civil case or in a criminal case in which the witness is not a defendant; and

    (B) must be admitted in a criminal case in which the witness is a defendant, if the probative value of the evidence outweighs its prejudicial effect to that defendant; and

(2) for any crime regardless of the punishment, the evidence must be admitted if the court can readily determine that establishing the elements of the crime required proving—or the witness's admitting—a dishonest act or false statement.

Rule 609(a)(1)

What: | A criminal conviction when the crime—in the convicting jurisdiction—was punishable by death or imprisonment for more than one year. *Note: The rule does not require that the person actually served for more than one year in prison—only that the punishment could have been for more than a year.* [FRE 609(a)(1)]

When: | In a civil case—the evidence *must* be admitted—if it survives a Rule 403 analysis. [FRE 609(a)(1)(A)]

In a criminal case—if the witness is not the defendant—the evidence must be admitted if it survives a Rule 403 analysis. [FRE 609(a)(1)(A)]

In a criminal case—if the witness is the defendant—the evidence *must* be admitted if the probative value outweighs its prejudicial effect to that defendant. [FRE 609(a)(1)(B)] Notice that this rule gives us what we call a "reverse 403" analysis because it is similar to Rule 403, but the requirement is flipped.

How:	The evidence can be in any form: testimonial or documentary.

* * *

Rule 609(a)(2)

What:	Any criminal conviction with elements of dishonesty or false statements regardless of the punishment. [FRE 609(a)(2)]

When:	In either a civil case *or* a criminal case—the evidence must be admitted—if the court can readily determine that establishing the elements of the crime required proving—or the witness's admitting—a dishonest act or false statement.

How:	Either testimonial or documentary evidence.

ii. Limitations Based on Time [609(b)]

The exceptions under Rule 609(a) have a specific limitation as to the admission of the evidence and the limitation is governed by Rule 609(b):

> **Rule 609.**
>
> **(b) Limit on Using Evidence After 10 Years.** This subdivision (b) applies if more than 10 years have passed since the witness's conviction or release from confinement for it, whichever is later. Evidence of the conviction is admissible only if:
>
> **(1)** its probative value, supported by specific facts and circumstances, substantially outweighs its prejudicial effect; and
>
> **(2)** the proponent gives an adverse party reasonable written notice of the intent to use it so that the party has a fair opportunity to contest its use.

a. Time Period

The limitation under 609(b) only applies if more than ten years have passed since: 1) the witness's conviction; or 2) the witness's release from confinement for it—whichever is later.

To understand this ten-year time period, let's look at an example:

John Doe is convicted of the crime of fraud:

Conviction	Imprisonment	Release	Date of Trial
01-31-05	01-31-06	01-31-09	05-15-17

The conviction is more than ten years old; however, the date of release is less than ten years old. Therefore, the limitations of

609(b) would not apply, and the prior conviction would be admissible. You might be wondering; how could the date of conviction ever be the date we would look at? After all, you couldn't be convicted after your release, could you? There are (at least) two circumstances when the date of conviction may be the date we apply under the rule: 1) a defendant may be sentenced to "time served," which might have ended before the actual conviction date (the date of the conviction is the later date of the two); 2) a defendant may not have to serve any time, so the conviction date is all that would matter. Remember that under Rule 609(a)(1), the crime must be "punishable by . . . imprisonment for more than one year," not actually *imprisoned* for more than one year (or even imprisoned at all).

b.　Admissibility

Assuming the time period for the conviction applies, then the court *must* admit the evidence subject to the limitations set forth in the applicable subparts under Rule 609(a)(1)(and (2).

When 609(b) applies, things are very different. Under this subpart, the evidence will only be admissible if two conditions are met:

1)　The probative value of the evidence (supported by specific facts and circumstances) substantially outweighs the prejudicial effect of the evidence (another Reverse 403); and

2)　The proponent of the evidence gives the adverse party written notice of the intent to use it so that the party has a fair opportunity to contest its use.

iii. Limitations Based on Pardon, Annulment, or Certificate of Rehabilitation [609(c)]

Rule 609(c) sets forth additional limitations. If Rule 609(c) applies, then evidence of the conviction will *not* be admissible.

Evidence of the conviction will not be admissible when:

Evidence not admissible per 609(c)(1)

1) The conviction has been the subject of a pardon;

2) The conviction has been the subject of an annulment;

3) The conviction has been the subject of a certificate of rehabilitation; or

4) The conviction has been the subject of a procedure that is the equivalent of a pardon, annulment or certificate of rehabilitation;

AND

• The person has not been convicted of a later crime punishable by death or imprisonment for more than one year;

OR

Evidence not admissible per 609(c)(2)

• The conviction has been the subject of a pardon, annulment, or other equivalent procedure based on a finding of innocence.

iv. Limitations Based Adjudication as a Juvenile [609(d)]

The next limitation is set out in Rule 609(d). Under this limitation, evidence of the previous conviction shall not be admissible if all four conditions are met:

1) The evidence is offered in a criminal case only;

2) The adjudication being offered into evidence is of a witness other than the defendant in the criminal case in which it is offered;

3) A conviction for the same offense for which an adult would be convicted, is admissible to attack any person's credibility; and

4) Admission of the evidence is necessary to fairly determine guilt or innocence. (*This last one is a bit subjective; for now, just make sure you learn the rule!*)

v.   Limitation Based on Pendency of Appeal [609(e)]

Rule 609.

(e)   Pendency of an Appeal. A conviction that satisfies this rule is admissible even if an appeal is pending. Evidence of the pendency is also admissible.

The last limitation under Rule 609 is not a limitation at all. Although a conviction is on appeal, the appeal does not affect the admissibility of the conviction. However, evidence of the pendency of the appeal would also be admissible.

G. Let's Get Visual—Again

Let's take a look at another visual representation of where we have been:

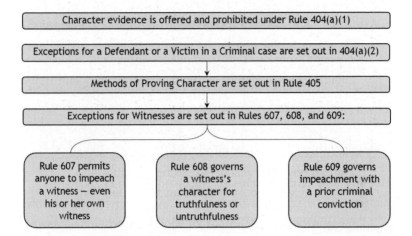

The rules you have just covered (404, 405, 607, 608, and 609) are the basic Character Evidence rules—the foundation of Character Evidence. Unfortunately, we are not done yet.

H. Crimes, Wrongs, or Other Acts [404(b)]

1. The Prohibition [404(b)(1)]

While 404(a) addresses "Character Evidence" such as reputation and opinion concerning a person's honesty and integrity, Rule 404(b) addresses specific conduct.

> **(b)   Crimes, Wrongs, or Other Acts.**
>
> (1)   Prohibited Uses. Evidence of a crime, wrong, or other act is not admissible to prove a person's character in order to show that on a particular occasion the person acted in accordance with the character.

This is a different prohibition. In other words, Rule 404(b)(1) addresses specific instances of conduct—as opposed to opinions or reputations addressed by Rule 404(a)(1). This prohibition covers almost anything. It provides that

> **Attention!**
> Both the 3rd and 10th Circuits have held that evidence which is admitted under Rule 404(b) may relate to conduct occurring either before or after the charged offense.

evidence of a 1) crime; 2) wrong (how vague is that?); or 3) other act (there we go with a broad term again) is not admissible. For anything? No, no, no! This evidence is not admissible to "show that on a particular occasion the person acted in accordance with the character."

Now we can go back to our example with Judy the jewel thief. You may remember that Judy had been convicted of theft (stealing diamonds) on four prior occasions. Currently, Judy is on trial for theft—of diamonds. As a prosecutor, you want the jury to hear about the four prior convictions, right? Sure! The reasoning being that if Judy committed four previous diamond thefts she, more likely than not, committed this one. A prosecutor would try to use those prior convictions to aid in obtaining this conviction. However, Rule 404(b)(1) prohibits the admissibility of those prior crimes if the prosecution is trying to show that, because Judy committed those prior crimes, she must have committed this jewel heist for which she is currently on trial.

While this is an example of the prohibition of 404(b)(1), guess what? There are exceptions.

2. *The Exceptions [404(b)(2)]*

Rule 404(b)(2) sets out the exceptions to the prohibition, which apply to both criminal and civil cases. Rule 404(b)(2) provides a list of exceptions, but they are only examples. That is, the list is not an exclusive list of exceptions to admit evidence otherwise prohibited by Rule 404(b)(1). When evidence is offered for any other purpose such as proving: 1) motive; 2) opportunity; 3) intent; 4) preparation; 5) plan; 6) knowledge; 7) identity; 8) absence of mistake; or 9) lack of accident, then the Rule does not prohibit its admission.

What exception may apply to Judy so that her four prior theft convictions are admissible? Suppose that at all of Judy's previous thefts, she left a long-stemmed white rose behind, as her "signature." On the most recent occasion, the thief also left a long-stemmed white rose. Evidence of the previous thefts and the "signature" roses would suggest that Judy also committed this theft. The roses would help prove "identity." Does this mean that it was definitely Judy? Certainly not. A "copy-cat" might have left the white rose to throw the police off of her trail to implicate Judy. Nevertheless, under the Rule, the evidence of the previous thefts would be admissible as an exception.

i.   The Notice Requirements

There are notice requirements when seeking to admit evidence based on the exceptions listed under Rule 404(b)(2), but the notice requirements apply only in criminal cases. For this evidence to be admissible in a criminal case, if requested by the defendant, the defendant must be given:

1)   Reasonable notice of the general nature of any such evidence that the prosecution intends to offer at trial; and

2)   The notice must be given before trial—or during trial if the court, for good cause, excuses lack of pretrial notice.

There you have it, that's Character Evidence. No—not really. There is still more. Sorry.

I.   The Rape Shield Law

In the "old" days—(sarcasm alert) nobody does this now—criminal defense attorneys would often stop at nothing to defend their client. In cases involving sexual assault, defense lawyers would, on occasion, go on the "attack" of the victim and attempt to make her out as the aggressor. The idea being that whatever may have happened on the occasion in question in the current trial should be considered in light of past relationships. If, for example, a woman was sexually active then on the occasion in question, her lack of consent should be considered in light of her past sexual exploits.

The rule-makers figured out that a rule was needed to stop this tactic. And now we have it—Rule 412. Its unofficial title is the "Rape Shield Law." The intent is, under appropriate circumstances, to "shield" the victim. Now, let's turn to the rule.

1.   *Sex-Offense Cases [Rule 412]*

i.   The Prohibition [412(a)]

In both civil and criminal cases involving alleged sexual misconduct, Rule 412 prohibits evidence to prove:

1)   That a victim engaged in other sexual behavior; or

2)   A victim's sexual predisposition.

You can see how this prohibition goes right to the heart of the tactics employed by defense counsel—in the "old" days.

ii.   The Exceptions in Criminal Cases [412(b)(1)]

In criminal cases, Rule 412(b)(1) provides three circumstances in which evidence may be admitted:

1)   Evidence of specific instances of a victim's sexual behavior if offered to prove that someone other than the defendant was the source of semen, injury, or other physical evidence. [Rule 412(b)(1)(A)]

> *Example:* Johnny offers evidence from Tim that Jenny had "rough sex" with him the night before she had sex with Johnny. Therefore, the bruises she suffered came from Tim, not Johnny.

2)   Evidence of specific instances of a victim's sexual behavior with respect to the person accused of the sexual misconduct, if offered by the defendant to prove consent or if offered by the prosecutor. [Rule 412(b)(1)(B)]

> *Example:* Johnny offers evidence that he and Jenny had been intimate for the past six months. He offers this evidence to prove that the intercourse between Jenny and Johnny was consensual.

3)   Evidence which exclusion would violate the defendant's constitutional rights. [Rule 412(b)(1)(C)]

> *Explanation:* The exclusion of any evidence which violates the constitutional rights of the defendant would be improper. This provision merely sets out that premise in black and white.

iii. The Exceptions in Civil Cases [412(b)(2)]

While the exceptions [412(b)(1)(A)-(C)] apply only to criminal cases, Rule 412(b)(2) sets out the exception in civil cases:

> "In a civil case, the court may admit evidence offered to prove a victim's sexual behavior or sexual predisposition if its probative value substantially outweighs the danger of harm to any victim and of unfair prejudice to any party."

Quite specific, isn't it? No, not really. But, it's the rule. The exception does not stop there, however. First, go back and read it again. That portion of the rule applies only to "a victim's sexual behavior or sexual predisposition." It does not apply to a victim's sexual reputation. The last part of the rule addresses that:

> "The court may admit evidence of a victim's reputation *only if the victim* has placed it in controversy."[3]

There is a bit more to the rule—as to procedure, etc., but you can read those portions in the Appendix. Happy reading.

J. Sexual-Assault and Child-Molestation Cases

You may recall that the reason we have prohibitions on Character Evidence is because we don't want—for example—a jury convicting a defendant of the accused crime simply because he committed a similar crime previously. That policy does not hold true in cases involving sexual-assault and child-molestation cases.

1. Sexual Assault Cases—Criminal [Rule 413]

Rule 413 governs character evidence in sexual assault cases. Unlike the previous rules, this is a permissive rule, not a prohibition.

---

[3]   FRE 412(b)(2) (emphasis added).

Also, it only applies to criminal cases. Here is a breakdown of the rule:

<u>Requirements</u>

1)   Criminal case; and

2)   Defendant accused of sexual assault.

<u>Result</u>

- Court may admit evidence that the defendant committed any other sexual assault.

As you can see, this rule is almost the "opposite" of the former rules prohibiting character evidence.

You will find that the rule does not have a time limit as to how old the former sexual assaults must be to prevent admission. In fact, the Second Circuit touches on this and held that a sexual assault which occurred 16 to 20 years before the trial was not too old to be admissible.[4]

2.   *Child-Molestation Cases—Criminal [Rule 414]*

Rule 414 is much like Rule 413.

<u>Requirements</u>

1)   Criminal case; and

2)   Defendant accused of child molestation.

<u>Result</u>

- Court may admit evidence that the defendant committed any other child molestation.

---

[4]   *U.S. v. O'Connor*, 650 F.3d 839, 853 (2nd Cir. 2011).

The Fourth Circuit held that when analyzing evidence to be admitted under per Rule 414, under a Rule 403 analysis, a court should consider a number of factors, including:

1)   The similarity between the previous offense and the charged crime;

2)   The temporal proximity between the two crimes;

3)   The frequency of the prior acts;

4)   The presence or absence of any intervening acts; and

5)   The reliability of the evidence of the past offense.[5]

While Rules 413 and 414 address the admission of these kinds of evidence in criminal cases, Rule 415 addresses the admission of both types of evidence in civil cases.

3.   *Sexual Assault or Child Molestation Cases— Civil [Rule 415]*

This rule addresses evidence of sexual assault *and* evidence of child molestation. This rule has requirements that are similar to Rules 413 and 414.

Requirements

1)   Civil; and

2)   Case involves a claim for relief based on a party's alleged:

a.   sexual assault; or

b.   child molestation.

Result

•   Court may admit evidence that the defendant committed any other sexual assault or child molestation.

---

[5]   *U.S. v. Kelly,* 510 F.3d 433, 437 (4th Cir. 2007).

CHAPTER VI

Hearsay

A. Overview

Hearsay is likely to be the most difficult area of Evidence that you will study. It's just hard. So, what *is* hearsay? The rules define it and govern when hearsay will and will not be admissible. But what *is* it?

Hearsay refers to an out-of-court statement. Yes—it's a little more complicated than that, but it's a start. Assume that Tina says she saw you steal cash from a cash register. Next thing you know, you are being prosecuted for theft based on Tina's statement. However, Tina is not in court; she is not a witness; and she is nowhere to be found. Nevertheless, you are prosecuted and convicted for theft—all based on Tina's out-of-court statement. This "crazy" hypothetical is rooted in a real case that happened many, many years ago in England[1] and forms the basis of what we now call the "hearsay" rule.

The foundation of the hearsay rule is that *out-of-court statements* generally should not be used, unless there is a likelihood

---

[1] *The Trial of Sir Walter Raleigh*, 2 How. St. Tr. 1, 27 (1603).

that the statements are accurate. Accuracy means more than just "telling the truth." The reliability of out-of-court statements has to do with the degree to which believing the evidence requires unsupported reliance upon the four *things* we call the "testimonial capacities" of the person making the statement. These are known as: sincerity, perception, narration, and memory. In fact, the hearsay rule and its exceptions are designed to overcome or redress these capacities when the testimony would otherwise be reliable.

By way of example, consider Tina's statement about stealing cash from the cash register. Let's examine the testimonial capacities in light of her hearsay statement:

1) Sincerity ------- Maybe she lied; (she wanted you to get into trouble)

2) Perception ---- Maybe her vision was bad; (she thought she saw you but she actually saw someone else that looked like you)

3) Narration ------ Maybe she said it was you; (but she really meant to say Bob); or

4) Memory -------- Maybe she remembered that you took the cash (but it was really Bob that stole from the register).

In theory, when statements that would otherwise be excluded under the hearsay rule are admitted, they are admitted on the basis that the exceptions have "safeguards" against these testimonial capacities' proclivities for inaccuracy.

An understanding of hearsay requires that you be very familiar with the rules governing hearsay and also recognize the process for analyzing hearsay.

Hearsay gives us another perfect opportunity for a flowchart. To begin with, hearsay is governed by Article VIII, Rules 801–805 and 807.

Consider this *very basic* overview of a hearsay analysis. Take the time to read, and try to understand each step. After you read the steps, and think about the "flow," then move onto the next section.

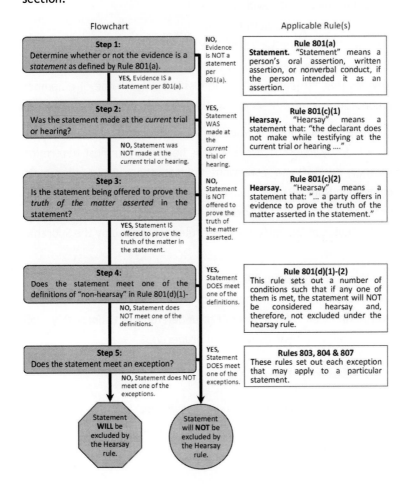

Flowchart

Step 1:
Determine whether or not the evidence is a *statement* as defined by Rule 801(a).

YES, Evidence IS a statement per 801(a).

NO, Evidence is NOT a statement per 801(a).

Step 2:
Was the statement made at the *current* trial or hearing?

NO, Statement was NOT made at the *current* trial or hearing.

YES, Statement WAS made at the *current* trial or hearing.

Step 3:
Is the statement being offered to prove the *truth of the matter asserted* in the statement?

YES, Statement IS offered to prove the truth of the matter in the statement.

NO, Statement is NOT offered to prove the truth of the matter asserted.

Step 4:
Does the statement meet one of the definitions of "non-hearsay" in Rule 801(d)(1)-

NO, Statement does NOT meet one of the definitions.

YES, Statement DOES meet one of the definitions.

Step 5:
Does the statement meet an exception?

NO, Statement does NOT meet one of the exceptions.

YES, Statement DOES meet one of the exceptions.

Statement **WILL** be excluded by the Hearsay rule.

Statement will **NOT** be excluded by the Hearsay rule.

Applicable Rule(s)

Rule 801(a)
Statement. "Statement" means a person's oral assertion, written assertion, or nonverbal conduct, if the person intended it as an assertion.

Rule 801(c)(1)
Hearsay. "Hearsay" means a statement that: "the declarant does not make while testifying at the current trial or hearing ...."

Rule 801(c)(2)
Hearsay. "Hearsay" means a statement that: "... a party offers in evidence to prove the truth of the matter asserted in the statement."

Rule 801(d)(1)-(2)
This rule sets out a number of conditions such that if any one of them is met, the statement will NOT be considered hearsay and, therefore, not excluded under the hearsay rule.

Rules 803, 804 & 807
These rules set out each exception that may apply to a particular statement.

B. The Rule Against Hearsay

Now that you have seen an overview, let's break down the hearsay rule into discreet parts. The starting point in any analysis is a determination of whether a particular piece of evidence is hearsay by using the definition in the rule. But why do we care? The

> **Attention!**
> Remember, even if you determine that the hearsay rules do not exclude a piece of evidence, you must make sure there is no other rule that could exclude the evidence.

answer lies in Rule 802. This is the "rule against hearsay." This rule provides that "[h]earsay is not admissible unless" one of a number of conditions is met.

The starting point is whether the piece of evidence *is* hearsay as defined by Rule 801. Next, if it is hearsay, you must determine whether one of the conditions is met that would permit its admission. Rule 802 tells us that hearsay will not be admissible unless any of the following provide otherwise: a federal statute, the Federal Rules of Evidence, or other rules prescribed by the Supreme Court.

Don't worry about 802 yet. Let's spend some time with 801. The first four steps in the above flowchart all address Rule 801. It's a very important rule. If you fail to understand 801 thoroughly, you cannot analyze a hearsay question properly.

C. Defining Hearsay

Before you can determine what is *not* hearsay (Section D below), you must determine what *is* hearsay. At the most basic level, for evidence to be considered hearsay, it must satisfy four requirements of Rule 801:

(1) It must be a statement [Rule 801(a)];

(2) The statement must have been made by a declarant [801(b)];

(3) The statement must have been made out of court [Rule 801(c)(1)]; and

(4) It must be offered for the truth of the matter asserted in the statement [Rule 801(c)(2)].

If all four (4) of these requirements are not met, then the statement is not considered hearsay. Now, let's look at each requirement in turn:

1. *The Requirement of a Statement [801(a)]*

Rule 801(a) defines a statement as "a person's oral assertion, written assertion, or nonverbal conduct if the person intended it as an assertion." This is a fairly straightforward rule, although it can—under the right circumstances—be tricky. The rule may be broken down into three parts:

(1) Who made the statement?

(2) What kind of statement is it? and

(3) Is it intended as an assertion?

(1) From where does the statement come?

The first inquiry, "Who made the statement?" is usually easy to ascertain. The "who" must be a person. That means that a parrot, that repeats what a human said, cannot produce hearsay. What about a printout? It comes from a computer, doesn't it? Yes, but if it was generated by a person and the printout reflects the statement of the person, then it would be considered a statement by a person. Don't get me wrong, you might be able make the same argument about a parrot but, it won't work. Now back to printouts. Does this mean that all printouts are statements? No. Consider automated printouts; maybe a stock report or measurements from a weather station. These examples would not be considered statements. They do not come from a "person" as required by the rule.

What about testimony of an animal's actions? For example, dogs that are trained to detect drugs or explosives are also trained to indicate what they encounter. In airports, drug sniffing dogs are trained to sit when they find something. That way no one is the wiser, but the dog has signaled to its handler that something has been found. However, because only persons can make statements, or in this case, an assertion, testimony as to the action of the dog would not be hearsay.

(2) What kind of statement is it?

The next inquiry is, "What kind of statement is it?" One can usually discern whether we are dealing with an oral, written, or non-verbal communication. The more difficult part is discerning whether the statement meets the final requirement of 801(a), which we discuss next.

(3) Is it intended as an assertion?

The last requirement of this part of the rule is that the statement be intended as an assertion. An assertion is an intent to communicate something. Determining whether an assertion has been made can be challenging. If Tom says, "I saw the dog bite the child," then the assertion intended by Tom is pretty clear. He is

> **Attention!**
> Do not make the mistake of thinking that questions can never be assertions. Some questions, particularly rhetorical questions, do not seek information but rather, are intended to be assertions.

trying to convey what he saw. What if Tom says, "What time is it?" Some might say that he is asserting that he does not know the time. But that's incorrect. There is no assertion there.

By definition, the determination of whether or not something is an assertion is subjective. The rule defines a statement as one in which the person *intends* it to be an "assertion." Suppose a person gets a paper cut and in the process, screams "Aggghhhh!" At first blush, you might think that the person is intending an assertion that he is in pain. But, in fact, there is likely no assertion here because it was more reactive or reflexive. There was no intent to communicate. The fact that someone screamed reactively (pain), does not mean she *intended* that scream to be a communication.

Now, consider nonverbal communication. The obvious example is a person communicating through the use of sign language. But sometimes, nonverbal communication can be less obvious. Has your mother ever given you the "look" that tells you she is mad? That is an example of nonverbal communication. She is communicating something, and you know quite well, what is being communicated.

Once you have determined that there was a statement made, it is necessary to identify who was the declarant. Rule 801(b) defines the declarant as the person making the statement in question. Assume Officer Jones wrote a police report. The report said that Sam, the victim, told Officer Jones that "The truck rear-ended me." At trial, Officer Jones testifies as to what Sam told him at the scene of the accident. The declarant is Sam, not the police officer. Why? Because we are concerned with who made the statement being offered. In this case, Sam's statement, "The truck rear-ended me" is being offered, so he is the declarant per Rule 801(b).

Now if you have determined that the evidence in question is a statement and have determined who the declarant is, the next step is to determine whether or not the statement was made outside of the current court proceeding where it is being offered. For this, we turn to Rule 801(c)(1).

2. *The* **Out of Court** *Requirement [801(c)(1)]*

This rule provides that in order for the evidence to be hearsay, it must be a statement that was not made at the current trial or hearing. This frequently confuses people so here is an example.

Suppose there is a wreck involving two people at an intersection. Immediately after the wreck, a witness named Judy is standing next to her friend Cindy. The following dialogue occurs at the scene of the accident:

Consider the following two scenarios based on the above example:

> Scenario 1:
>
> At trial, Cindy is on the witness stand and says: "The light was green when the little silver car went through the intersection."
>
> Scenario 2:
>
> At trial, Judy is on the witness stand and says: "Cindy told me the little silver car had the green light."

In Scenario 1, the statement contained in quotations would *not* meet the definition of a hearsay statement per Rule 801(c)(1) because Cindy made that statement at the trial. That is, Cindy testified as to what she personally observed at the time of the accident. Therefore, because her statement was not made out of court, as required by the definition, it is not hearsay and would not be excluded by the hearsay rule (Rule 802 only excludes hearsay).

However, in Scenario 2, Judy's statement is considered hearsay. Why? Because she is not testifying as to what she saw at the accident scene. Rather, she is testifying as to what Cindy had told her at the scene. So, Cindy's statement to Judy was not made at the current trial or hearing. Therefore, Cindy's statement meets the definition of 801(c)(1).

Now consider the following scenario:

Scenario 3:

Cindy, a witness on the stand at trial says: "I told Judy that the light was green when the car went through the intersection."

It might seem like this would not meet the definition of hearsay since Cindy is testifying as to what she had told Judy at the time of the accident. However, this *is* considered a hearsay statement under 801(c)(1) because she was testifying at the trial about her statement outside of court to Judy. If Cindy had simply testified that she observed that the light was green when the silver car went through the intersection, her testimony would not be hearsay.

I know, it's a lot to digest. Go back and look at the three scenarios again. An understanding of this fundamental concept is necessary to understand the rule.

Once it has been determined that a particular statement does, in fact, meet the out-of-court statement requirements, you must then analyze whether the statement meets the final requirement under 801(c)(2).

3. The "Offered for Its Truth" Requirement [801(c)(2)]

For many students, this rule is often the most difficult to analyze. Rule 801(c)(2) provides that for a statement to be hearsay, it must be offered "in evidence to prove the truth of the matter asserted in the statement." Consider the following:

Scenario 4:

Cindy, a witness on the stand at trial says: "The light was green when the car went through the intersection."

The critical question you must be able to answer is *why* a particular statement is being offered. Why would you be offering the statement in Scenario 4 above? Suppose this is a lawsuit and your client has been sued for negligence. A key fact might be the color of the light when your client drove through the intersection. If so, it is imperative that the color of the light, at the time your client drove through the intersection, be admitted into evidence. That color was green. You would be offering the statement, "The light was green when the car went through the intersection" for its truth; the light was, in fact, green.

Any case has certain fundamental issues:

(1) If civil, the essential elements of the cause of action;

(2) If criminal, the elements of the crime charged;

(3) The elements of any defense or affirmative defense; and

(4) The credibility of each witness.

Knowing why (the purpose) a particular statement is offered is essential to the determination of whether the statement is being offered to prove the substance of the statement. So, in Scenario 4, the color of the light is essential to prove the defense in a negligence case (that the light was, in fact, green), thus the statement is hearsay because it is being offered for the truth of the matter asserted.

4. *Statements Not Offered for Their Truth*

There are many reasons that a statement may be offered that have nothing to do with the truth of the matter asserted in the statement. There are six basic reasons (or purposes) that a statement might be offered for a reason other than the truth of the matter asserted: 1) to show the effect on the listener; 2) as a verbal act; 3) as verbal parts of an act; 4) for impeachment purposes; 5) as circumstantial proof of state of mind; and 6) to prove knowledge. Let's take a look at each of these and see if we can make some sense out of them.

Suppose you are challenging the credibility of a witness. Consider the following scenario:

> Scenario 5:
>
> Wally witnesses a shooting. After the shooting, he tells his friend Trent, "The shooter was wearing a grey sweatshirt and a baseball cap."
>
> At trial, Wally testifies that the shooter was "wearing a green sweatshirt."

Now you might want to offer the statement from Wally to Trent for different purposes. But suppose you want to demonstrate that Wally's testimony about the shooter wearing a green sweatshirt is not to be believed. In that case, you would be offering the testimony to *impeach* the witness. Maybe it was dark out, maybe Wally's vision was not so great. Regardless of the reason, you want to demonstrate that the testimony of Wally at the trial (that the shooter was wearing a green sweatshirt) is inaccurate. One way to impeach him is to demonstrate that he told someone outside of court something completely different. This out-of-court statement (that the "the shooter was wearing a grey sweatshirt") is being offered to impeach Wally. In that scenario, it is NOT hearsay because it is not being offered for the truth of the matter asserted. That is, you are not offering to prove that the shooter was wearing a grey sweatshirt but rather to demonstrate the inaccuracy (for whatever reason) of Wally's description.

> **Reality Check**
>
> There may be many reasons to attack the credibility of a witness that have nothing to do with lying. That is, the witness may not be trying to intentionally be deceptive. It could be the witness has poor memory, poor vision or poor hearing. Maybe the witness was impaired at the time. Lying does not need to be the only reason to impeach a witness.

Let's look at another example. Suppose you represent a client who has a grandfather with mental faculties on the decline. You wish to get him help, but state law requires a finding of incompetency before the state will provide help. As your client's lawyer, you must prove that your client's grandfather has mental issues. As part of your case, you have evidence that each morning your client's grandfather would walk outside of his home and greet passersby with a bow and introduce himself as King Henry, IV. You might find it hard to believe, but your client's grandfather is not King Henry, IV. His name is John Anderson. At trial, you wish to introduce the testimony of a neighbor who would walk his dog every morning in front of John's home. He will testify that every morning, John would bow and say, "Greetings from the Kingdom, I am King Henry, IV." It is your position that the statement will provide some evidence as to John's mental state.

Now let's look at the rule and how we would analyze this statement. The statement "Greetings from the Kingdom, I am King Henry, IV" was made in front of John's house which is outside of the current trial or hearing. So, the next question is, for what purpose is it offered? Is it offered for the truth of the matter asserted? If so, what is the assertion? The assertion is that "I (John) am King Henry, IV." So, if you are offering it for the truth of the matter asserted, you would be offering it to prove that John was, in fact, King Henry, IV. But you are not. You are offering it to prove only that he made such a statement. Period. Therefore, it cannot be hearsay.

Whether or not he actually believed it is a wholly different matter completely unrelated to the *hearsay* analysis. Maybe he was

> **Attention!**
> Bar Examiners love to test Hearsay. Hearsay questions are frequently found on the Multistate Bar Examination as well as many state exams. So, learn the rule!

kidding; maybe he was trying to drive the neighbor nuts; or maybe he believed it. None of that matters for purposes of the hearsay analysis. All that matters is for you to determine "for what purpose" the statement is offered. You are not offering it for the *truth* of the matter asserted. You are offering the statement because you want the court to find that John believed it. If he believed the statement, it would constitute some evidence that he was mentally incompetent. Again, none of that has anything to do with the hearsay analysis. Why? Because a statement can only be hearsay if it is offered for the truth of the matter asserted.

i.   To Show the Effect on the Listener

This is probably the easiest example of a statement offered for something other than the truth of the matter asserted. This is the

easiest because the description means what it says. When offering a statement not for the truth of the matter asserted, but rather, for the effect on the listener then—by definition—the statement is not hearsay. Let's illustrate this purpose

> **Attention!**
> You cannot perform a proper hearsay analysis unless you can answer the question: "For what purpose is the statement being offered?"

by example. Suppose John walks into a bar holding a gun, points it at Darrell and says, "I'm going to kill you." Before John can pull the trigger, Darrell pulls a gun and shoots John. At Darrell's trial for the murder of John, he seeks to introduce the statement that John made. In this case, it is being offered not for its truth—that John was going to kill Darrell. Rather, it's being offered to show the effect on Darrell (the listener)—that he was in fear for his life when he shot John (which would be important if he was pleading "self-defense").

ii.   **Verbal Acts (Legally Operative Words) and Verbal Parts of an Act**

This one is somewhat difficult. The term "Verbal Acts" refers to statements to which the law attaches rights or obligations simply because they were spoken. The fact that *the statement was made* has legal significance; when statements are offered for their truth, the relevance of the statement is tied to its veracity. When a statement is offered as a verbal act, whether or not it is true is irrelevant. The only thing that matters is whether or not the words were spoken.

The verbal part of an act consists of an act which includes both a conduct-part and a verbal-part. The verbal-part may compliment, or complete, the conduct-part. The conduct and the verbal utterance must be made by the same person.

a.   **Examples**

(1)   **Statements with Legal Significance**

David says to Peter, "I will mow your lawn for $65." Peter says, "Deal!" At the trial for breach of contract, Peter offers David's statement. Would this statement be hearsay? No because David's statement was a verbal act; it was an offer. There is legal significance attached to the speaking of the words, so David's statement does not constitute hearsay.

(2) Statements Made During the Course of a Criminal Act

Donny walks into a bank and says, "I have a gun. Give me all of the money in the till." Legal significance attaches to the words being spoken. Whether or not he actually had a gun (the truth of the matter asserted) does not matter. Rather, Donny's spoken words constitute a criminal act and are not hearsay.

(3) Legal Instruments

Checks that have been written on a bank account have been held to "fall squarely in this category of legally-operative verbal acts that are not barred by the hearsay rule."[2] When offering checks into evidence, they will not be considered hearsay.

(4) Ambiguous Acts

Words which accompany ambiguous acts might be verbal acts. For example, assume that Drew is on trial for trespass because he spent the night, unannounced, at Paula's house. Drew testifies that once, when visiting Paula, she said, "Whenever you are in town, feel free to stay at my place." Drew is offering the statement of Paula as a defense to the trespass case. Under these circumstances, Paula's statement would be an example of a verbal act and would not be hearsay.

Other examples of verbal acts may include statements regarding: making of a gift, offering of a bribe, fraud, perjury, and defamation.

iii. Impeachment (Prior Inconsistent Statements)

On occasion, out-of-court statements may be offered to impeach the testimony of a live witness. The critical inquiry here is, "what am I trying to prove here?" Or, to put it another way, "for

---

[2] *U.S. v. Benitez-Avila*, 570 F.3d 364, 367-68 (1st Cir. 2009).

what purpose is the evidence offered?" It could be that you believe the witness is untruthful, has a poor memory, has terrible vision or hearing, or a myriad of other reasons that the witness's testimony is not accurate. So, if you are trying to demonstrate that the witness's testimony is not accurate, then you are offering an out-of-court statement to prove that—inaccuracy (impeachment), not for the truth of the matter asserted. Let's look at an example.

a.   Example

Suppose that Witness testifies that the man running down the back alley was wearing a blue sweatshirt. And suppose that she previously told a friend that the man was wearing a green sweatshirt. You offer into evidence the statement that Witness told her friend. It's an out-of-court statement, so hearsay might be implicated. But *why* are you offering the statement? If you are offering it to prove the sweatshirt was green, then it would be considered hearsay because you *are* offering it for the truth of the matter asserted. On the other hand, if you are offering it to show that her testimony about the color of the sweatshirt is inconsistent— then it is not hearsay because you are offering it to impeach the witness's testimony with her prior inconsistent statement.

iv.   Circumstantial Proof of State of Mind

Statements which are used to show a person's state of mind are not hearsay— because—they are not offered for the truth of the matter asserted.

Let's say your neighbor, David Smith, goes around telling everyone that he is the famous movie star, Jean Claude Van Damme. Of course, he isn't. I know that, you know that, but unfortunately, he doesn't know that.

> **Caution**
>
> Do not confuse Circumstantial Proof of State of Mind with the Hearsay Exception under Rule 803(3) which is a statement being offered for the truth of the matter asserted.

Your neighbor's kids are trying to get him committed (so he can get help). They have to prove he's a bit "nuts." As evidence that David Smith is leaning towards the coo-coo side of things, the kids offer the statement that he told you (remember, *you* are the neighbor), "I'm Jean Claude Van Damme. You should see me in my most recent movie." So, *why* is the statement offered? It would likely not be offered for the truth of the matter asserted, because if it was it would be offered to prove that your neighbor is, in fact, Jean Claude Van Damme. However, it is more likely that being offered to prove his state of mind at the time he made the statement. Therefore, the statement would not be hearsay.

5. Who Is the "Declarant"?

Now we turn back to Rule 801(b) that defines "declarant." Recall that 801(c) requires that the declarant's statement be made somewhere other than at the current trial or hearing. So, what does "declarant" mean? Rule 801(b) defines a "declarant" as "the person who made the statement." This is a fairly straightforward rule. However, be cognizant of a few things. As previously discussed, animals cannot be declarants. If a talking parrot makes a statement, that statement will not be hearsay because, by definition, a statement must come from a *person*. This example reminds me of a story.

> One evening a burglar broke into a home. While he was ransacking the home, he heard a voice call out, "Jesus is watching you." A chill went down his spine. He stood frozen for a few minutes. Hearing nothing more he continued his thievery. Then, he heard it again, "Jesus is watching you." He swept his flashlight all around the room and eventually spotted a parrot. The burglar asked, "Did you say that?" The parrot squawked, "I'm just trying to warn you." The burglar replied, "Warn me? What's your

name little parrot?" The bird replied "Moses." The burglar laughed, "Moses—what kind of people would name a parrot Moses?" The parrot said, "The same kind of people that would name their Rottweiler Jesus."

Come on, that was funny! This rule also means that certain computer-generated printouts cannot be statements because they do not come from persons. Wait, but what about email, you ask? Email comes from a computer, so are they not statements? Yes, they *are* statements, but the distinction whether a person or automated system generates the ultimate statement. A person who inputs data that comes out of a computer in some form or fashion would ultimately be a statement. Emails, text messages, and any other sort of printout—even computer-generated—would be considered statements made by a declarant so long as a human generated it. On the other hand, a computer that takes readings, such as temperature or other types of data and generates a report, would not be hearsay because there no person (declarant) who generated the report.

6. *What Is a "Statement"?*

We now turn to 801(a). This portion of the rule defines a "statement" as "a person's oral assertion, written assertion, or nonverbal conduct, if the person intended it as an assertion." Believe it or not, there is more to break down here than meets the eye. Let's begin with discussing the *types* of assertions:

> **Attention!**
> Like the book? Dislike the book? Have suggestions, thoughts, ideas or questions? Please drop me a line at HappyEvidence@ gmail.com.

Oral

The rule provides that assertions may be oral. The spoken word is the most obvious, but realize that recorded statements also qualify as "oral" assertions.

Written Assertions

Written assertions can come in virtually any form. The rule does not distinguish between languages or methods of conveyance. A printout, a handwritten document, a typed document, or even words on a tablet or computer screen. Stone tablets would also qualify but would be quite heavy to carry into a courtroom.

Non-Verbal Conduct

Non-verbal conduct can be extremely challenging to analyze under the rule. Sign language would be considered non-verbal conduct. That's an easy example. But many examples are not as easy. Other non-verbal conduct can be used to convey messages. The critical question is whether or not the conduct is intended to convey a message (an assertion). Consider the following scenario.

> Back in 2014, the city of Flint, Michigan, changed its water source from the municipal system to the Flint River. Unfortunately, water from the river was apparently toxic from lead, which leached from old pipes. The Environmental Protection Agency (EPA) claimed that the river water, if properly filtered, was safe to drink.
>
> After the release of the EPA report, people were still weary of drinking the water, even filtered. To combat the concerns, the Mayor of Flint invited the press to his home. With cameras rolling, he removed a clear glass from his kitchen cabinets, filled it with filtered water from his tap, and immediately consumed it.

There is clearly non-verbal conduct. The drinking of the water from the tap is the conduct.

The crucial question for the non-verbal conduct and, for that matter, any conduct evaluated under this rule, is whether or not the declarant intended the conduct as an assertion. Do you think that the Mayor's invitation to the press and his drinking the water was intended as an assertion? Most definitely yes. *Any* non-verbal conduct, if intended as an assertion, meets the requirement of Rule 801(a).

i. What Is an "Assertion"?

Do not forget that, in addition to non-verbal conduct, oral, and written statements must also be intended as an assertion to qualify under the rule. Let's look at some examples.

If your partner, significant other, or spouse writes "XOXOXOXO" on a card and gives it to you, is that an assertion? Sure, it means hugs and kisses. If an emoji comes across your screen that resembles a happy face, is that an assertion? It might be. It all depends upon the declarant's intentions. Suppose that you accidentally cut yourself, and in the process of cutting yourself, you let out a scream—"Ahhhhh." Your scream is undoubtedly *verbal* conduct. However, it is very unlikely that in the act of screaming you intended to assert something. You might be thinking, "I was asserting that I am in pain." Of course, the verbal act reflected that you were in pain, but it is unlikely you made the sound to convey something via oral communication; or, in the words of Rule 801(a), you did not intend your scream as an assertion.

ii. Can a Question Be an Assertion?

Some questions may not be hearsay, while others may be hearsay. The critical determination is whether the person making the statement intended the question as an assertion. "[T]he grammatical form of a verbal utterance does not govern whether it fits within the definition of hearsay. . . . [T]he term 'matter asserted' . . . includes *both* matters directly expressed and matters the declarant *necessarily implicitly intended* to assert."[3]

---

[3]   *U.S. v. Torres*, 794 F.3d 1053, 1059 (9th Cir. 2015).

This means that when you ask your son, "Did you eat that piece of chocolate cake?"—you intended to make an assertion.

7. *Bringing 801(a), (b) and (c) Together*

You have now deciphered the first portion of Rule 801(a)-(c). This part of the rule must always be your starting point in any hearsay analysis:

i. Determine what the statement is (801(a));

ii. Determine who the declarant is (801(b));

iii. Determine if the statement was made other than at the current trial or hearing (801(c)(1); and

iv. Determine whether the statement is offered into evidence to prove the truth of the matter asserted in the statement (801(c)(2).

If a statement meets all of the above conditions, then that statement is hearsay. Now you must analyze the statement in light of 801(d). We will look at that part of the rule next but, until then, consider each of the examples set forth in the next section.

D. **Examples of Statements That Are and Are Not Hearsay**

Consider the following examples of statements:

- On the issue of breach of contract, a written contract executed by both parties. **✗ Not Hearsay**
  - ❖ This would not be hearsay because the contract is a legally operative fact.

- On the issue of whether the traffic light was red or green when the car traveled through the intersection, the witness **✓ Hearsay** testified that he was told by Wilma that the light was green.

❖ This would be **oral** hearsay because the statement is being offered to prove the truth of the matter asserted in the statement (the color of the light).

- On the issue of whether the transfer of Disney stock from Adam to Brandy was a gift or a sale, Brandy offers a statement made at the time of the transfer: "I'm giving you this share of stock as an employee bonus for your performance."

| ✖ | Not Hearsay |

❖ This would not be hearsay because the statement offered encompasses legally operative words of a gift and is not offered to prove the truth of the matter asserted.

- On the issue of whether the plastic baggie found on the Defendant contained methamphetamine, the prosecutor offers the report from the crime lab, which states that the baggie contained methamphetamine.

| ✓ | Hearsay |

❖ This would be **written** hearsay because the statement (the report) is being offered to prove the truth of the matter asserted in the statement (that the contents of the baggie was methamphetamine).

E. Statements That Are Not Hearsay

Once you have determined that a particular statement is "hearsay" as defined by Rule 801(a)-(c), you must then determine whether or not it is considered "not hearsay" under Rule 801(d). What?!?!?! Confused? Don't be. Certain statements that meet the definition of hearsay will still be considered *not hearsay* because of the rules. Historically, academics frequently call these kinds of statements "non-hearsay." However, the rule uses the phrase "not hearsay." Unfortunately, that phrase causes all kinds of confusion. Many states simply call this part of Rule 801(d) "exceptions." So, it might help to think of them as exceptions.

> **I'm Confused**
>
> It may be easier to think of statements that fall under 801(d) as "exceptions." Academics often call these statements "non-hearsay." The Federal Rules call them "Not Hearsay." Just figure out what your Professor calls them and use that term.

1. Recap

Let's recap. Once you determine that a statement is hearsay as determined by Rules 801(a)-(c), your next step is to analyze the statement under Rule 801(d). If—and only if—the statement meets one of the sections of 801(d), then that statement will be considered "non-hearsay." [Please read the *I'm Confused* box now!]

F. Breaking Down Rule 801(d)

There are two major subsections to 801(d) which define certain statements as "not hearsay." Subsection 801(d)(1) addresses statements which are made by a witness who was also the declarant; subsection 801(d)(2) governs statements which are made by an opposing party.

1. A Declarant-Witness's Prior Statement [801(d)(1)]

There are four different types of statements that will be considered "non-hearsay" under Rule 801(d)(1). Each of these is a statement that was made *by the witness* prior to the trial at which they are being offered: (A) inconsistent statements; (B)(i) statements used to rebut a charge of recent fabrication, (B)(ii) to rehabilitate a witness; or (C) statements of identification. These types of statements are categorized as "declarant-witness's prior statements."

> **I'm Confused**
>
> Why would we use the term "non-hearsay" when the rule uses the phrase "not hearsay?" The answer is this; when you refer to a statement as "not hearsay" most people would assume you meant that it did not meet one of the requirements of 801(a)-(c). But if you use the term "non-hearsay," then we will assume that you mean the statement DOES meet the requirements of 801(a)-(c) AND meets one of the exceptions in 801(d). This will make more sense after you have studied 801(d).

i.   Prior Inconsistent Statement

The first type of statement is found in Rule 801(d)(1)(A):

Rule 801(d)(1)(A).

➤   The declarant testifies at the current trial or hearing; *[801(d)(1)]*

➤   The declarant is subject to cross-examination; *[801(d)(1)]*

➤   The statement is *inconsistent* with the declarant's in-court testimony; and *[801(d)(1)(A)]*

> ➢ The statement was given under penalty of perjury at: *[801(d)(1)(A)]*
>   - a trial;
>   - a hearing;
>   - another proceeding; or
>   - a deposition.

Remember the statement being analyzed was given somewhere other than *this* court proceeding. The fact that it may have been given in a courtroom would not exclude it from meeting the requirements of 801(a)-(c). However, once (a) through (c) have been met, if the conditions of 801(d)(1)(A) are met, then the statement would be *non-hearsay*.

ii.   Prior Consistent Statement

The second type of statement is found in Rule 801(d)(1)(B)(i):

> **Rule 801(d)(1)(B)(i).**
> ➢ The declarant testifies at the current trial or hearing; *[801(d)(1)]*
> ➢ The declarant is subject to cross-examination; *[801(d)(1)]*
> ➢ The statement is consistent with the declarant's in-court testimony; and *[801(d)(1)(B)]*
> ➢ The statement is offered to rebut an express or implied charge that the declarant recently fabricated it or acted from a recent improper influence or motive in so testifying. *[801(d)(1)(B)(i)]*

This Rule is best explained by example. Suppose Husband and Wife are involved in a hotly contested divorce case. *(Yes, I realize that this is the study of the federal rules, and federal courts do not hear divorce cases. But, stick with me. It's a good example.)* Wife alleges that Husband has been abusive. Husband alleges that Wife is making up the allegations and has never made these allegations prior to this case (an express or implied charge that declarant (wife) recently fabricated the allegations). In response to the charge of recent fabrication, the Wife offers statements that she had previously made to a counselor, where she told the counselor that her Husband was abusive.

These statements, which would otherwise be considered hearsay under 801(a)–(c), would now be considered "non-hearsay" because the wife's prior statement to her counselor is consistent with her in-court testimony (801(d)(1)(B)(i)).

iii. Prior Consistent Statement to Rehabilitate Declarant's Credibility

The third type of statement is found in Rule 801(d)(1)(B)(ii):

Rule 801(d)(1)(B)(ii).

(1)   The declarant testifies at the current trial or hearing; *[801(d)(1)]*

(2)   The declarant is subject to cross-examination; *[801(d)(1)]*

(3)   The statement is consistent with the declarant's in-court testimony; and *[801(d)(1)(B)]*

(4)   The statement is offered to rehabilitate the declarant's credibility as a witness when attacked on another ground. *[801(d)(1)(B)(ii)]*

This type of statement is a prior consistent statement that is being used to rehabilitate a witness who has been attacked, based on a matter other than a recent fabrication or improper influence or motive. Examples that would apply would be factors including an alleged inconsistency in the witness's testimony or an allegation that the witness has some sort of sensory deficiency, such as vision or hearing.

iv. Prior Statement of Identification

The fourth type of statement is found in Rule 801(d)(1)(C):

Rule 801(d)(1)(C).

(1) The declarant testifies at the current trial or hearing; *[801(d)(1)]*

(2) The declarant is subject to cross-examination; and *[801(d)(1)]*

(3) The statement is one which identifies a person as someone the declarant perceived earlier. *[801(d)(1)(C)]*

The type of statement implicated by this rule is typically one of a photo identification, but can be other types of identification, such as a live visual line-up.

While statements that fall within the provisions of 801(d)(1)(A)-(C) are considered "non-hearsay", Rule 801(d) has an additional part that applies to statements made by an opposing party. (801(d)(2)).

2. *Statements by Opposing Party*

Rule 801(d)(2) sets out five different types of statements, any of which will be considered "non-hearsay." Each type has the same requirement—that the statement is offered *against an opposing party*. The subparts to the rule are variations of what legally constitutes a statement by an opposing party.

> **Rule 801(d)(2).**
>
> The statement is offered against an opposing party and:
>
> **(A)** was made by the party in an individual capacity;
>
> **(B)** is one the party manifested that it adopted or believed to be true;
>
> **(C)** was made by a person whom the party authorized to make a statement on the subject;
>
> **(D)** was made by the party's agent or employee on a matter within the scope of that relationship and while it existed; or
>
> **(E)** was made by the party's co-conspirator during and in furtherance of the conspiracy.
>
> The statement must be considered but does not by itself establish the declarant's authority under (C); the existence or scope of the relationship under (D); or the existence of the conspiracy or participation in it under (E).

i.   Made by a Party in an Individual or Representative Capacity [801(d)(2)(A)]

Statements that comply with this rule have historically been called an "admission by a party-opponent." The change to the current title, "statements by opposing party," reflects the fact that the statements need not actually be any kind of "admission." This rule provides that if a *party* to the lawsuit makes an out-of-court statement, and that statement is *offered against that party,* then the statement is not hearsay.

Note that although these are not necessarily "admissions," they can be. Regardless—commentators, academics, lawyers, etc., will frequently refer to statements that fall under this rule as "admissions." Any statement that meets a definition under the Rule qualifies.

There are only two requirements for admissibility under Rule 801(d)(2)(A): "a statement was made by a party, and the statement was offered against the party."[4]

a.   Personal Knowledge Not Required

A statement that falls under this rule will not be excluded based on a lack of personal knowledge because "trustworthiness is not the touchstone for admissibility of party admissions."[5]

b.   Person Cannot Offer His or Her Own Statement

Rule 801(d)(2)(A) does not "extend to a party's attempt to introduce his or her own statements through the testimony of other witnesses. . . . [I]f such statements were deemed admissible under [this rule], parties could effectuate an end-run around the adversarial process by, in effect, testifying without swearing an oath, facing cross-examination, or being subjected to firsthand scrutiny by the jury."[6]

ii.   Adoptive Admissions [801(d)(2)(B)]

A party adopts the statement of another person as his or her own. This adoption may be express or implied.

a.   Adoption by Silence

Under certain circumstances, a party may adopt the statement of another by silence. This adoption is an inference that may arise when the following facts occur:[7]

> (1)   "A statement is made in the [adopting] party's presence;

---

[4]   *Jordan v. Bivins*, 712 F.3d 1123 (7th Cir. 2013).

[5]   *Jordan v. Bivins*, 712 F.3d 1123, 1128 (7th Cir. 2013).

[6]   *U.S. v. McDaniel*, 398 F.3d 540, 545 (6th Cir. 2005).

[7]   *U.S. v. Miller*, 478 F.3d 48, 51 (1st Cir. 2007).

{this means that the adopting party *heard and understood* the statement}

(2) The nature of the statement is such that it normally would induce the [adopting] party to respond; and {this means that a reasonable person would have denied the statement under the circumstances}

(3) The [adopting] party nonetheless fails to take exception."
{this means that the person did not deny the statement}

b. Adoption of Written Statement

A party may adopt a written statement if the party uses the statement, or takes action in compliance with the statement. The adopting party need not have actually reviewed the document, but courts look to see "whether the surrounding circumstances tie the possessor and the document together in some meaningful way."[8]

iii. Vicarious Admissions [801(d)(2)(C)–(E)]

Admissions may also take the form of vicarious statements. These are statements which the party does not actually make but, instead, is made *for* him or her. In cases such as these, the statement will be considered as though it was made by the party whom it is offered against. Rules 801(d)(2)(C)-(E) cover these vicarious admissions made under the following circumstances: the statement was made by a person whom the party authorized to make a statement on the subject [801(d)(2)(C)]; the statement was made by the party's agent or employee [801(d)(2)(D)]; or the statement was made by a co-conspirator [801(d)(2)(E)]. We will look at a few different relationships to help understand this rule.

---

[8] *Transbay Auto Serv. v. Chevron*, 807 F3d 1113, 1119 (9th Cir. 2015).

a. Authorized Spokesperson

When a person is specifically authorized to speak on behalf of another person, then that statement may be offered against that party. [801(d)(2)(C)]

b. Agent/Employee

A statement made by ". . . a party's agent or employee on a matter within the scope of that relationship and while it existed" will be deemed an admission under 801(d)(2)(D). However, the "employee's [position] within the organization is not [a factor in] the Rule 801(d)(2) analysis."[9] The foundation to establish the agency relationship under Rule 801(d)(2)(D) is:

1) The existence of the agency relationship;

2) That the statement was made during the course of the relationship; and

3) That it relates to a matter within the scope of the agency [employment].[10]

c. Partners

Business partners may also be considered agents if, once a partnership is shown to exist, the proponent shows that the statement relates to matters within the scope of the partnership. If both of those requirements are met, one partner's statement will be binding on the other partners.

d. Co-Conspirators

Statements of co-conspirators are also considered "non-hearsay" [801(d)(2)(E)] when the following requirements are met:[11]

---

[9] *McDonough v. City of Quincy*, 452 F.3d 8, 21 (1st Cir. 2006).

[10] *Marcic v. Reinauer Transp.*, 397 F.3d 120, 128-29 (2nd Cir. 2005).

[11] *U.S. v. Bobb*, 471 F.3d 491, 498 (3rd Cir. 2006).

1) The conspiracy existed;

2) Both the defendant and the declarant were members of the conspiracy;

3) The statement was made in the course of the conspiracy; and

4) The statement was made in furtherance of the conspiracy.

The statement itself may be considered when determining whether or not the statement meets the requirements. However, "casual conversation" between two or more co-conspirators would not satisfy the "in furtherance of the conspiracy" requirement.[12]

(1) Criminal Activity Not Required

A reading of the co-conspirator rule [801(d)(2)(E)] might lead you to think that a conspiracy only involves a criminal activity. After all, doesn't "conspiracy" make you think of criminal endeavors? However, the rule itself demands no such requirement.

"[A]dmissibility under Rule 801(d)(2)(E) does not turn on the criminal nature of the endeavor. Instead, a statement may be admissible under [the Rule] if it is made in furtherance of a lawful joint undertaking. One can qualify as a joint venture for the purposes of [the Rule] merely by engaging in a joint plan—distinct from the criminal conspiracy charged—that was non-criminal in nature. Pursuant to this joint venture theory, a statement is not hearsay if it was made during the course and in furtherance of a common plan. . . with a party, regardless of the non-criminal nature of that endeavor."[13]

---

[12] *U.S. v. Holt*, 777 F.3d 1234, 1267 (11th Cir. 2015).

[13] *U.S. v. El-Mezain*, 664 F.3d 467, 502 (5th Cir. 2011).

Let's take another look at a simplified version of the flowchart reviewed in Section A based on what we know so far:

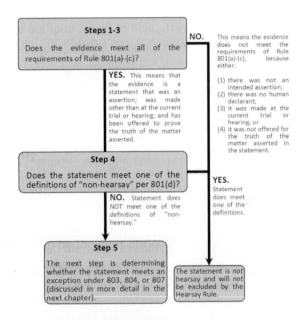

3.   *Hearsay Within Hearsay [805]*

Hearsay statements that *contain* hearsay statements are *hearsay within hearsay*. What? You may recall the previous scenario there was a wreck involving two people at an intersection. Immediately after the wreck, witnesses Judy and Cindy engaged in the following dialogue at the scene of the accident:

After the wreck, a police officer arrives and takes down a report. The report includes the following dialogue:

Police Officer   Cindy

The police officer writes a comprehensive report. At trial, the police report is offered into evidence to prove the truth of the matter asserted in the statements; this means that each statement is offered for the truth as to the color of the light. This scenario has multiple levels of hearsay:

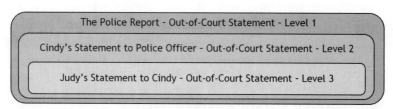

Why do we care about hearsay within hearsay? Because Rule 805 provides that "[h]earsay within hearsay is not excluded by the rule against hearsay if *each* part of the combined statements conforms with an exception to the rule." Put another way, where multiple levels of hearsay exist, each level must undergo a separate hearsay analysis. Each level must be: not hearsay, "non-hearsay," or meet an exception under Rules 803, 804 or 807.

Let's see how this would apply to the police report. The content in the report would be offered for the truth of the matter asserted, and would need to meet an exception (i.e., The business records exception) (See Chapter VIII). Assume that it does, in fact, meet an exception. The report would not be excluded by the hearsay rule! But—you are not finished. Although the report is not excluded—parts of the report *might* be excluded. Why? Because the report contains multiple levels of hearsay. This means that each statement in the report might contain another level of hearsay (in this case the statement from Cindy to the Police Officer and the statement from Judy to Cindy) that must be analyzed separately to determine whether each statement also meets an exception (which are discussed in detail in Chapter VII).

4. *Hearsay Terminology*

Now that you have a fundamental basis of the hearsay rules, it is a good idea to make certain you are comfortable with the terminology of the rules:

Type of Statement	*Description*
Not Hearsay	Statements that do not meet all of the parts of 801(a)-(c).
Hearsay	Statements that meet all of the parts of 801(a)-(c) but do not meet any of the "non-hearsay" definitions of 801(d). Note, these statements might be subject to an exception under 803, 804, or 807.
Non-hearsay	Statements that meet one of the definitions in either 801(d)(1) or (d)(2). The Rules refer to statements that meet one of these definitions as "not hearsay," which makes things confusing. Accordingly, this book (and some scholars) refer to statements that meet one of the definitions under 801(d)(1) or (d)(2) as "non-hearsay." It might help to think of these statements as meeting an exception.

| Exceptions | Hearsay statements that meet an exception under either 803, 804, or 807. These are covered in detail in the next chapter. |

CHAPTER VII

Hearsay Exceptions

A. Overview

Hearsay exceptions are exactly what they seem to be: exceptions to inadmissible hearsay pursuant to Rule 802 which prohibits the admission of hearsay unless the Federal Rules of Evidence (or a Federal Statute or the United States Constitution) provide otherwise. Well, here we have Federal Rules of Evidence that do, in fact, provide otherwise (Rules 803, 804, and 807). If a statement would otherwise be excluded under the hearsay rule and, if that statement meets one of these exceptions, then the evidence is excepted from the hearsay rule and is not excluded.

The federal rules have exceptions broken down into three primary categories. Unofficially, these are called the "strong" exceptions, the "weak" exceptions, and the residual exception. The strong exceptions are those listed in Rule 803, and are called "strong" because these exceptions will apply regardless of the declarant's availability to testify. The "weak" exceptions are set out in Rule 804 and apply *only* if the declarant is unavailable to testify. We will look at both rules in detail but, before we do, look at some visual cues to help you remember the differences.

"Strong" Exceptions	**Remember**	"Weak" Exceptions

Availability of declarant is not required.		The declarant *must* be unavailable to testify.

Finally, there is the residual exception, which is also referred to as the "catch all" exception, found under Rule 807. The residual exception is the "kitchen sink" exception. It's like throwing in everything you can think of, in an attempt to keep the hearsay from being excluded. It is rarely used, and can be considered the "weakest" exception. It is weak because courts will rarely find that a statement meets the requirements of the rule.

Now—let's begin by looking first at the "strong" exceptions.

B. "Strong" Exceptions to the Rule

Rule 803 contains 23 "strong" exceptions. The theory behind these exceptions is that the statements are reliable when they have been made under the circumstances set out in each exception. Whether you agree or not, it is part of the hearsay challenge to attack a statement and keep it out of evidence. Likewise, it is challenging to see how you might get a statement in evidence under one of these "strong" exceptions.

Rule 803 provides that "[t]he following [kinds of statements] are not excluded by the rule against hearsay, regardless of whether the declarant is available as a witness." As mentioned above, the part of the rule that says, "regardless of whether the declarant is available as a witness" is what makes the rule "strong." And when I say "strong," I'm talking Arnold Schwarzenegger strong (in his younger days). Therefore, the only real requirement is that a statement specifically meet the requirements of the individual exception. Although there are 23 exceptions found in Rule 803, this book covers only the ones commonly taught and tested.

1. *Present Sense Impression [803(1)]*

> *"A statement describing or explaining an event or condition, made while or immediately after the declarant perceived it."*

The key to applying this exception is realizing that it has a temporal requirement; that is, the statement must be made "while or immediately after" perceiving whatever happened. If one afternoon, a car runs a red light, and the declarant immediately says "Oh my, the car just ran that red light," then the statement would meet the requirement of 803(1). But, if the declarant had said hours later at dinner, "This afternoon, a car ran a red light," then the statement would not meet the requirements of 803(1). Why? Because the temporal requirement is not met. The declarant didn't make that statement "while" perceiving the incident, nor did she make it "immediately after" perceiving it. Instead, she made it hours later at dinner, so the exception does not apply.

i. The Requirements

This exception has only two requirements:

(1) The statement must describe, or explain, the event or condition; and

(2) The statement must be made:

    1. While the declarant perceived it; or

    2. Immediately after the declarant perceived it.

ii.   The Rationale

Some of the concerns with hearsay are not present with statements made under this exception. For example, a person may have a poor memory. It is believed that because the statement is made "while" or "immediately after" perceiving the event, any memory issues would not be present; the same is true with veracity. The odds are that the declarant didn't lie because she made the statement so close in time to the event. One court held that "[t]he theory underlying [this] exception is that substantial contemporaneity of event and statement negate the likelihood of deliberate or conscious misrepresentation."[1]

2. *Excited Utterance [803(2)]*

> *"A statement relating to a startling event or condition, made while the declarant was under the stress of excitement that it caused."*

The Excited Utterance exception is often confused with the Present Sense Impression exception. Do not be fooled—they are very different. Unlike the previous exception, this one does not have a temporal requirement. Instead, it has an emotional requirement. Specifically, the statement must have been made while the declarant was "under the stress of excitement that [the startling event or condition] caused." This could be hours or, potentially, days later.

---

[1]   *U.S. v. Boyce*, 742 F.3d 792, 796 (7th Cir. 2014).

i. The Requirements

This exception has three requirements:

1. There was a startling event;

2. The statement related to the startling event; and

3. The statement was made while under the stress of the excitement that it caused.

One court noted that for the exception to apply "the declarant's state of mind at the time that the statement was made [must] preclude conscious reflection on the subject of the statement."[2] Translation: The declarant was so "stressed" that she did not have time to *think* about her answer.

ii. The Rationale

"The rationale underlying [this exception] is that the excitement suspends the declarant's powers of reflection and fabrication, consequently minimizing the possibility that the utterance will be influenced by self-interest and therefore rendered unreliable."[3]

iii. Example

For example, consider the victim of a car wreck (a startling event). The victim could go into shock and at while in the hospital, maybe hours after having been admitted, blurt out that she "saw the car fly through the red light" (related to the startling event). If she was still under the stress of the excitement caused by the wreck, then the statement would qualify under the exception.

---

[2] *U.S. v. Alexander*, 331 F.3d 116, 122-23 (D.C. Cir. 2003).

[3] *Id.*

iv.   Distinction Between the Present Sense Impression [803(1)] and the Excited Utterance [803(2)]

Usually, there is not a significant delay between the statement and the event. Nevertheless, by its own terms, the rule does not dictate any time period. As one court noted, "[t]he excited utterance exception allows for a broader scope of subject matter coverage than the present sense impression [803(1)]. This is because the Federal Rules of Evidence provide that an excited utterance [803(2)] includes a statement "relating to" a startling event, . . . while the present sense impression exception [803(1)] is limited to 'describing or explaining' the event. . . ."[4] "[T]he temporal gap between the event and the utterance is not itself dispositive."[5]

3.   *Then-Existing Mental, Emotional, or Physical Condition [803(3)]*

> *"A statement of the declarant's then-existing state of mind (such as motive, intent, or plan) or emotional, sensory, or physical condition (such as mental feeling, pain, or bodily health), but not including a statement of memory or belief to prove the fact remembered or believed unless it relates to the validity or terms of the declarant's will."*

This is known, informally, as the "State-of-Mind" exception. Statements that meet the requirements of this exception should "mirror a state of mind, which, in light of all the circumstances, including proximity in time, is reasonably likely to have been the same condition" at the time the statement was made.[6]

---

[4] *U.S. v. Boyce*, 742 F.3d 792, 796 (7th Cir. 2014).
[5] *U.S. v. Alexander*, 331 F.3d 116, 122-23 (D.C. Cir. 2003).
[6] *Colasanto v. Life Ins. Co. of N. Am.*, 100 F.3d 203, 212 (1st Cir. 1996).

i. The Requirements

This exception has two requirements; the statements must:

1. Describe the state of mind, or the emotional, sensory, or physical condition of the declarant at the time the statement was made; and

2. Not be one of memory or belief to prove the fact remembered, unless it relates to the validity or terms of the declarant's will.

ii. The Rationale

It is believed that many of the traditional concerns with hearsay, such as incorrect perception, poor memory, etc., would not apply because the declarant would know his or her own state of mind.

iii. The Exception to the Exception

The rule itself provides an exception to the exception. That is, "a statement that would otherwise be admissible under [this exception] is *inadmissible* if it is a statement of memory or belief offered to prove the fact remembered or believed. . . . [A] witness may testify [that a declarant said] 'I am scared,' but not 'I am scared because the defendant threatened me.' "[7] The reason is that the first statement is simply the declarant's state of mind. The second encompasses much more; it expresses the declarant's belief that the defendant threatened her.

---

[7]   *U.S. v. Ledford*, 443 F.3d 702, 709 (10th Cir. 2005) (emphasis added).

4. Statement Made for Medical Diagnosis or Treatment [803(4)]

> "A statement that
>
> 1. is made for—and is reasonably pertinent to—medical diagnosis and treatment; and
>
> 2. describes medical history; past or present symptoms or sensations; their inception; or their general cause."

i. The Requirements

This exception has two requirements:

(1) The declarant's motive in making the statement is consistent with the purposes of promoting treatment; and

(2) The content of the statement must be one that would be reasonably relied upon by a physician for treatment or diagnosis.

ii. Exception Is Not Limited to Physicians

This exception has been extended to providers other than physicians including: psychotherapists, psychologists, therapists, and nurses. However, it would not apply to your mother treating your injury.

iii. The Rationale

The basis for this exception is the belief that persons seeking medical treatment (or diagnosis) do not have any motive to lie. Rather, they have a very strong motivate to tell the truth.

iv. Exceptions to the Exception

To be fair, the Rules do not actually have exceptions to 803(3). However, there are circumstances when statements you would think fall under the exception actually do not meet the exception because the evidence exceeds the realm of what is admissible under the Rule.

For example, statements which concern the *cause* of the injury will *frequently* meet the requirements for the exception, but statements which go beyond that and potentially identify an assailant would unlikely meet the requirements of the exception. If statements which identify the assailant are relevant to treating the victim's emotional or psychological injuries, then under those particular circumstances, those statements may meet the exception. Be cautious, however; such identifications would rarely have anything to do with a diagnosis or treatment.

5. *Record Recollection [803(5)]*

> *"A record that:*
>
> *(a) is on a matter the witness once knew about but now cannot recall well enough to testify fully and accurately;*
>
> *(b) was made or adopted by the witness when the matter was fresh in the witness's memory; and*
>
> *(c) accurately reflects the witness's knowledge.*
>
> *If admitted, the record may be read into evidence but may be received as an exhibit only if offered by an adverse party."*

The "I forgot" problem is one that my child experiences often. Apparently, the same problem happens to adults too—so much so, there is an exception for witnesses who need to can *refresh* their memory with virtually any kind of record when their recollection fails them.

i. The Requirements

This exception has a few requirements:

(1) The statement must be in a record (of some kind);

(2) The statement must be on a matter that the witness once knew about;

(3) The matter (contained in the statement) must be one that the witness cannot now recall well enough to testify fully and accurately;

(4) The statement was made at a time when the matter was fresh in the witness's memory; and

(5) The statement accurately reflects the witness's knowledge.

ii. The Rationale

It is believed that the record would be more accurate and reliable because it would have been made at a time when the facts were fresh in the witness's memory.

iii. The Procedure

This exception has an unusual provision as part of its procedures. If a statement from a record is admitted, then the witness may *only* read the statement at issue into the court record. The record used to refresh the witness's recollection would not be admitted as an exhibit unless the record is offered into evidence by the *adverse* party.

6. The Business Records Exception [803(6)]

To begin with, the name of this exception is *not* the Business Records Exception. It is actually called *"Records of a Regularly Conducted Activity."* So, why is it titled this way? Because it is common for practitioners to refer to it as the Business Records Exception.

> *"A record of an act, event, condition, opinion, or diagnosis if:*
>
> *(A) the record was made at or near the time by— or from information transmitted by—someone with knowledge;*
>
> *(B) the record was kept in the course of a regularly conducted activity of a business, organization, occupation, or calling, whether or not for profit;*
>
> *(C) making the record was a regular practice of that activity;*
>
> *(D) all these conditions are shown by the testimony of the custodian or another qualified witness, or by a certification that complies with Rule 902(11) or (12) or with a statute permitting certification; and*
>
> *(E) the opponent does not show that the source of information or the method or circumstances of preparation indicate a lack of trustworthiness."*

This exception is one of the most commonly used exceptions in trial. Under this exception, any writing (or record for that matter) which meets the requirements will not be excluded by the hearsay rule. However, this exception is full of pitfalls. One of the pitfalls is that records which fall into this category are frequently fraught with multiple levels of hearsay. Let's look at the requirements.

i.   **The Requirements**

This exception has a number of requirements:

(1)   The record must be of an act, event, condition, opinion, or diagnosis; [803(6)]

(2)   The record must have been made: [803(6)(A)]

   i.   *At the time* of the matter contained in the record; or

   ii.   *Near the time* of the matter contained in the record;

(3)   The record must have been made: [803(6)(A)]

   i.   *By someone with knowledge* of the matter contained in the record; or

   ii.   *Transmitted by someone with knowledge* of the matter contained in the record;

(4)   The record was *kept* in the course of a *regularly conducted activity* of the entity which made the record *(Note: The rule lists the various entities such as: business, organization, occupation, or calling, whether or not for profit);* [803(6)(B)]

(5)   It was a regular practice of that entity engaged in that activity to make that kind of record; *(Think about a nurse making notes on a chart in a hospital);* [803(6)(C)]

(6)   A qualified witness can testify that these requirements (1–5 above) were met; [803(6)(D)] and

(7)   The opponent does not show that the source of information or the method or circumstances of preparation indicate a lack of trustworthiness. [803(6)(E)]

ii.   Meeting the Requirements

It is important that *each* of the requirements is met for the exception to apply. Although this exception is traditionally, and informally, called the "business records exception" the exception is not limited to businesses. On the contrary, the exception applies to any "business, organization, or calling whether or not for profit." [803(6)(B)]. Does this mean that it could apply to your neighbor who makes teddy bears in her living room and sells them on eBay? Yes, it does.

When applying the requirements under the exception, it would be easier *not* to go through the subparts in numerical order. Actually, the requirements make more sense in this order:

STEP 1

(1)   Is the record sought to be admitted, one that is an "act, event, condition, opinion, or diagnosis?" [803(6)]

If so, then continue your analysis. If not, the exception would not apply.

STEP 2

(2)   Was the record "kept in the course of a regularly conducted activity of a business, organization, occupation, or calling, whether or not for profit?" [803(6)(B)]

This part of the exception is construed broadly. It could apply to hospitals, schools, universities, churches, restaurants, etc.

STEP 3

(3)   Was the making of the record "a regular practice of that activity?" [803(6)(C)]

Usually, this question is answered easily. But consider the case of *Palmer v. Hoffman*, where the railroad company prepared a report concerning an accident.[8] The United States Supreme Court held that the railroad was in the "railroad" business, not the business of preparing reports in preparation for litigation. Hence, the making of the record was *not* admissible because compiling an accident report was not a regular practice of that activity [running a railroad].

(4.1) Was the record made "at—or near—the time of the act, event, condition, opinion, or diagnosis?" [803(6)(A)] {Option 1}

STEP 4
(OPTION 1)

This part of the exception has an important temporal requirement. It has to be made either contemporaneously with the "act," etc. or near the time of the "act," etc. [803(6)(A)].

OR

(4.2) Was the record created from "information transmitted by someone with knowledge of the act, event, condition, or diagnosis." [803(6)(A)] {Option 2}

STEP 4
(OPTION 2)

If the information, that was ultimately documented, was obtained because someone with knowledge of the "act," etc. transmitted the information, then *this*

---

[8]   318 U.S. 109 (1943).

requirement has been met. If made at a time that is substantially later than the time when the "act," etc. occurred, then the information must have been transmitted by someone with knowledge.

If each of the four steps is met, then the record at issue must undergo one last analysis under this exception. Although the rule does not use the term "authentication," that is essentially what the final step does. Notably, most of the other hearsay exceptions do not have similar authentication provisions; however, this one does. And that leads us to step 5.

STEP 5

(5) Each of the above steps (1-4) must be shown by one of the following:

    i.   The testimony of the custodian of the records;

    ii.   The testimony of someone other than the custodian who is appropriately qualified;

    iii.   A certification that complies with 902(11);

    iv.   A certification that complies with 902(12); or

    v.   A statute that permits certification. [803(6)(D)]

Step five might seem challenging, but the custodian required by the rule "need not be the individual who personally gather[ed]. . . [the] business record[s]. The custodian of the records need not be in control of or have individual knowledge of the particular corporate records, but need only be familiar with the company's recordkeeping practices."[9]

STEP 6

(6)   The final analysis to this exception is Step 6, which it isn't really a step at all. It's more like a "what if" scenario when all of the previous steps are met. Can the opponent show that "the source of information or the method or circumstances of preparation indicate a lack of trustworthiness?" If so, the exception will not apply.

iii. The Rationale

Records that comply with this exception are thought to be reliable because "businesses depend on them to conduct their own affairs, so there is little if any incentive to be deceitful, and because the regularity of creating such records leads to the habits of accuracy."[10]

iv. Documents Which May Fall Short of the Exception

Some documents are more difficult to assess when viewed in light of this exception. Some of the more common problems are discussed below:

a.   Email Messages

E-mails create a number of challenges, and the application of the business records exception to email is no different. As the 4th Circuit held:

> "Courts are in disagreement on whether emails can, and should, fall under the business records hearsay exception.

---

[9]   *Thanongsinh v. Board of Educ.*, 462 F.3d 762, 777 (7th Cir. 2006).

[10] *Jordan v. Binns*, 712 F.3d 1123, 1135 (7th Cir. 2013).

The business records exception assumes that records containing information necessary in the regular running of a business will be accurate and reliable. E-mail, however, is typically a more casual form of communication than other records usually kept in the course of business, such that it may not be appropriate to assume the same degree of accuracy and reliability.

. . .

While properly authenticated emails may be admitted. . . under the. . . exception, it would be insufficient to survive a hearsay challenge simply to say that since a business keeps and receives e-mails, then *ergo* all those e-mails are business records falling within [Rule 803(6)]. An e-mail created within a business entity does not, for that reason alone, satisfy [Rule 803(6)]."[11]

b. Documents Prepared in Anticipation of Litigation

As discussed above, if an entity is not in the "business" of preparing records, then documents prepared in anticipation of litigation cannot meet the requirement of the business records exception. Why? Because 803(6)(C) requires that the making of the record was a regular practice of that activity. As the 7th Circuit recently held, "It is well established. . . that documents prepared in anticipation of litigation are not admissible under [Rule 803(6)]."[12]

c. Computer Records

"When dealing with computer records under Rule 803(6), it is not required that the qualified witness [referring to 803(6)(D)] be a computer programmer. . . or that she be the person who actually

---

[11] *U.S. v. Cone*, 714 F.3d 197, 219-220 (4th Cir. 2013).

[12] *Jordan v. Binns*, 712 F.3d 1123, 1135 (7th Cir. 2013).

prepared the record. The rule simply requires that the witness be one who can explain and be cross-examined concerning the manner in which the records are made and kept."[13]

d.   Hospital Records

Hospital records usually meet the requirements under the business records exception. Be cautious, however; at times hospital records contain information that exceeds the scope of what would typically fall within those regularly kept by hospitals. On the other hand, records related to medical diagnosis and treatment are quite likely to meet the exception.

v.   Hearsay Within Hearsay as It Relates to the Business Records Exception

Business records frequently contain hearsay within hearsay. Recall that each level of hearsay must meet an exception. Does this mean that the entire content of records that fall within the business records exception would not be excluded? To the contrary, hearsay within hearsay "in the context of business records exists when the record is prepared by an employee with information supplied by another person. If the person who provides the information is an outsider to the business who is not under a business duty to provide accurate information, the reliability rationale that underlies the business records exception ordinarily does not apply. Accordingly, the general rule is that any information provided by an outsider to the business preparing the record must fall within a [different] hearsay exception to be admissible."[14]

When not dealing with an "outsider," the requirement of a different exception may not apply. Hearsay within hearsay "in the context of a business record exists when the record is prepared by

---

[13] *U.S. v. Cameron*, 699 F.3d 621, 641 n.10 (1st Cir. 2012).
[14] *U.S. v. Blechman*, 657 F.3d 1052, 1065-66 (10th Cir. 2011).

an employee with information supplied by another person. If both the source and the recorder of the information, as well as every other participant in the chain producing the record, are acting in the regular course of business, the multiple hearsay is excused by Rule 803(6)."[15]

It might be best to understand these concepts with an example. Suppose that the business records in question are medical records. The medical records may contain records of a medical examination and a diagnosis. These records would likely fall squarely within the business records exception. But what if those medical records also contained statements by a patient that led to the diagnosis. Those statements would have been provided by an "outsider. . . who is not under a business duty to provide accurate information" and, therefore, would not be admissible under 803(6).[16] Those statements must also meet an exception to the hearsay rule. The patient's statements, in this example, would likely meet the exception set out in Rule 803(4), *(Statement Made for a Medical Diagnosis or Treatment)*. Therefore, the hearsay (patient's statements) within the hearsay (medical records) would not be excluded by the hearsay rule because they *each* meet an exception.

7. *Absence of a Record of Regularly Conducted Activity [803(7)]*

> Evidence that a matter is not included in a record described in paragraph (6) if:
>
> (A) the evidence is admitted to prove that the matter did not occur or exist;

---

[15] *Wilson v. Zapata Off-Shore Co.*, 939 F.2d 260, 271 (5th Cir. 1991).

[16] *U.S. v. Blechman*, 657 F.3d 1052, 1065-66 (10th Cir. 2011).

> (B) a record was regularly kept for a matter of
>   that kind; and
>
> (C) the opponent does not show that the possible
>   source   of   the   information   or   other
>   circumstances   indicate   a   lack   of
>   trustworthiness.

This exception is basically the "opposite" of the business records exception. Whereas the business records exception is trying to prove something—this is trying to prove *nothing*. For example, every time you rode your bike, you logged the date and time of your ride. Now, looking at your log for the past month, you notice that there is no date or time written down for one particular Saturday. With that absent entry, you could use the log to show that you did not ride your bike on that particular Saturday. That is what is meant under the "absence of a record of a regularly conducted activity" exception.

i.   The Requirements

The requirements for this exception are that you must demonstrate that:

(1)   all of the elements of 803(6) have been met;

(2)   that you are attempting to prove that a matter (otherwise documented in the records) did not occur or exist; and

(3)   that a record was regularly kept for what you are trying to prove did not occur or exist.

If these requirements are met, the documents will be admitted. But there is one additional provision in the rule.

(4)   The opponent of the evidence must *not* show that the possible source of the information or other circumstances indicate a lack of trustworthiness.

ii.   The Rationale

The rationale for this exception is the same as the previous exception. Records that comply with this exception are considered reliable because "businesses depend on them to conduct their own affairs, so there is little, if any, incentive to be deceitful, and because the regularity of creating such records leads to the habits of accuracy."[17]

iii.   Another Example

My favorite example of this rule is found in the movie, *A Few Good Men*. You do not need to be familiar with the movie to understand the example. In the movie there is a courtroom scene where defense counsel (a/k/a Tom Cruise) offers into evidence two log books from the airport runway towers. The tower log books detail each take-off and landing that occurred at the airport. He was using the logs to show that a particular flight did *not* exist. If the logs recorded *every* take-off and *every* landing, then the *absence* of a record of a take-off or landing would prove that a particular flight did not exist. Get it? If you haven't seen the movie, watch it.

8.   *Public Records [803(8)]*

> *A record or statement of a public office if:*
>
> *(A)   it sets out:*
>
> *(i)   the office's activities;*
>
> *(ii)   a matter observed while under a legal duty to report, but not including, in a*

---

[17]   *Jordan v. Binns*, 712 F.3d 1123, 1135 (7th Cir. 2013).

> *criminal case, a matter observed by law-enforcement personnel; or*
>
> *(iii) in a civil case or against the government in a criminal case, factual findings from a legally authorized investigation; and*
>
> *(B) the opponent does not show that the source of information or other circumstances indicate a lack of trustworthiness.*

i.   The Requirements

a.   Public Office

Unfortunately, neither the Rules nor the Advisory Committee Notes define "public office." Prior to the adoption of FRE 803(8), the admission of official records was governed by 28 U.S.C. § 1733(a) which provided, in part, that records of "any department or agency of the United States shall be admissible . . . ." Records of nonfederal agencies were not admissible under the rule. These nonfederal agencies included both state government entities and foreign government entities. When Rule 803(8) was adopted, it was clearly meant to be broader in scope than the former rule. The Advisory Committee noted that Rule 803(8) "makes no distinction between federal and nonfederal offices and agencies." See the "What Does This Mean" box on the next page.

b.   Duty to Report

The writing must have been made by, and within the scope of the duty of, the public employee. [803(8)(A)(ii)]

c.   What Is Reported

1.   The activities of the office or the agency; [803(8)(A)(i)]

or

2. Matters observed (by the office) while under a legal duty to report; [803(8)(A)(ii)]

or

3. In a civil case, factual findings from a legally authorized investigation; [803(8)(A)(iii)]

or

4. In a criminal case when used against the government, factual findings from a legally authorized investigation.

d. Exceptions

In a criminal case, matters observed by law-enforcement personnel will not be exempt under Rule 803(8)(A)(ii).

ii. Criminal v. Civil

The rule treats civil cases and criminal cases differently. The Advisory Committee noted that "[p]olice reports have generally been excluded except

What Does This Mean?

Although neither the rule, nor the courts, have defined "public office" as used in Rule 803(8), we might find some guidance in other authority. The Sixth Circuit has discussed the term "public office" by holding that "[g]iving the word 'office' the sovereignty of the state attaches for its technical qualities, five elements [that] would seem indispensable in order to make a public office of a civil nature. (1) It must be created by the Constitution or the Legislature, or by a municipality or other body with authority conferred by the Legislature. (2) There must be a delegation of a portion of the sovereign powers of government to be exercised for the benefit of the public. (3) The powers conferred and the duties discharged must be defined either directly or indirectly by the Legislature or through legislative authority. (4) The duties must be performed independently and without control of a superior power other than the law. (5) The office must have some permanency and continuity and the officer must take an official oath." *Pope v. Commissioner of Internal Revenue*, 138 F.2d 1006, 1009 (6th Cir. 1943).

to the extent to which they incorporate firsthand observations of the officer."

iii. The Rationale

Rule 803(8) is grounded on the assumption "that a public official will perform his duty properly and the unlikelihood that he will remember details independently of the record."[18]

iv. Example

An accident report is made by a police officer who describes the accident scene and comes to the conclusion that Danny Driver drove through a red light. The report also includes statements from witnesses who said Danny Driver drove through the red light.

In the civil case of *Plaintiff v. Danny Driver*

The police report would be admissible under 803(8)(A)(ii) [as to the description of the scene] and 803(8)(A)(iii) [as to the finding that Danny drove through the red light].

The statements from witnesses would not meet the exception under 803(8). They would need a separate basis for admission.

In the criminal case of the *State v. Danny Driver*

The police report would not be admissible against Danny Driver (unless the report can be admitted under another exception). If the police report is offered by Danny Driver against the State, then the police officer's conclusion would be admissible.

The statements from witnesses would not meet the exception under 803(8). They would need a separate basis for admission.

---

[18] *Zeus Enterprises, Inc. v. Alphin Aircraft, Inc.*, 190 F.3d 238 (4th Cir. 1999).

9. *Absence of a Public Record [803(10)]*

> *Testimony—or a certification under Rule 902—that a diligent search failed to disclose a public record or statement if:*
>
> > *(A) the testimony or certification is admitted to prove that*
> >
> > > *(i) the record or statement does not exist; or*
> > >
> > > *(ii) a matter did not occur or exist, if a public office regularly kept a record or statement for a matter of that kind; and*
> >
> > *(B) in a criminal case, a prosecutor who intends to offer a certification provides written notice of that intent at least 14 days before trial, and the defendant does not object in writing within 7 days of receiving the notice— unless the court sets a different time for the notice or the objection.*

Much like the Rule 803(7) exception (absence of a business record), Rule 803(10) is the same exception but applied to a public record. If Jane Doe says she was born in a hospital in Lexington, Kentucky, and the custodian of records cannot find (after a "diligent search") any birth certificate, then one might appropriately infer that Jane Doe was not, in fact, born in a hospital in Lexington, Kentucky.

10. *Statements in Ancient Documents [803(16)]*

Although not frequently tested, it is worth mentioning the exception for "Statements in Ancient Documents" because this exception was significantly revised as of December 1, 2017. This exception formerly permitted an exception for statements in documents which were at least 20 years old and whose authenticity is established. However, as of December 1, 2017, the revised Rule 803(16) provides an exception for statements "in a document that was prepared before January 1, 1998, and whose authenticity is established." The reason for the change is that modern-day documents are usually created and stored electronically which permits tampering of such documents in ways those documents could not be before current technology.

11. *The Remaining Exceptions*

Although there are twenty-three (23) "strong" exceptions, most law school courses (and bar examinations) only teach (or test) the ones listed above. The remaining exceptions that are not elaborated in this book are listed below. The complete rules are set out in the Appendix.

803(9):	Public Records of Vital Statistics.
803(11):	Records of Religious Organizations Concerning Personal or Family History.
803(12):	Certificates of Marriage, Baptism, and Similar Ceremonies.
803(13):	Family Records.
803(14):	Records of Documents That Affect an Interest in Property.
803(15):	Statements in Documents That Affect an Interest in Property.
803(17):	Market Reports and Similar Commercial Publications.
803(18):	Statements in Learned Treatises, Periodicals, or Pamphlets.

803(19): Reputation Concerning Personal or Family History.

803(20): Reputation Concerning Boundaries or General History.

803(21): Reputation Concerning Character.

803(22): Judgment of a Previous Conviction.

803(23): Judgments Involving Personal, Family, or General History, or a Boundary.

803(24): [Other Exceptions.] [Transferred to Rule 807.] This exception, 803(24), has become the residual exception, Rule 807.

It would certainly be worth your time to read each one in its entirety. After all, you never know when one of them might rear its head—in court, on an exam, or on the bar. Remember, these twenty-three exceptions are the "strong" ones—that is—the declarant's availability is immaterial. However, unavailability is the critical predicate to the application of the "weak" exceptions which we will examine next.

C. "Weak" Exceptions to the Rule

Exceptions under Rule 804 apply only if the declarant is unavailable. "Unavailability" is defined by Rule 804(a) so no other definitions matter.

A word of caution: Consider these exceptions only if no "strong" exceptions under 803 apply.

1. Defining Unavailability

Rule 804(a) defines "unavailability" and restricts the applicability of this definition to five specific circumstances.

> **Rule 804. Hearsay Exceptions; Declarant Unavailable**
>
> **(a) Criteria for Being Unavailable.** A declarant is considered to be unavailable as a witness if the declarant:
>
> **1.** is exempted from testifying about the subject matter of the declarant's statement because the court rules that a privilege applies;
>
> **2.** refuses to testify about the subject matter despite a court order to do so;
>
> **3.** testifies to not remembering the subject matter;
>
> **4.** cannot be present or testify at the trial or hearing because of death or a then-existing infirmity, physical illness, or mental illness; or
>
> **5.** is absent from the trial or hearing and the statement's proponent has not been able, by process or other reasonable means, to procure:
>
> > **(A)** the declarant's attendance, in the case of a hearsay exception under Rule 804(b)(1) or (6); or
> >
> > **(B)** the declarant's attendance or testimony, in the case of a hearsay exception under Rule 804(b)(2), (3), or (4).
>
> But this subdivision (a) does not apply if the statement's proponent procured or wrongfully caused the declarant's unavailability as a witness in order to prevent the declarant from attending or testifying.

Now let's look at each of these circumstances of unavailability in greater depth.

i. A Privilege Applies [804(a)(1)]

> **(a) Criteria for Being Unavailable.** A declarant is considered to be unavailable as a witness if the declarant:

> **1.** is exempted from testifying about the subject matter of the declarant's statement because the court rules that a privilege applies.

"Unavailability" does not necessarily mean physical unavailability. This first definition of unavailability is a great illustration of this fact.

So, for example, if a reporter refused to testify because his testimony is protected by privilege, and the court ruled that a privilege does, in fact, apply, then the reporter would be treated as unavailable under the definition. Although the Federal Rules of Evidence do not specifically set forth privileges, the federal courts do recognize many privileges. The chapter on privileges (Chapter XI) discusses these in greater detail. But for now, here is a list of the most common privileges: Accountant-Client; Attorney-Client; Clergy-Penitent; Governmental; Journalist; Physician-Patient; Psychotherapist/Social Worker; Self-Incrimination; and Spousal (Husband/Wife) Privileges. The invocation of any privilege (that is sustained by a court) would qualify the witness as being unavailable under Rule 804(a)(1).

ii. Refusal to Testify [804(a)(2)]

> **(a) Criteria for Being Unavailable.** A declarant is considered to be unavailable as a witness if the declarant:
> **(2)** refuses to testify about the subject matter despite a court order to do so.

If a declarant refuses to testify about the subject matter of the statement, then the witness would be considered "unavailable" under the Rule. However, the necessary prerequisite is that the judge must have ordered the witness to testify. The inference of this rule is that the declarant be the witness. Without that, the court could not be in a position to order the witness to testify. Also, do not be misled into thinking that the witness must blatantly refuse to testify for the exception to apply. The definition only requires that the witness "refuse to testify about the subject matter."

iii. Bad Memory [804(a)(3)]

> (a) **Criteria for Being Unavailable.** A declarant is considered to be unavailable as a witness if the declarant:
>
>   (3) testifies to not remembering the subject matter.

The critical requirement of this exception is that the declarant not remember *the subject matter* of the statement. If the declarant cannot remember actually making the statements, the requirement of the exception is not met.[19]

iv. Death or Illness [804(a)(4)]

> (a) **Criteria for Being Unavailable.** A declarant is considered to be unavailable as a witness if the declarant:
>
>   (4) cannot be present to testify at the trial or hearing because of death or a then-existing infirmity, physical illness, or mental illness.

Unlike the previous definitions, to meet *this* definition of unavailability, the declarant must be unable to be physically present at the hearing. However, the basis for the lack of presence must be because of death, infirmity, or physical or mental illness. A word of caution, however; a judge will usually require some form of proof that comports with the definition of unavailability (i.e., a note from a physician).

---

[19] *Lamonica v. Safe Hurricane Shutters, Inc.*, 711 F.3d 1299, 1317 (11th Cir. 2013).

v. Absent from Trial [804(a)(5)]

> **(a)** **Criteria for Being Unavailable.** A declarant is considered to be unavailable as a witness if the declarant:
>
> **(5)** is absent from the trial or hearing and the statement's proponent has not been able, by process or other reasonable means, to procure:
>
> **(A)** the declarant's attendance, in the case of a hearsay exception under Rule 804(b)(1) or (6); or
>
> **(B)** the declarant's attendance or testimony, in the case of a hearsay exception under Rule 804(b)(2), (3), or (4).

The last recognized circumstance requires the declarant to be absent from the trial. However, unlike the previous definition, this one requires there being an *inability to require* the declarant to be physically present—such as through a subpoena. If the witness, for example, refused to testify voluntarily and was outside the subpoena range of the court, then the witness might be considered unavailable.

a. Rules 804(b)(1) or 804(b)(6)

If the declarant could not be subpoenaed, then the declarant would be "unavailable" in cases with the following hearsay exceptions: 804(b)(1)—the Former Testimony exception; or, 804(b)(6)—the exception for a Statement Offered Against a Party That Wrongfully Caused the Declarant's Unavailability.

b. Rules 804(b)(2)–804(b)(4)

If the declarant could not be subpoenaed, *and* the proponent offering the witness could not otherwise procure the declarant's attendance or testimony, then the declarant would be "unavailable" with the following hearsay exceptions: 804(b)(2)—

Statement Under the Belief of Imminent Death; 804(b)(3)—
Statement Against Interest; or 804(b)(4)—Statement of Personal or
Family History.

In a recent case, (well, 2008—maybe not so recent) the
proponent of a statement argued that he could not procure the
attendance of some prisoners who were incarcerated more than 100
miles away; instead, he tried to submit the depositions of the
prisoners. The court did not permit him to use the depositions
because the proponent should have tried to comply with the
bureaucratic red tape sooner for the prisoners to be present. The
judge didn't actually use the term "bureaucratic red tape" but you
get my meaning. The court found that the prisoners were *not*
"unavailable" as defined by the rule. Oops![20] This is not something
you want to happen to you as a lawyer.

2. *When Unavailability Criteria Does Not Apply*

When the proponent of the testimony caused the unavailability
of the witness, then the rule provides that: ". . . this subdivision (a)
does not apply if the statement's proponent procured or wrongfully
caused the declarant's unavailability as a witness in order to
prevent the declarant from attending or testifying." [804(a)]

This part of the rule has two requirements:

1)   it must be shown that the proponent procured, or
     wrongfully caused, the declarant's unavailability,
     and;

2)   the procurement, or cause of the unavailability, was
     done to prevent the declarant from attending or
     testifying.

---

[20] *Pierce v. County of Orange,* 526 F.3d 1190, 1201-02 (9th Cir. 2008).

3. The Exceptions [804(b)(1)–(6)]

Rule 804(b) sets out five different instances when hearsay will not be excluded by the Hearsay Rule [802]. As you now know, these exceptions are not available *unless* the declarant is unavailable as defined above (in 804(a)).

Before looking at the exceptions under Rule 804, make sure of the following:

1) Hearsay is present [801(a)-(c)];

2) Non-hearsay does not apply [801(d)];

3) Hearsay exceptions under Rule 803 do not apply; and

4) The declarant is "unavailable" under Rule 804(a).

Once you have completed each of these steps, then determine whether one of the exceptions under Rule 804(b) apply:

i.   Former Testimony [804(b)(1)]

> **(b)(1)   Former Testimony.** Testimony that:
>
> **(A)** was given as a witness at a trial, hearing, or lawful deposition, whether given during the current proceeding or a different one; and
>
> **(B)** is now offered against a party who had—or, in a civil case, whose predecessor in interest had—an opportunity and similar motive to develop it by direct, cross-, or redirect examination.

This exception has strict requirements. The statement must be:

(1) Testimony that was given [by] a witness at a trial—or hearing—or deposition; and

(2)   Offered against a party who had an opportunity and similar motive to develop the testimony.

The former statement could have been made in either the current case or in another case. The challenging part of this exception is determining whether or not the party against whom it is offered had "an opportunity and similar motive to develop" the testimony. Although many of the types of evidence that fall under the exception are easy, some can be quite difficult.

For example, suppose you represent the Plaintiff and take the deposition of Jane Doe as part of the case. At trial, Jane Doe is "unavailable" by definition. Now, you want to offer parts of her deposition at trial. In this example, the deposition was "[t]estimony that was given as a witness at a. . . lawful deposition. . . during the current proceeding. . . . ; and is now offered against [the defendant]." Assuming the defendant, or her lawyer, was present at the deposition then the defendant would have "had—an opportunity and similar motive to develop [the testimony] by direct, cross-, or redirect examination." Why? Because she was present at the deposition, and since the deposition was in the same case, she had the opportunity and motive to develop the testimony.

On the other hand, one could imagine that the defendant wanted to save the "juicy" questions for trial and not ask them at a deposition. In this case, the defendant would have the motive to develop the testimony but chose not to do so.

Another difficult example involves testimony from a different hearing or trial. The problem is being able to convince the court that the party against whom the statement is offered had an opportunity and motive—when the original testimony was given—to develop the testimony.

ii. Statement Under Belief of Imminent Death [804(b)(2)]

> **(b)(2)** **Statement Under Belief of Imminent Death.** In a prosecution for homicide or in a civil case, a statement that the declarant, while believing the declarant's death to be imminent, made about its cause or circumstances.

This exception is informally known as the "dying declaration." It is a narrow exception.

a. In a Criminal Case

The only criminal case to which this exception applies is homicide. So, a case of attempted homicide or assault won't cut it. (By the way, murder *is* homicide).

b. In a Civil Case

The exception applies in all civil cases.

c. The Requirements

1) It must be a statement made while the declarant believed that his or her death was imminent; and

2) The statement must be about the cause or circumstances.

The requirements of this rule occasionally cause some confusion. First, it is important to recognize that the exception *does not* require the declarant to actually be dead. Yes, she must be unavailable and certainly—if she is dead then she is unavailable. But—death is not a requirement.

Second, the statement *must* be about the cause or circumstances of what the declarant believes is her end! Consider a police officer who was shot and says, "Sammy shot me." If he believed that his death was imminent and he was unavailable for trial, then the statement would fit squarely within the hearsay exception (if it was a civil trial or a prosecution for homicide).

iii. Statement Against Interest [804(b)(3)]

> **(b)(3)**   **Statement Against Interest.** A Statement that:
>
> **(A)** a reasonable person in the declarant's position would have made only if the person believed it to be true because, when made, it was so contrary to the declarant's proprietary or pecuniary interest or had so great a tendency to invalidate the declarant's claim against someone else or to expose the declarant to civil or criminal liability; and
>
> **(B)** is supported by corroborating circumstances that clearly indicate its trustworthiness, if it is offered in a criminal case as one that tends to expose the declarant to criminal liability.

This exception is frequently confused with Rule 801(d)(2) ("An Opposing Party's Statement.") While the fundamental requirement of Rule 801(d)(2) is for the person making the statement be a party to the case, Rule 804(b)(3), has no such requirement. And, frankly, if the statement sought to be admitted fits Rule 801(d), you would not need to consider Rule 804 exceptions. Unfortunately, if you get to Rule 804 in your analysis, you are reaching the "bottom of the exception barrel"—so to speak.

a. The Requirements

The statement applies in all civil or criminal cases and must be one that:

(1) A reasonable person in the declarant's position (situation) would only have made the statement if he or she thought it was true; **and**

(2)

(a) When the statement was made, it was so contrary to the declarant's proprietary or pecuniary interest; **or**

(b) When the statement was made, it had so great a tendency to invalidate the declarant's claim against someone else; **or**

(c) When the statement was made, it exposed the declarant to civil or criminal liability; **and**

If offered in a criminal case:

In *addition* to the above requirements, if it is offered in a criminal case as a statement that tends to expose the declarant to criminal liability, then it must:

(3) Be supported by corroborating evidence that clearly indicate its trustworthiness.

As you can see, this exception is intended to be used with a statement that is so "bad" no one would have actually said it unless it were true!

b. Interpreting the Exception

There are a fair number of cases that address this exception. Here are some important points to understand:

Non-self-inculpatory Statements

Statements that are not self-inculpatory, even when made with statements that are self-inculpatory, are not admissible under this exception.[21] Courts "may not just assume. . . that a statement is self-inculpatory because it is part of a fuller confession. . . ."[22]

Corroboration in Criminal Cases

"[A] clear degree of corroboration is required. . . that clearly indicates that the statements are worthy of belief, based upon the circumstances in which the statements were made."[23]

c.   The Rationale

"[This exception] is based on the common-sense notion that reasonable people, even reasonable people who are not especially honest, tend not to make self-inculpatory statements unless they believe them to be true."[24]

iv.   Statement of Personal or Family History [804(b)(4)]

> **(b)(4)   Statement of Personal or Family History.** A Statement about:
>
> **(A)**   the declarant's own birth, adoption, legitimacy, ancestry, marriage, divorce, relationship by blood, adoption, or marriage, or similar facts of personal or family history, even though the declarant had no way of acquiring personal knowledge about that fact; or
>
> **(B)**   another person concerning any of these facts, as well as death, if the declarant was related to the

---

[21] Self-inculpatory statements are those which tend to show that the declarant was involved in an act or guilty of something.

[22] *Williamson v. U.S.*, 512 U.S. 594, 600-01 (1994).

[23] *U.S. v. Ocasio-Ruiz*, 779 F.3d 43, 46-47 (1st Cir. 2015).

[24] *U.S. v. Lozado*, 776 F.3d 1119, 1125 (10th Cir. 2015).

> person by blood, adoption, or marriage or was so intimately associated with the person's family that the declarant's information is likely to be accurate.

a. The Requirements

There are two different scenarios in which this exception will apply: (1) a statement about the declarant; and (2) a statement about another person.

(1) A Statement About the Declarant

This scenario has two basic requirements:

1. The statement must be *about* the declarant; and

2. The statement must concern one (or more) of the following topics:

   a. Birth;

   b. Adoption;

   c. Legitimacy;

   d. Ancestry;

   e. Marriage;

   f. Divorce;

   g. Relationship by Blood;

   h. Relationship by Adoption;

   i. Relationship by Marriage; or

   j. Similar Facts of Personal or Family History.

(2) A Statement About Another Person

This scenario has three basic requirements:

1. The statement must be about someone *other than* the declarant;

2. The declarant *must be related* to the person (about which the statement was made) by:

    a. blood, adoption, or marriage; or

    b. be so intimately associated with the person's family that the declarant's information is likely to be accurate; and

3. The statement must concern one (or more) of the following topics:

    a. Birth;

    b. Death; *[Note: For obvious reasons this is not included above]*

    c. Adoption;

    d. Legitimacy;

    e. Ancestry;

    f. Marriage;

    g. Divorce;

    h. Relationship by Blood;

    i. Relationship by Adoption;

    j. Relationship by Marriage; or

    k. Similar Facts of Personal or Family History.

(3) Personal Knowledge

The rule does not require personal knowledge. Say what? Yes—it's true.

b. Rationale

This exception is "premised on the view that certain categories of statements are free enough from the risk of inaccuracy and trustworthiness such that the test of cross-examination would be of marginal utility. [This exception] assumes that the statements of family history are likely to be informed by knowledge shared in common among family members on the basis of customs and understandings that are likely to be true."[25]

v. Statement Offered Against a Party That Wrongfully Caused the Declarant's Unavailability [804(b)(6)]

> **(b)(4)** **Statement Offered Against a Party That Wrongfully Caused the Declarant's Unavailability.** A statement offered against a party that wrongfully caused—or acquiesced in wrongfully causing—the declarant's unavailability as a witness, and did so intending that result.

The informal name for this exception is "Forfeiture by Wrongdoing." The informal name results from the belief that the party's wrongdoing forfeits the right to use the statements.

---

[25] *Porter v. Quarantillo*, 722 F.3d 94, 98 (2nd Cir. 2013).

a.   The Requirements

This exception has four basic requirements and is rarely used:

1) The statement must be offered against a party;

2) That party must have wrongfully caused (or acquiesced in wrongfully causing) the declarant's unavailability as a witness;

3) The party intended that the declarant be unavailable; and

4) The declarant was, in fact, rendered unavailable.

b.   The Rationale

Isn't the rationale obvious?

D. The Residual Exception [807]

The residual exception is the "catch-all" exception. That is, when none of the other exceptions apply—this one might fit. This exception was formerly listed under *both* the "strong" and the "weak" exceptions. Fortunately, the drafters realized that listing the identical exception under both made no sense at all—because the availability of the declarant did not impact the exception.

1. The Requirements

Rule 807. The Residual Exception

(a) **In General.** Under the following circumstances, a hearsay statement is not excluded by the rule against hearsay even if the statement is not specifically covered by a hearsay exception in Rule 803 or 804:

   (1) the statement has equivalent circumstantial guarantees of trustworthiness;

> **(2)** it is offered as evidence of a material fact;
>
> **(3)** it is more probative on the point for which it is offered than any other evidence that the proponent can obtain through reasonable efforts; and
>
> **(4)** admitting it will best serve the purposes of these rules and the interests of justice.
>
> **(b) Notice.** The statement is admissible only if, before the trial or hearing, the proponent gives an adverse party reasonable notice of the intent to offer the statement and its particulars, including the declarant's name and address, so that the party has a fair opportunity to meet it.

2. Interpreting the Exception

Oddly, there are not a large number of cases reported to interpret this exception. In truth, courts rarely use this exception because of the requirement of 807(a)(1) that the statement has equivalent circumstantial guarantees of trustworthiness of those in rules 803 or 804. Nevertheless, some cases help us identify when the application of the exception is appropriate.

i. Exceptional Circumstances

This exception is "necessary to permit courts to admit evidence in exceptional circumstances where the evidence [is] necessary, highly probative, and [carries] a guarantee of trustworthiness equivalent to, or superior to, that which underlies the other recognized exceptions."[26]

---

[26] *U.S. v. End of Horn*, 829 F.3d 681, 686 (8th Cir. 2016).

ii. Reliability

"The purpose of Rule 807 is to make sure that reliable, material hearsay evidence is admitted, regardless of whether it fits neatly into one of the exceptions enumerated in the Rules of Evidence."[27]

iii. Almost Fits

"[W]here a statement 'almost fit[s]' into other hearsay exceptions, the circumstance cuts in favor of admissibility under the [FRE 807] residual exception. We [do] not, however, hold the factor [to be] determinative. . . ."[28]

iv. Fits 803 or 804 Exceptions

Most courts interpret Rule 807 to mean that "if a statement is admissible under one of the hearsay exceptions, that exception should be relied on instead of the residual exception."[29]

3. The Notice Requirement

Unlike the exceptions found in Rules 803 and 804, this exception has a notice requirement. The proponent of the statement must give her opposing party reasonable notice of her intent to offer the statement and its particulars, including the declarant's name and address. This permits the opposing party to have a fair opportunity to be prepared for the possibility of admission or, if desired, to argue against admission.

---

[27] *U.S. v. Moore*, 824 F.3d 620, 624 (7th Cir. 2016).

[28] *U.S. v. Bonds*, 608 F.3d 495, 501 (9th Cir. 2010).

[29] *U.S. v. Laster*, 258 F.3d 525, 530 (6th Cir. 2001).

E. Recap

If you have made it this far, you should have a basic grasp of how the hearsay rule and its exceptions work. Let's review the process with another flowchart:

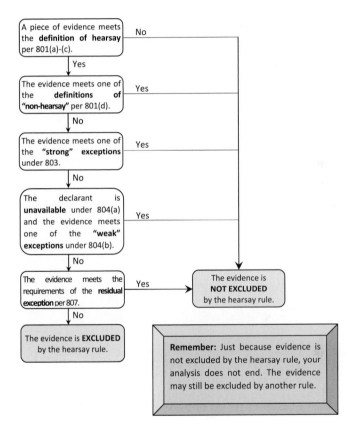

CHAPTER VIII

The Hearsay Rule and the Confrontation Clause

A. Overview

When a defendant is on trial and a hearsay statement is to be used against that defendant, then the defendant has the right to confront—and cross-examine—the witness who made the statement against her. This is referred to as the Confrontation Clause issue. The Confrontation Clause only applies in criminal cases.

However, if the declarant is present in the courtroom—and subject to cross-examination—then there is no Confrontation Clause issue.

B. The *Crawford* Case

The 6th Amendment Confrontation Clause in the United States Constitution, and its impact on hearsay in criminal cases, arose with the case of *Crawford v. Washington.*[1] I don't usually give you a

---

[1] *Crawford v. Washington*, 541 U.S. 36 (2004).

189

miniature case-brief, but the fundamentals of the *Crawford* case are necessary to understand the rest of the chapter.

In *Crawford*, the defendant was charged with assault and attempted murder after stabbing a man who allegedly tried to rape his wife. At trial, the prosecution sought to introduce into evidence a recorded statement by the wife describing the stabbing to police. The trial court allowed the tape to be played for the jury and convicted Mr. Crawford. The wife was unavailable to testify at trial because of the state's marital privilege. The Washington Court of Appeals reversed the conviction, holding that the taped statement violated Crawford's Sixth Amendment confrontation right. The Washington Supreme Court reversed, agreeing with the trial court that the statement bore guarantees of trustworthiness and reinstated the conviction.

The United States Supreme Court held that under the 6th Amendment, a defendant has the right to confront the witnesses who provide "testimonial" statements against him and cross-examine those witnesses.

Testimonial statements are those that the declarant would reasonably expect to be used by the prosecution.

Crawford left us with the rule that testimonial statements of unavailable witnesses are admissible only where the defendant had a prior opportunity for cross-examination. In this case, the wife's taped statement against Mr. Crawford was considered testimonial because it was made to law enforcement officials in an interrogation and the wife knew, or should have known, that the statement was going to be used at the subsequent trial. Thus, because the wife is unavailable at trial based upon the marital privilege, and because Mr. Crawford did not have an opportunity to cross-examine the wife as to the statement, its admission would violate the Confrontation Clause. Therefore, the statement was held to be inadmissible.

C. Hearsay Versus the 6th Amendment to the United States Constitution

The determination of whether a statement is excluded by the hearsay rule and the determination as to whether a statement is excluded by the United States Constitution are separate analyses. Nonetheless, if the hearsay rules exclude a statement, then there is no reason to evaluate the statements under the 6th Amendment. Likewise, if a statement violates the 6th Amendment, it cannot be admitted, and a hearsay analysis is unnecessary. Nevertheless, it makes sense to follow an order. The simplified process, below, is one way to proceed.

D. Simplified Process—Chart

This chart illustrates a simplified *Crawford* analysis.

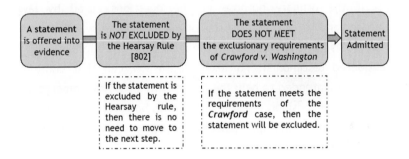

E. The Confrontation Clause

1. The Requirements

Each of the following requirements must be met before the Confrontation Clause exclusion applies. Note, however, that even though a statement meets an exception to the hearsay rule, if the following requirements are met, then the statement will *not* be admitted:

i.   The case is criminal;

ii.   The statement is offered against the defendant;

iii.   The declarant is unavailable;

iv.   The statement was testimonial in nature; and

v.   The defendant had no opportunity to cross-examine the declarant as to the "testimonial statement" prior to trial.

2. *Testimonial Statements*

The critical question is whether or not a statement is considered testimonial. While *Crawford* did not define "testimonial," subsequent cases have provided some guidance.

i. Police Investigations

If the primary purpose of the questions asked by law enforcement is to address an ongoing emergency, then the statements made in response to the questions will generally *not* be considered testimonial. For example, a 911 call that contains statements intended to help the police with an existing emergency would *not* be considered testimonial. Note, however, that 911 calls often consist of multiple statements, some of which could be testimonial in nature, while others may not.

If the primary purpose of the questions asked by law enforcement is to investigate—i.e., establish past facts relevant to a criminal investigation—then the statements are testimonial. For example, in one case, also handed down by the Supreme Court, statements that were given after a domestic violence incident were evaluated as to whether or not they were testimonial.[2] The court determined that once the immediate threat was neutralized, or

---

[2] *Davis v. Washington,* 547 U.S. 813 (2006).

otherwise no longer existed, statements from the victim to the police officers, which described the incident, were testimonial.

ii. Written Reports

Many written reports are easier to evaluate. Reports that summarize findings, or that provide an analysis, are frequently testimonial in nature. Examples would include a report from a forensic analysis of fingerprints, or a lab report indicating that the drug found was an illegal narcotic. These reports would be testimonial in nature, so the declarant would have to be present for cross-examination.

Be aware, however, that these reports may be offered for a purpose that would not violate the 6th Amendment, such as establishing the bias of a witness.

3. Forfeiture by Wrongdoing

The protection offered by the 6th Amendment is not absolute. When a defendant causes the declarant to be unavailable, she cannot then "hide" behind the protections of the 6th Amendment. Under this circumstance, the statements would not be excluded if the defendant *intended* to keep the witness from testifying at trial.

4. Right to Physical Confrontation

The 6th Amendment also includes the right to confront the accuser—or, in this case—to physically confront the declarant. In one case, a screen was used to separate the defendant from a child victim; the Supreme Court held that this violated the 6th Amendment. The Supreme Court has held, however, that the right of confrontation is not an absolute right. In another child-victim case, the Court found it appropriate to permit the child to testify via a one-way closed-circuit television. In that latter case, the Court found the additional safeguards were appropriate and would not violate the right to confrontation if the trial court made specific findings of possible trauma to the child if the child were to testify in the presence of the defendant.

F. Due Process

The Supreme Court has held that hearsay and other exclusionary rules cannot be applied when doing so would effectively deprive a defendant of her 14th Amendment due process right to a fair trial.[3]

---

[3]　*Chambers v. Mississippi*, 410 U.S. 284 (1973).

CHAPTER IX

Documentary Evidence

A. Overview

Documentary evidence is frequently referred to in other resources as "writings." It is, in fact, significantly broader than just writings. Documentary evidence includes photographs, audio recordings, video recordings, etc. As with other forms of evidence, documentary evidence must "check all the boxes" with regard to admissibility—relevance, hearsay exceptions, best evidence, and other applicable rules. But with documentary evidence also comes the need for authentication. This is an issue that does not arise with testimonial evidence.

When faced with the admissibility of documentary evidence, you should always consider three areas of the rules that impact admissibility: Authentication (see Sections B & C below), Hearsay (see Chapters VII-VIII), and Best Evidence (see Section D below).

B. Authentication—Generally

Authentication is required before documentary evidence may be admitted. The term "authentication" in the context of the rules simply means that the evidence "is what the proponent claims it is." [Rule 901(a)] There are two types of document that fall under the authentication rules: documents which require evidence as to their authenticity, and documents which are considered "self-authenticating" and, therefore, do not require additional evidence for authentication.

C. Authentication—Methods

Rule 901 requires that evidence (which is not self-authenticating) be authenticated with "evidence to support a finding that the item is what the proponent claims it is." Rule 902, on the other hand, sets forth an exclusive list of evidence which is considered self-authenticating.

1. *Documents Which Require Evidence of Authenticity*

Rule 901. Authenticating or Identifying Evidence

(a) **In General.** To satisfy the requirement of authenticating or identifying an item of evidence, the proponent must produce evidence sufficient to support a finding that the item is what the proponent claims it is.

The first part of the rule sets the stage. It requires that all evidence must be supported by evidence that the item—is what it is. But "how" is that done? There are no specific requirements as to how authentication is accomplished. Nevertheless, Rule 901(b) sets out a series of examples which would satisfy the requirement of authentication.

It is important to note that the list is non-exclusive and only sets out examples. Any evidence which would support the authentication of a document will suffice.

2. Examples Under the Rule

(b) **Examples.** The following are examples only—not a complete list—of evidence that satisfies the requirement:

    (1) **Testimony of a Witness with Knowledge.** Testimony that an item is what it is claimed to be.

Rule 901(b)(1) is the most common method of authentication. It frequently manifests itself through oral testimony from a witness who will testify about the document. For example, suppose you are seeking to introduce evidence of Jane Doe's Federal Income Tax Return. Jane Doe could testify that the document is, indeed, her tax return.

(b)(2) **Nonexpert Opinion About Handwriting.** A nonexpert's opinion that handwriting is genuine, based on a familiarity with it that was not acquired for the current litigation.

Do not be misled into thinking that only experts can compare handwriting. Is there anyone whose handwriting you can recognize? Maybe a parent, a child, a sibling, or a spouse? The law permits a lay person (a nonexpert) to testify that she can recognize someone's handwriting.

> **(b)(3)   Comparison by an Expert Witness or the Trier of Fact.** A comparison with an authenticated specimen by an expert witness or the trier of fact.

It wouldn't make sense to let a layperson testify as to the identification of someone's handwriting but not an expert, would it? No, of course not. The rules permit an expert witness to testify as to such identification.

> **(b)(4)   Distinctive Characteristics and the Like.** The appearance, contents, substance, internal patterns, or other distinctive characteristics of the item, taken together with all the circumstances.

Do you know what a Fabergé egg looks like? If not, *Google* it. I would have included a picture but you know—copyright and all. Okay, how about a different example? Do you know what a Corvette looks like? Could you, based on the appearance, distinctive characteristics, etc. identify a car as a Corvette? You probably could. Now, I know what you are thinking; a Corvette is not documentary evidence (unless it's a photo of a Corvette); and you are probably thinking that a Corvette is not likely going to make an appearance in a courtroom. You are correct on both accounts. But, I needed an example and a Corvette came to mind. Let's just go with that.

> **(b)(5)   Opinion About a Voice.** An opinion identifying a person's voice—whether heard firsthand or through mechanical or electronic transmission or recording— based on hearing the voice at any time under circumstances that connect it with the alleged speaker.

Maybe it was a phone call; maybe it was a recording; maybe it was some new-fangled technology that has not been invented when I sat down to write this book. It doesn't matter. If a person can identify the voice of another person, then she can testify to that. For example, you could authenticate the voice of someone you are very familiar with such as a parent, spouse, sibling, or child. You can do this because under the rules, your familiarity means that you can most likely be able to recognize the voice of one of these individuals. Do not, however, confuse this rule with Rule 901(b)(6) below.

> **(b)(6)** **Evidence About a Telephone Conversation.** For a telephone conversation, evidence that a call was made to the number assigned at the time to:
>
> **(A)** a particular person, if circumstances, including self-identification, show that the person answering was the one called; or
>
> **(B)** a particular business, if the call was made to a business and the call related to business reasonably transacted over the telephone.

This is not the same as voice recognition. Using this rule, a person can identify a particular person—or a business—based on a telephone call. Let's say you call 1-800 Flowers and a person answers the phone and says, "Hello, this is Jason's diner." Assuming the person was not kidding, it is likely that you did not call the flower shop. On the other hand, if you called 1-800 Flowers and ordered a bouquet of roses to be delivered to your spouse, then you could reasonably authenticate that the telephone conversation occurred with the flower shop.

3. *The Remaining Examples*

The remaining examples are self-explanatory. Review them with the understanding that these are merely examples set out by the rule. They are not an exclusive list.

(b)(7)   **Evidence About Public Records.** Evidence that:

      (A) a document was recorded or filed in a public office as authorized by law; or

      (B) a purported public record or statement is from the office where items of this kind are kept.

(b)(8)   **Evidence About Ancient Documents or Data Compilations.** For a document or data compilation, evidence that it:

      (A) is in a condition that creates no suspicion about its authenticity;

      (B) was in a place where, if authentic, it would likely be; and

      (C) is at least 20 years old when offered.

(b)(9)   **Evidence About a Process or System.** Evidence describing a process or system and showing that it produces an accurate result.

(b)(10)   **Methods Provided by a Statute or Rule.** Any method of authentication or identification allowed by a federal statute or a rule prescribed by the Supreme Court.

4. Self-Authenticating Documents

Rule 902 sets out an exclusive list of items of evidence which are self-authenticating. The importance of this list is two-fold: first, it is exclusive. That is, absent another rule or statute to the contrary, only the items listed are self-authenticating; second, no other evidence is required to authenticate these items of evidence. Pay special attention to Rules 902(13) and (14) because they are the two newest rules that were effective December 1, 2017.

Rule 902. Evidence That Is Self-Authenticating

The following items of evidence are self-authenticating; they require no extrinsic evidence of authenticity in order to be admitted.

(1) Domestic Public Documents That Are Sealed and Signed. A document that bears:

    (A) a seal purporting to be that of the United States; any state, district, commonwealth, territory, or insular possession of the United States; the former Panama Canal Zone; the Trust Territory of the Pacific Islands; a political subdivision of any of these entities; or a department, agency, or officer of any entity named above; and

    (B) a signature purporting to be an execution or attestation.

(2) Domestic Public Documents That Are Not Sealed but Are Signed and Certified. A document that bears no seal if:

    (A) it bears the signature of an officer or employee of an entity named in Rule 902(1)(A); and

    (B) another public officer who has a seal and official duties within that same entity certifies under seal—or its

---

equivalent—that the signer has the official capacity and that the signature is genuine.

(3) Foreign Public Documents. A document that purports to be signed or attested by a person who is authorized by a foreign country's law to do so. The document must be accompanied by a final certification that certifies the genuineness of the signature and official position of the signer or attester—or of any foreign official whose certificate of genuineness relates to the signature or attestation or is in a chain of certificates of genuineness relating to the signature or attestation. The certification may be made by a secretary of a United States embassy or legation; by a consul general, vice consul, or consular agent of the United States; or by a diplomatic or consular official of the foreign country assigned or accredited to the United States. If all parties have been given a reasonable opportunity to investigate the document's authenticity and accuracy, the court may, for good cause, either:

(A) order that it be treated as presumptively authentic without final certification; or

(B) allow it to be evidenced by an attested summary with or without final certification.

(4) Certified Copies of Public Records. A copy of an official record—or a copy of a document that was recorded or filed in a public office as authorized by law—if the copy is certified as correct by:

(A) the custodian or another person authorized to make the certification; or

(B) a certificate that complies with Rule 902(1), (2), or (3), a federal statute, or a rule prescribed by the Supreme Court.

(5) **Official Publications.** A book, pamphlet, or other publication purporting to be issued by a public authority.

(6) **Newspapers and Periodicals.** Printed material purporting to be a newspaper or periodical.

(7) **Trade Inscriptions and the Like.** An inscription, sign, tag, or label purporting to have been affixed in the course of business and indicating origin, ownership, or control.

(8) **Acknowledged Documents.** A document accompanied by a certificate of acknowledgment that is lawfully executed by a notary public or another officer who is authorized to take acknowledgments.

(9) **Commercial Paper and Related Documents.** Commercial paper, a signature on it, and related documents, to the extent allowed by general commercial law.

(10) **Presumptions Under a Federal Statute.** A signature, document, or anything else that a federal statute declares to be presumptively or prima facie genuine or authentic.

(11) **Certified Domestic Records of a Regularly Conducted Activity.** The original or a copy of a domestic record that meets the requirements of Rule 803(6)(A)-(C), as shown by a certification of the custodian or another qualified person that complies with a federal statute or a rule prescribed by the Supreme Court. Before the trial or hearing, the proponent must give an adverse party reasonable written notice of the intent to offer the record—and must make the record and certification available for inspection—so that the party has a fair opportunity to challenge them.

(12) **Certified Foreign Records of a Regularly Conducted Activity.** In a civil case, the original or a copy of a foreign record that meets the requirements of Rule 902(11), modified as follows: the certification, rather than complying with a federal statute or Supreme Court rule,

> must be signed in a manner that, if falsely made, would subject the maker to a criminal penalty in the country where the certification is signed. The proponent must also meet the notice requirements of Rule 902(11).
>
> **(13) Certified Records Generated by an Electronic Process or System.** A record generated by an electronic process or system that produces an accurate result, as shown by a certification of a qualified person that complies with the certification requirements of Rule 902(11) or (12). The proponent must also meet the notice requirements of Rule 902(11).
>
> **(14) Certified Data Copied from an Electronic Device, Storage Medium, or File.** Data copied from an electronic device, storage medium, or file, if authenticated by a process of digital identification, as shown by a certification of a qualified person that complies with the certification requirements of Rule (902(11) or (12). The proponent also must meet the notice requirements of Rule 902 (11).

Yes, the rule is fairly long, but it is also straight-forward. Documents that fit squarely within the rule are self-authenticating. Problems arise when lawyers attempt to exceed the rules and apply the concept of self-authentication too broadly.

For example, Rule 902(7) provides that trade inscriptions are self-authenticating. Under the rule, the trade inscription—itself—is what is self-authenticating. In one case, a lawyer tried to introduce an owner's manual as self-authenticating because the cover contained a trade inscription. The court held that "[t]he owner's manual is not a trade inscription and admitting the manual because it had a trade inscription on its cover does not comport with the rule."[1]

Before leaving this rule, we must take a moment to discuss Rule 902(11). This is an important rule because the business records exception to the hearsay rule is frequently used. Don't worry—we are still talking about authentication. However, Rule 902(11) provides that domestic documents that meet the requirements of 803(6)(A)-(C) will be self-authenticating. As one court noted, "Rule 902(11) is a powerful and efficient short-cut, but it includes important built-in safeguards that cannot be taken lightly. Those safeguards include providing opposing counsel with advance notice of any Rule 902(11) certifications to give that party a fair opportunity to challenge the certifications. . . . [T]he Rule does not give a party license to dump business records into evidence without giving an adverse party an opportunity to question the certificate's signer where such questioning may be warranted."[2] Documents that comply with this rule for self-authentication do not bypass the hearsay rule; they are simply meeting the requirements of both rules that share the same requirements. These documents are simply "killing two birds with one stone" so to speak.

D. The Best Evidence Rule

This rule frequently gives people heartburn. It infrequently comes up in "real life," but bar examiners love to test on it and make it one of your multiple-choice answer selections. And, probably because of this, law professors often like to test on it. It's really not that hard—but please—do not skip it. Now, let's look at the rules. Yes—plural—there is more than one rule that needs to be discussed.

---

[1] *Whitted v. General Motors Corp.*, 58 F.3d 1200, 1204 (7th Cir. 1995).

[2] *U.S. v. Green*, 648 F.3d 569, 579 (7th Cir. 2011).

First, much like the "Business Records Exception," the "Best Evidence Rule" is NOT actually titled the "Best Evidence Rule." The actual title of Rule 1002 is: "Requirement of the Original." Many years ago, the 9th Circuit wrote in an opinion that "it is more accurate to refer to Rule 1002 as the 'Original Document rule,' not the Best Evidence rule."[3] But nobody listened. Here is what the text of the rule looks like:

Rule 1002. Requirement of the Original

An original writing, recording, or photograph is required in order to prove its content unless these rules or a federal statute provides otherwise.

---

1. *Applying the Rule*

Rule 1002 is commonly misunderstood, as many interpret the rule literally. The misunderstanding is that a copy is not as good as an original and, therefore, a court will not admit a copy. You might be thinking "But that *is* what the rule says." Not exactly; it says ". . . unless these rules. . . provide[ ] otherwise." And the rules *do* permit copies. I will go over this in greater detail in section *D.4. Copies*, later in this Chapter.

To apply the rule, you must determine whether the contents of the writing, recording or photograph are sought to be proved. As noted by the Advisory Committee, "[A]n event may be proved by nondocumentary evidence, even though a written record of it was made. If, however, the event is sought to be proved by the written record, the rule applies. For example, payment may be proved without producing the written receipt which was given. Earnings

---

[3] *U.S. v. Mayans*, 17 F.3d 1174, 1185 (9th Cir. 1994).

may be proved without producing books of account in which they are entered."[4]

But before we get into more detail, let's look at an example of the rule in use. Suppose that you wish to prove that John paid Suzy $60 for mowing his lawn. A few weeks later, Suzy forgets that John paid her. She ultimately sues John. At trial, John says, "I paid Suzy, and she signed a receipt." Suzy objects, asserting the "Best Evidence" rule. She argued that receipt of proof of payment would be the "best evidence," not John's testimony. She would be correct!

2. Photographs

The Advisory Committee offered wisdom, specifically on photographs and the Best Evidence Rule. We are told that "[t]he assumption should not be made that the rule will come into operation on every occasion when use is made of a photograph. . . . On the contrary, the rule will seldom apply to ordinary photographs. . . . [Usually] a witness on the stand identif[ies] the photograph or motion picture as a correct representation of events which he saw or of a scene with which he is familiar. In fact, he adopts the picture as his testimony or, in common parlance, uses the picture to illustrate his testimony. Under these circumstances, no effort is made to prove the contents of the picture, and the rule is inapplicable."[5]

3. Recordings of Conversations

The 9th Circuit addressed the issue of how to evaluate a recording of a conversation when a person is called to testify about the conversation: "[A]. . . recording cannot be said to be the best evidence of a conversation when a party seeks to call a participant

---

[4] Fed. R. Evid. 1002 cmt.

[5] Fed. R. Evid. 1002 cmt. *citing* Pierre R. Paradis, *The Celluloid Witness*, 37 U. Colo. L. Rev. 235, 249-51 (1965).

in, or observer of, the conversation to testify to it. In that instance, the best evidence rule has no application at all."[6]

4. *Copies*

As mentioned above, a common misconception is that Rule 1002 requires an actual original, as opposed to a copy, to be admissible. Practically speaking, this is just silly. For example, where is the original deed? Filed with the County! Where is the original digital photograph? It's stored electronically on a hard drive somewhere or, these days, deep inside someone's cell phone. Where is the original of an email, or a Facebook page or a Snapchat? The concept of requiring an actual original is almost impossible these days. Oh, and we also have a rule that says we don't need it! Here it is:

> ### Rule 1003. Admissibility of Duplicates
> A duplicate is admissible to the same extent as the original unless a genuine question is raised about the original's authenticity or the circumstances make it unfair to admit the duplicate.

What does *this* rule mean? First, it means copies are just as good as an original. Second, it means that *if* there is a question about the authenticity of the original, then the admission of a copy is inappropriate. Why? Because a court (or an expert) might need the original to determine its authenticity. There also may be facets of a copy that would prevent a court (or an expert) from being able to determine its actual authenticity.

Under certain circumstances, it may be unfair to admit a duplicate, but of course, that would be up to the judge. Consider the following example: Suppose that an attorney offers a copy of a witness's Federal Income Tax Return into evidence. Unfortunately,

---

[6]　*U.S. v. Workinger*, 90 F.3d 1409, 1415 (9th Cir. 1996).

when the copy was made, the person making the copy forgot to remove a large sticky note that was on top of one of the schedules. With the copy there is no way to determine what was underneath the sticky note. So, in this instance, the admission of the copy would be "unfair."

And by the way, copies of copies are still copies and, therefore, admissible, as recognized by the 9th Circuit: "[A] duplicate of a duplicate is a duplicate for purposes of [FRE] 1003."[7]

5. *Missing Originals*

Occasionally an original cannot be produced for a variety of reasons. In those case, the rules also provide some relief:

Rule 1004. Admissibility of Other Evidence of Content

An original is not required and other evidence of the content of a writing, recording, or photograph is admissible if:

(a) all the originals are lost or destroyed, and not by the proponent acting in bad faith;

(b) an original cannot be obtained by any available judicial process;

(c) the party against whom the original would be offered had control of the original; was at that time put on notice, by pleadings or otherwise, that the original would be a subject of proof at the trial or hearing; and fails to produce it at the trial or hearing; or

(d) the writing, recording, or photograph is not closely related to a controlling issue.

This rule, in effect, is a "fairness" rule. "Once the terms of Rule 1004 are satisfied, the party seeking to prove the contents of

---

[7] *In re Griffin*, 719 F.3d 1126, 1127 (9th Cir. 2013).

the recording. . . may do so by any kind of secondary evidence."[8] After all, if the original is gone, then secondary evidence should be offered in fairness, right?

But, there is a small caveat. Rule 1004(c) prohibits the extrinsic evidence if "the proponent lost or destroyed the original in bad faith."[9]

E. Parol Evidence Rule

Call this a "pet peeve," call this whatever you want, but the parol evidence rule is *not* a rule of evidence. It *is* a rule, and it *does* govern evidence, so maybe I should just "let it go"—so to speak. However, this rule usually is taught, and tested, in Contracts—not Evidence. Nevertheless, it could be on the bar examination, so let's take a quick look at it.

The 10th Circuit once said that "[t]he parol evidence rule is as much one of substantive contract law as it is an evidentiary rule."[10] At least they got it half right. Anyway, as they said, "[t]he parol evidence rule bars the court from considering evidence of terms outside of an integrated written agreement."[11] Under the rule, "extrinsic evidence may not be admitted to contradict the terms of a binding integrated agreement or to add terms of [an]. . . agreement. . . . An integrated agreement exists when the parties to a contract have reduced to a final written expression one or more terms of their agreement."[12]

It is also important to note that the rule is actually a common law rule. Federal courts apply this state rule when there is a need to apply the rule in a contract dispute. Nevertheless, there are some

---

[8] *U.S. v. Ross,* 33 F.3d 1507, 1513 (11th Cir. 1994).

[9] *Id.*

[10] *U.S. v. Rockwell Int'l Corp.,* 124 F.3d 1194 (10th Cir. 1997).

[11] *Id.*

[12] *Id.*

commonalities with regard to the application of the parol evidence rule across the states.

1. When the Parol Evidence Rule Excludes Evidence

When does this rule apply? It applies when someone is trying to break the rule! In other words, parol evidence kicks in when a party is trying to prove the terms of the document by offering evidence outside the "four corners" of the document. The rule prevents prior and contemporary oral agreements from being admitted. That old— "but he promised me. . . blah blah blah." Sorry, those statements are not coming in.

2. When the Parol Evidence Rule Cannot Exclude Evidence

There are occasions when the Parol Evidence rule does not apply. Certain circumstances that may make oral agreements (statements) admissible are set forth below:

i. A Contract That Is Ambiguous or Incomplete

If a court finds that a contract is ambiguous or incomplete, then parol evidence may be admitted. However, this extrinsic evidence may not contradict, or vary, the terms of the contractual agreement.

ii. Mutual Mistake

When one party to an agreement alleges that the contract contains a mutual mistake, parol evidence may be admitted, although it may contradict the terms of the agreement. The evidence admitted would give insight as to the intent of the parties.

iii. Void or Voidable Contract

When one party alleges that a contract is void, or voidable, then evidence may be admitted to prove:

1) Fraud, duress, or undue influence used to induce agreement;

2) Lack of consideration;

3) Illegality of the subject matter; or

4) Failure to comply with a condition precedent for the contract to be effective.

There are other matters as well but, again, this issue is a state law issue applied in a federal forum. Because of this, the rule and its application (and exceptions) vary from state to state. If you are required to know specifics in your Evidence class, your professor will let you know.

CHAPTER X

Privileges

A. Overview

Wealth, power, and fame are all associated with privilege. None of them have anything to do with the kind of privileges we are discussing in this chapter. In the context of Evidence, privileges provide the "legal" right to refuse to testify on certain matters or, to prevent someone else from testifying on certain matters.

There are many types of privileges. Some are recognized at the federal level, some at the state level, and some at both. In diversity cases, state law governs privileges while federal law governs privileges in cases where jurisdiction is based on a federal question. Because there are several privileges, this guide will address only the privileges most often encountered.

The Federal Rules of Evidence do not specifically set forth independent privileges, but they do contain rules that relate to, and recognize, certain privileges. We begin with Rule 501:

> **Rule 501. Privilege in General**
>
> The common law—as interpreted by United States courts in the light of reason and experience—governs a claim of privilege unless any of the following provides otherwise:
>
> - the United States Constitution;
> - a federal statute; or
> - rules prescribed by the Supreme Court
>
> But in a civil case, state law governs privilege regarding a claim or defense for which state law supplies the rule of decision.

Privileges may arise at the federal and state levels. At the federal level, they are created by common law, federal statute or the Constitution, which is recognized by Rule 501. At the state level, rules are usually created by the State's Supreme Court.

1. Who May Assert the Privilege?

Privileges are held by the individuals to whom they apply. What does that mean? It means that, for example, with the attorney-client privilege, the privilege belongs to the *client*, not the attorney. This means that the client is the one who holds the privilege and may assert the privilege. Let me be more specific. Assume that a client is discussing his case with his attorney. The client admits that he robbed a convenience store. This information is protected by the attorney-client privilege. The client "owns" the privilege. This means that the attorney cannot reveal this information unless permitted by the client. It's the client's privilege. The attorney must, absent client consent, take the information to his grave. Of course, there are exceptions to this too. But you will learn more about that in your professional responsibility course.

2. Confidentiality

For the privilege to apply, the communications must be made in confidence. If you tell your lawyer, across a crowded restaurant, that you robbed the convenience store then—sorry—there is no privilege. Some states recognize a rebuttable presumption that communications made in certain relationships are made in confidence. But—shouting across a crowded room would easily rebut the presumption of confidentiality.

3. Comment on Privilege

Neither the lawyers nor the judge may comment on the fact that a person exercised his or her privilege. For instance, in the presence of a jury, commenting on a person's choosing not to testify so as not to possibly incriminate herself (5th Amendment) may—*not shall*—*may* constitute reversible error.

4. Waiver

Privileges may be waived—intentionally or otherwise. Here are ways in which someone may waive a privilege:

i. Failure to Claim a Privilege

When evidence, which would otherwise be protected by the privilege, is offered into evidence and no objection is made then—guess what? The privilege is waived. You *did* guess that, right?

ii. Intentional Waiver

Recall that the privilege is owned by the person to whom it applies. That person (i.e., the client) may waive the privilege. It belongs to the client to do with as she desires; therefore, she can waive it if she wants to.

iii. Written Agreement

A person may waive her privilege, in advance, in writing.

iv. Carelessness

A party may inadvertently waive a privilege if the party is careless. For example, in one case, a party did not take precautions to make sure that documents he gave to his lawyer remained confidential. Some of the papers were co-mingled with other documents that could be reviewed by a third-party. In that case, the court found that "if a client wishes to preserve the [attorney-client] privilege. . . he must take some affirmative action to preserve confidentiality."[1]

5. *Expectation of Privacy*

What if someone overheard the communication that would, otherwise, be privileged? This is similar to the carelessness waiver previously discussed. If someone overhears information that would otherwise be privileged, the surrounding circumstances become the critical question. If the—lawyer and client (for example)—take appropriate precautions to maintain confidentiality, then the privilege will hold, and the client can prevent the person who heard the information from revealing it. On the other hand, if the conversation takes place at lunch in a crowded restaurant, then the privilege would likely be waived.

B. The Privileges

So, let's take a look at some commonly recognized privileges. The privileges are listed alphabetically.

---

[1] *In re Grand Jury Subpoena Served Upon Horiwitz*, 482 F.2d 72, 82 (2nd Cir. 1973).

With regard to each privilege listed below, you will find two boxes: the first box indicates whether federal common law recognizes the privilege and, the second box indicated whether state law recognizes the privilege. (Note: You will need to research specific jurisdictions to determine whether or not a privilege is recognized by a particular state.)

Remember: In diversity cases, state law governs privileges; in federal question cases, federal law governs.

1. *Accountant-Client*

Recognized Under: Federal Common Law: **No** | State Jurisdictions: **Yes**

This is somewhat similar to the attorney-client privilege discussed below except the accountant-client privilege *is not* recognized under federal common law like the attorney-client privilege does.

2. *Attorney-Client*

Recognized Under: Federal Common Law: **Yes** | State Jurisdictions: **Yes**

This privilege is probably the most common, most heavily used, most well-recognized (next to the 5th Amendment privilege) and certainly one of the most often tested. There are certain requirements which, if met, permit the client to exercise the privilege. The United States Supreme Court has recognized the privilege and, in fact, described it as "the oldest of the privileges for confidential communications known to the common law."[2] Unfortunately, the Supreme Court has not given us precise elements

---

[2]   *Upjohn Co. v. United States*, 449 U.S. 383, 389 (1981).

as to what is protected by this privilege. However, many state courts have required these elements for the privilege to apply:[3]

1. *Legal advice* of any kind is sought;

2. From a *legal professional* in his or her capacity as such;

3. The *communication* relates to that purpose; and

4. The communication is made in *confidence*.

i. Legal Advice of Any Kind Is Sought

This element might seem pretty simple. Usually, it is. You might think that the typical scenario is a client seeking advice from his lawyer in the lawyer's office. However, legal advice can be sought under many different circumstances. It could happen anywhere—even a bar. Wait!!! A bar? Sure—*this* element. But if you examine the fourth element—the communication must be made in confidence—the environment of the bar may undermine or destroy *that* element.

ii. From a Legal Professional in His or Her Capacity as Such

So, what does *this* element mean? The Seventh Circuit tells us that "[t]he privilege is limited to situations in which the attorney is acting as a legal advisor. Business advice does not count, and is not protected."[4] That is, giving business advice is not acting in the capacity of a legal professional. If you are discussing sports scores with your lawyer, then the communication is not protected. Seriously, a communication between lawyer and client can consist of many kinds; those related to the client's seeking of legal advice will be protected; those unrelated will not be protected.

---

[3] *United States v. Graf*, 610 F.3d 1148, 1156 (9th Cir. 2010).

[4] *Burden-Meeks v. Welch*, 319 F.3d 897, 899 (7th Cir. 2003).

iii. The Communication Relates to That Purpose

Remember the sports scores reference above? It applies here—but a bit differently. In the reference above, the attorney must be acting in his or her capacity as a legal professional. Here, the communication must relate to the purpose of seeking legal advice. Sports statistics? Not so much; unless you are a sports agent, the scores are your client's, and you are speaking to your client about his upcoming contract.

iv. The Communication Is Made in Confidence

The communication must be made in confidence. Although usually not a problem, certain situations can create problems with confidentiality. Consider the client who brings in his, or her, spouse for support. If the spouse is not a client *also*, then—oops—we might have a breach in confidence. If the communication occurs in a crowded restaurant—again, we might have a problem.

What about personnel at law firms. Communication to, or with, them does not breach the confidentiality requirement. Associates, para-professionals, and staff are all appropriate individuals to communicate with, and to be part of, any communication with clients. Without the protections extending to these individuals, the job of an attorney would be virtually impossible.

3. *Attorney-Work Product*

Recognized Under: > Federal Common Law: **Yes**   State Jurisdictions: **Yes**

This is—similar to the attorney-client privilege, but it is not the same thing. While the attorney-client privilege protects communications with clients, what about the attorney's work product? There is another privilege, the attorney-work product privilege. For example, if he interviews a witness, the witness is not a client. Therefore, the communication is not protected by the attorney-client privilege. However, the communication might be protected under the work product privilege because the attorney is performing work on behalf of her client. The United States Supreme Court has told us that work product is not subject to discovery except in the very rare circumstance where it is a necessity and cannot otherwise be obtained by other means.[5]

4. *Clergy-Penitent*

Recognized Under: | Federal Common Law: Yes | State Jurisdictions: Yes

"American common law. . . compels the recognition of a clergy-penitent privilege. . . ."[6] "The privilege[ ] between [clergy] and penitent. . . [is] rooted in the imperative need for confidence and trust. The . . . privilege recognizes the human need to disclose to a spiritual counselor, in total and absolute confidence, what are believed to be flawed acts or thoughts and to receive priestly consolation and guidance in return."[7]

i.　The Requirements

For a communication to be protected, and for the privilege to apply:

a.　The communication must be made with a reasonable expectation of confidentiality;

b.　The communication be made to a member of the clergy; and

c.　The clergy must have been acting in his or her professional or spiritual capacity.

---

[5] *Hickman v. Taylor*, 329 U.S. 495 (1947).

[6] *In re Grand Jury Investigation*, 918 F.2d 374, 384 (3rd Cir. 1990).

[7] *Trammel v. U.S.*, 445 U.S. 40, 51 (1980).

ii. Who Qualifies as Clergy

A clergy member is "a minister, priest, rabbi, or other similar functionary of a religious organization, or an individual reasonably believed so to be by the person consulting him."[8]

iii. Who May Claim the Privilege?

The privilege may be claimed by the clergy member or by the penitent, the penitent's guardian or conservator, or by the penitnent's personal representative if the penitent is deceased.[9]

iv. Confidential Communication

Much like the attorney-client privilege, this privilege requires confidential communication. The communication will be considered confidential if it was made privately and if not intended for further disclosure except to third-parties present in furtherance of, or essential to, the purpose of the communication.[10] In one case, a letter to a cleric was not subject to the privilege because there was no indication that it was intended to be confidential. Nor did the letter indicate that it was seeking religious counsel or spiritual advice, etc.[11]

v. Clergy in Capacity of Spiritual Adviser

The communication must be made in the clergy's capacity as a spiritual advisor. Some examples of what *not* to do: A communication was made to a cleric seeking help in avoiding taxes. This would *not* fall within the privilege. Yes, it really happened.[12] In another case, a guy had an employee who happened to be a

---

[8] *In re Grand Jury Investigation*, 918 F.2d 374, 380 (3rd Cir. 1990) (citing proposed FRE 506).

[9] *Id.*

[10] *Id.*

[11] *U.S. v. Wells*, 446 F.2d 2, 4 (2nd Cir. 1971).

[12] *U.S. v. Dube*, 820 F.2d 886, 889-90 (7th Cir. 1987).

priest. His communications to his employee were not protected because the priest was not employed as a priest.[13] (But you can't blame a guy for trying.)

5. *Journalist*

Recognized Under: | Federal Common Law: **No** | State Jurisdictions: **Yes**

At the federal level the Supreme Court has not recognized a privilege for a journalist's sources. At the state level, some (but not all) jurisdictions have recognized a journalist's privilege.

    i.   The privilege often has the following requirements:

        a.   It may only be claimed by the journalist—not another witness;

        b.   The journalist need not be credentialed for an established press entity; and

        c.   The person acting as a journalist must have intended to gather the information for the purpose of dissemination and should independently seek the information (as opposed to serving or promoting the interests of another).

    ii.   The following information is protected by the privilege:

        a.   A journalist's confidential sources; and

        b.   Potentially, a journalist's non-confidential sources, depending on the Circuit and the nature of the proceedings in which the privilege is invoked.

---

[13] *U.S. v. Gordon*, 655 F.2d 478, 486 (2nd Cir. 1981).

iii. To assert the privilege:

    a. The party claiming the privilege has the initial burden to prove that at the beginning of the investigation, she had intended to disseminate to the public the information obtained through the investigation; and

    b. The party claiming the privilege must do more than assert it; she must provide the court with particularized allegations or facts that support the claim of privilege.

iv. To overcome the privilege:

    a. A court must weigh the First Amendment concerns against the opposing need for disclosure in light of the facts of the case.

    b. A three-part test for overcoming the privilege has been followed by many courts:

        (1) Whether the information is relevant to the underlying cause of action;

        (2) Whether the information can be obtained by alternative means; and

        (3) Whether there is a compelling interest in the information.

6. *Physician-Patient*

Recognized Under: Federal Common Law: **No** | State Jurisdictions: **Yes**

Although this privilege is not recognized by federal law, most state-court jurisdictions recognize some form of this privilege. The elements commonly used require the communication to be:

i.   Made to a medical professional (need not be the actual doctor);

ii.   Acquired while attending to the patient; and

iii.   Related to the treatment.

Federal common law, however, protects a patient's limited right to privacy regarding medical records.

7. *Psychotherapist/Social Worker*

Recognized Under: Federal Common Law: **Yes**   State Jurisdictions: **Yes**

Individuals have limited rights to refuse to disclose, and to prevent another person from disclosing, confidential communications made to a psychotherapist, or persons who are participating in the diagnosis or treatment under the direction of a psychotherapist, to diagnose or treat:

i.   A mental condition;

ii.   An emotional condition; or

iii.   A drug addiction.

8. *Self-Incrimination (5th Amendment)*

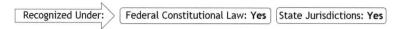

Recognized Under: Federal Constitutional Law: **Yes**   State Jurisdictions: **Yes**

The privilege against self-incrimination is constitutional. Specifically, it is an absolute right provided by the 5th Amendment to the United States Constitution. This means that a witness (any witness—not just a party) may refuse to answer any question which might elicit information that might subject him or her to criminal prosecution. Additionally, a defendant in a criminal case may—under this privilege—refuse to take the stand at all and it cannot be legally held against her for exercising this privilege.

i. When the Privilege Applies

This privilege always applies. That is, it can be claimed in any federal or state proceeding whether criminal or civil.

ii. "Incrimination" Defined

Testimony is considered incriminating when "answers. . . would. . . support a conviction under a. . . criminal statute [and] embraces those which would furnish a link in the chain of evidence needed to prosecute the [witness] for a. . . crime.[14]

9. Spousal Privileges

Recognized Under: Federal Common Law: Yes   State Jurisdictions: Yes

 i. Under federal common law, two types of spousal privileges exist:

  a. The marital confidential-communications privilege; and

  b. The spousal testimonial privilege.

 ii. The Marital Confidential-Communications Privilege:

  a. Generally:

   (1) Protects confidential communications between spouses;

   (2) Is held by both spouses; and

   (3) Applies in both civil and criminal cases.

  Both spouses jointly hold this privilege and either may refuse to disclose a confidential communication made between the spouses while they were married. In some jurisdictions, the

---

[14] *Hoffman v. United States*, 341 U.S. 479, 486 (1951).

privilege also permits one spouse to prevent the other spouse from testifying as to the confidential communication.

b. The privilege has two elements. The communication must have been made:

(1) During a valid marriage; and

(2) In reliance upon the intimacy of the marital relationship.

c. Waiver/Inapplicability of the privilege:

(1) If the communication is made in the presence of a stranger, then the privilege will be waived;

(2) The privilege does not apply in actions (lawsuits) between spouses (i.e., divorces);

(3) The privilege does not apply in criminal cases against the testifying spouse; and

(4) The privilege does not apply to actions against either of the spouse's children (i.e.: assault and battery, incest, bigamy, child abuse, child endangerment or neglect, etc.).

iii. The Spousal Testimonial Privilege

1. Generally

This privilege protects a married criminal defendant. The defendant's spouse may not be called to testify and cannot be compelled to testify against the defendant in any criminal proceeding. In this context, criminal proceeding includes a grand jury proceeding.

2.   To Whom Does the Privilege Belong?

In federal courts, the privilege is held by the witness-spouse; it is not held by the defendant. So, if the witness-spouse chooses not to invoke the privilege, then she may testify.

In state courts, the person holding the privilege may vary from jurisdiction to jurisdiction. It can be held only by the witness-spouse or, in some states, it can be held by both parties. Therefore, in the latter situation, the defendant could prevent the witness-spouse from testifying.

3.   The privilege has two elements:

   (1)   There must be a valid marriage; and

   (2)   The privilege lasts only while the marriage is valid.

CHAPTER XI

Judicial Notice

A. Overview

Judicial Notice is the recognition, by the court, of an undisputable reasonable fact. For example, a court could take judicial notice of the fact that there are 365 days in a year (except for leap year, of course). Rule 201 governs when a court can and cannot take judicial notice of a fact.

Rule 201. Judicial Notice of Adjudicative Facts

(a) **Scope.** This rule governs judicial notice of an adjudicative fact only, not a legislative fact.

(b) **Kinds of Facts That May Be Judicially Noticed.** The court may judicially notice a fact that is not subject to reasonable dispute because it:

    (1) is generally known within the trial court's territorial jurisdiction; or

    (2) can be accurately and readily determined from sources whose accuracy cannot reasonably be questioned.

(c) Taking Notice. The court:

   (1)   may take judicial notice on its own; or

   (2)   must take judicial notice if a party requests it and the court is supplied with the necessary information.

(d) Timing. The court may take judicial notice at any stage of the proceeding.

(e) Opportunity to Be Heard. On timely request, a party is entitled to be heard on the propriety of taking judicial notice and the nature of the fact to be noticed. If the court takes judicial notice before notifying a party, the party, on request, is still entitled to be heard.

(f)   Instructing the Jury. In a civil case, the court must instruct the jury to accept the noticed fact as conclusive. In a criminal case, the court must instruct the jury that it may or may not accept the noticed fact as conclusive.

B. Judicial Notice of Facts

1. Facts Eligible for Judicial Notice

Only facts which are considered "adjudicative facts" may be recognized under Rule 201. Facts that are not "adjudicative facts" are "legislative facts." What in the world is an "adjudicative fact" you ask? Well, let me tell you.

"Adjudicative facts" are facts which:

1)   are generally known within the trial court's territorial jurisdiction; or

2)   can be accurately and readily determined from sources whose accuracy cannot reasonably be questioned.

The 8th Circuit described the difference between *adjudicative facts* and *legislative facts* as this: "Adjudicative facts are facts that normally go to the jury in a jury case. They relate to the parties, their activities, their properties, their businesses. By contrast, legislative facts do not relate specifically to the activities or characteristics of the litigants."[1]

i.   Common Knowledge

The phrase "generally known within the trial court's territorial jurisdiction" in Rule 201(b)(1) translates—loosely—into "common knowledge." When a fact, or facts, are generally known by "everybody" then they are the type of facts which are appropriate for "judicial notice."

Although examples would certainly include facts such as "there are twelve months in a year," or "Austin is the Capital of Texas," other facts which are much more localized may also be appropriate for judicial notice. Localized examples might be that all of the numbered streets in a certain city run East/West, while alphabetical streets run North/South.

ii.   Verifiable Facts

The phrase "can be accurately and readily determined from sources whose accuracy cannot reasonably be questioned" in Rule 201(b)(2) translates—loosely—into "easily verifiable." These facts, while not common knowledge, would be easily confirmed through appropriate sources.

Suppose that Broad Street was closed for repair last week. This could, likely, be verified through public records. A fact that is easily verified would be subject to judicial notice.

iii.   Scientific Principles

The Rule does not set out specific authority for a court to take judicial notice of scientific principles. On the contrary, with regard

---

[1]   *Qually v. Clo-Tex Int'l*, 212 F.3d 1123, 1128 (8th Cir. 2000).

to specific cases, it would seem that a party should prove whatever they hope to prove scientifically, right? Actually—yes. However, what one seeks to prove scientifically is different from a scientific principle.

Whether or not the defendant is a DNA match to the blood found at the crime scene is an example of what one party might seek to prove, scientifically, through evidence at trial. It's an adjudicative fact but subject to reasonable dispute and, therefore, not subject to judicial notice. However, the accuracy of DNA testing would reflect scientific principles.

Should a party be required to prove the scientific principles behind every theory he wishes to advocate? Courts will take judicial notice of scientific principles if they are easily verifiable. As noted by the 9th Circuit, "[A] high degree of indisputability is the essential prerequisite to taking judicial notice. . . ."[2]

Courts readily recognize scientific principles such as: the accuracy of radar gun results; blood test results for paternity testing; ballistic tests; etc.

iv. Knowledge Within Purview of Judge

Just because a judge might be aware of a fact, her knowledge (in and of itself) does not permit her to take judicial notice of the fact. Any judicial notice taken by the court must meet the requirements of the rule.

C. Judicial Notice of Law

This concept does not fit the rule. That is, the ability of courts to take judicial notice of applicable law is not addressed by the Federal Rules of Evidence.

---

[2] *Rivera v. Philip Morris, Inc.*, 395 F.3d 1142, 1151 (9th Cir. 2005).

D. Procedural Requirements

A court may take judicial notice on its own without a motion (*sua sponte*) or, in response to a party's request.

E. Effect of Judicial Notice

1. Bench Trial

Once the court takes judicial notice of a fact, that fact is taken as true, and proof is not necessary. A court can choose not to take judicial notice of a fact, thereby requiring additional proof.

2. Jury Trial—Civil

Under Rule 201(f), instructions are necessary in civil jury trials. Specifically, the court must instruct the jury to accept the fact as conclusive. [Rule 201(f)]

3. Jury Trial—Criminal

Jury instructions in criminal trials are different from civil trials. In criminal cases, the court must instruct the jury that *it may, or may not,* accept the noticed fact as conclusive.

F. Example of Facts Subject to Judicial Notice

1. The price of a stock on a certain day (e.g., Apple stock closed at 139.79 on March 1, 2017);

2. The location of a residence based on Google maps and a satellite image (e.g., it's on the north side of town);

3. The Consumer Price Index;

4. Matters of public record including the filing of a complaint;

5. Factual information on commercial internet sites (e.g., taking judicial notice of some statistics about a professional football team found on the team's website);

6. Proceedings in other courts, but not findings-of-fact from other courts;

7. Government data and publications;

8. Historical information contained in authoritative publications;

9. The time of the sunrise or sunset;

10. Definitions of words; and

11. Distances (e.g., the distance of a hospital from another hospital).

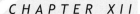

CHAPTER XII

Procedural
Considerations

A. Overview

The Rules of Evidence are, of course, the foundation of virtually all evidentiary issues and challenges in a courtroom. There are, however, procedural rules and considerations that occasionally impact an evidentiary analysis.

B. Burdens of Proof

The term "burden of proof" actually has two meanings that lay people don't recognize but, as a law student, you don't get to claim a "lay person" privilege. In the context of evidence, burden of proof can mean either: (1) the burden of production; or (2) the burden of persuasion.

1. Burden of Production

The party who has the burden on the case has the burden of production. What does this mean? This is best explained by example. Suppose Polly Plaintiff has sued Walmart for negligence claiming that Walmart failed to clean one of their aisles and, as a result, Polly slipped and fell resulting in serious injuries to Polly. It's a civil case, so the burden of persuasion (see below) is a *preponderance of the evidence*. But what in the world is the burden of production?

It basically means that Polly must produce enough evidence to prevent her case from being dismissed; she must produce enough evidence that a jury would be able to deliberate on the evidence. This may include documentary evidence or witness testimony.

Once the plaintiff meets her burden of production, then the burden of production shifts to the defendant who then must present evidence that it was not negligent. Textbooks often talk about these burdens like a see-saw going back and forth. In practice, it doesn't really happen that way.

2.   *Burden of Persuasion*

Individuals often confuse "Burden of Proof" with the "Burden of Persuasion." However, the Burden of Persuasion is standard of proof imposed upon the parties which will be discussed below in greater detail.

i.   Who Has the Burden?

It is possible for each party to have a burden depending on the type of case (criminal v. civil), the issues, and the types of claims and defenses. For example, in a negligence case, Polly has the burden of proof to show, by a *preponderance of evidence*, that Walmart was negligent. The burden does not shift to the opponent unless an affirmative defense has been raised. In the end, Polly either meets her burden of proof, or she doesn't.

ii.   Standards of Proof

There are three standards (burdens) of proof (or persuasion): 1) preponderance of the evidence; 2) clear and convincing evidence;

and 3) beyond a reasonable doubt. The nature of the lawsuit defines the burden.

Graphically, it looks something like this:

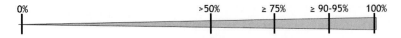

a.   Preponderance of the Evidence (> 50%)

This standard applies in most civil cases (such as personal injury and breach of contract cases), and defenses, as well as most (but not all) affirmative defenses in civil and criminal cases. This standard is often described as any amount greater than fifty-percent (50%). It requires convincing a fact-finder that the occurrence of a particular fact is more likely than not (i.e., greater than 50%).

b.   Clear and Convincing Evidence (≥ 75%)

Some civil cases require a measure of proof that is clear and convincing. This standard is higher than the Preponderance of the Evidence standard. Although there is no formal percentage tied to this standard, is has been described as greater than, or equal, to seventy-five percent (≥75%). This applies to a small number of civil cases usually involving issues such as: civil fraud, will contests, and administrative hearings. At the state level, some child support enforcement actions require a clear and convincing burden of proof.

c.   Beyond a Reasonable Doubt (≥ 90–95%)

This is the highest and most challenging standard and applies only to criminal cases. This standard, also, has no formal percentage

> **Attention!**
>
> A criminal defendant may elect not to offer any evidence if the defendant believes that the prosecution failed to meet its burden. However, if the defendant has an affirmative defense, the defendant's standard of proof is not the same as the prosecutor's burden. The defendant must prove his affirmative defense with a burden that is usually preponderance of the evidence.

tied to it but it has been described as requiring greater than, or equal to, ninety to ninety-five percent ($\geq$90–95%).

In a fairly recent criminal trial, a defendant was charged with murder, but argued he was acting in self-defense. When giving his closing statement to the jury, the defense attorney used a visual aid to demonstrate the standard of proof the prosecution must meet to prove that the Defendant is guilty of murder. It was similar to this:

Not Guilty	←	Self-Defense
Not Guilty	←	Self-Defense Highly Likely
Not Guilty	←	Self-Defense Likely
Not Guilty	←	Probably Self-Defense
Not Guilty	←	Suspected Self-Defense
Not Guilty	←	Perhaps Self-Defense
Not Guilty	←	May Not Be Self-Defense
Not Guilty	←	Possibly Not Self-Defense
Not Guilty	←	Unlikely Self-Defense
Not Guilty	←	Probably Not Self-Defense
Not Guilty	←	Less Than Likely Self-Defense
Not Guilty	←	Highly Unlikely Self-Defense
Guilty	←	Proven Murder Beyond a Reasonable Doubt

The purpose of the chart was to visually illustrate to the jury that **any** doubt, however slight, as long as it was reasonable, meant that the prosecution had not met **its** burden of proof.

C. Presumptions

A presumption is a starting point. It's a rule that requires a particular inference be drawn from a particular set of facts. It's basically a shortcut. It means that if a fact is presumed, then you do not have to prove it.

> *Example:* In some jurisdictions, there is a presumption that in a rear-end collision, the driver of the rearmost vehicle is at fault. The presumption is rebuttable, which we will discuss in a moment.

1. *Where Presumptions Are Found*

Most presumptions are created by statute, while other presumptions are created by case law. Presumptions are not found in the Federal Rules of Evidence. Rule 301 simply regulates the effect of evidentiary presumptions.

2. *Effect and Rebuttal of a Presumption*

Per Rule 301, in a civil case, the party against whom a presumption is directed has the burden of rebutting that presumption. In the above example, the driver of the rearmost vehicle would have the burden of proving that the accident was not his fault.

Rule 301 also provides that the rule does not shift the burden of persuasion. What does this mean? It means that if the driver of the vehicle in front (let's call her Pricilla) sues the driver of the rearmost vehicle (let's call him Dave) then, as the plaintiff, Pricilla has the burden of production **and** the burden of persuasion (which is a preponderance of the evidence standard). Because the presumption is that Dave was at fault, Pricilla must offer evidence of the collision, and proof that Dave was driving the rearmost vehicle. Then, Dave has the burden to rebut the presumption that he was not at fault.

When the opponent produces some evidence which contradicts the presumed fact, then the presumption is overcome (poof!—into the air it goes). What this means is that the presumption is of no effect at all—when sufficient evidence is admitted which is contrary to the presumption.

In our example, the burden of persuasion does not shift to Dave. But—when the jury deliberates—the question to be decided is whether or not Pricilla proved, by a preponderance of the evidence, that Dave acted negligently.

3. *How Much Evidence Is Needed?*

The amount of evidence needed to rebut the presumption is not clear. There is authority which has required "enough evidence to support a finding of the nonexistence of the presumed fact,"[1] and there is also authority which had required "minimal evidence."[2]

4. *Presumptions v. Inferences*

Inferences are not presumptions and are, occasionally, confused with presumptions. Black's Law Dictionary defines an "inference" as "[a] conclusion reached by considering other facts and deducing a logical consequence from them."[3] This is contrary to a presumption, which requires a fact to be taken as true unless rebutted.

5. *Presumptions in Criminal Cases*

There are certain presumptions that always exist in criminal cases.

i. **Presumption of Innocence**

Criminal defendants are presumed innocent unless, and until, they are proven guilty beyond a reasonable doubt. There is no

---

[1] *In Re Yoder*, 758 F.2d 1114, 1118 (6th Cir. 1985).

[2] *Cappuccio v. Prime Capital Funding, LLC*, 649 F.3d 180, 189 (3rd Cir. 2011).

[3] Black's Law Dictionary (10th ed. 2014).

burden shifting in criminal cases. The beginning point, the presumption of innocence, remains the "fact" unless the prosecution produces enough evidence to convince the fact-finder (judge or jury) that the defendant is guilty beyond a reasonable doubt.

ii.   Facts Presumed Against Accused

In criminal cases, a judge is not permitted to instruct the jury that it must find a presumed fact against the defendant. When a case involves a presumed fact, a jury *may* find the fact against the defendant. If a presumed fact establishes guilt or an element of an offense then that presumed fact must be established beyond a reasonable doubt.

D. Specific Presumptions

The law is rife with presumptions. The vast majority of presumptions are derived from state law although there are some federal presumptions (such as the presumption of innocence discussed above). Here are some presumptions which are frequently encountered:

1. *Against Suicide*

In civil cases, when the cause of death is in dispute, a presumption arises that the death was not suicide. As one court noted, ". . . the presumption against suicide is not evidence at all, but is a rule of law which. . . requires the conclusion, in the event of an unexplained death by violent injury, that the death was not suicidal until credible evidence of self-destruction is offered. When such evidence is offered. . . the presumption as a rule of law disappears from the case and the trier of facts passes upon the issues in the usual way."[4]

2. Bailee's Negligence

When evidence is offered that goods were loaned to a party in a particular condition, and the goods were not returned in the same condition, then there is a presumption that the Bailee was negligent.

3. Car Ownership

Many states have a presumption with regard to car ownership, that the owner is presumed the agent and responsible party.

4. Death from Absence

Persons are presumed dead, with regard to actions involving their property, if two requirements are met:

a. The person has been missing for at least seven (7) continuous years; and

b. The person has not been heard from by those with whom the person would normally be expected to communicate.

5. Legitimacy

You should be aware that various jurisdictions use a number of terms to describe legitimacy. Regardless, the presumption is that every person born during lawful wedlock is legitimate. Many states have created statutes which create the presumption of legitimacy, under certain conditions, even when a child is born out of wedlock—

---

[4]   *Jefferson Standard Life Ins. Co. v. Clemmer*, 79 F.2d 724, 729 (4th Cir. 1935).

such as the father being named on the birth certificate. The burden of proof for overcoming the presumption is "clear and convincing."

6. *Mail Delivery*

You probably remember something like this from your Contracts class. If a letter has been properly addressed, stamped, and placed in the mailbox, it is presumed to have been properly delivered. This is similar to the "mailbox" rule. An acceptance is considered effective when properly addressed, stamped and placed in the mailbox.

7. *Marriage*

If a ceremonial marriage has been performed, there is a presumption that the marriage is valid. Of course, many factors can rebut this presumption such as: bigamy, incompetence, fraud, age restrictions, failure to follow the state's requirements, etc.

8. *Regularity*

The presumption of regularity provides that courts are to presume, in the absence of clear evidence to the contrary, public officers have properly discharged their official duties.

9. *Sanity*

Individuals are presumed sane in both civil and criminal cases. (Of course, this is a terrible presumption not based in reality).

10. *Solvency*

There is a presumption that individuals are solvent and all debts are presumed to be collectible. (The more realistic presumption would seem to be one of insolvency).

11. Undue Influence in a Fiduciary Context

In some jurisdictions, when a fiduciary relationship exists between two or more parties, and the fiduciary obtains an advantage as a result of the relationship, a presumption arises that the fiduciary gained the advantage by undue influence or unfairness.

E. Conflicting Presumptions

Occasionally, presumptions will conflict. In those cases, judges are supposed to pick between the two presumptions by choosing which presumption should yield by determining from the evidence and inferences, which is the least probable to sustain.

Example: Recall that marriages are presumed to be valid if a ceremonial marriage has been performed. What if there is an issue as to a person with two marriages? One marriage is from many years ago and a current marriage. Which one is valid, given the presumptions?

In one case, following the rule, the court found that there was no extrinsic evidence of the first marriage, while there were two "strong reasons" which supported the validity of the second marriage. The court found that the evidence strengthened the presumption of the second marriage, and while that did not "destroy" the first presumption, it effectively led to the court yielding the presumption of the first marriage and, instead, recognizing the second.[5]

---

[5] *Cupler v. Secretary of Health, Education and Welfare,* 252 F.Supp. 178 (W.D. Pa. 1966).

CHAPTER XIII

Tying It All Together

If you have read this entire guide, you should have a pretty good handle on the basics of the Federal Rules of Evidence. Although complex, the Federal Rules of Evidence are fairly logical. Reading the rules in their entirety, along with relevant cases interpreting the rules and Advisory Committee Notes assisting with their explanation, the Rules of Evidence can be readily understood; at least, more than the "average bear" might understand them.

Attention!

Yes, I know you have seen a box before, but I really mean what I say. If you liked the book, disliked the book or have any suggestions, thoughts, ideas or questions, please drop me a line at HappyEvidence@gmail.com. I will try to respond to everyone. I can't promise I will be able to—but I will try.

Hopefully by now, you realize that any evidentiary analysis is a process and can follow, somewhat, a formula. Just like traveling down the dungeon path, each hurdle is an Orc you must kill. Kill all of the Orcs and the evidence is admitted. If an Orc kills you, then the evidence is excluded. To wrap things up, it makes some sense to revisit the flowchart from Chapter I, although now somewhat expanded.

Now that you have studied most of the rules, examine the flowchart carefully from the beginning to the end, considering what analysis is needed for each piece of evidence. Some evidence may require more than one analysis, while others may not.

A. The Comprehensive Evidence Flowchart

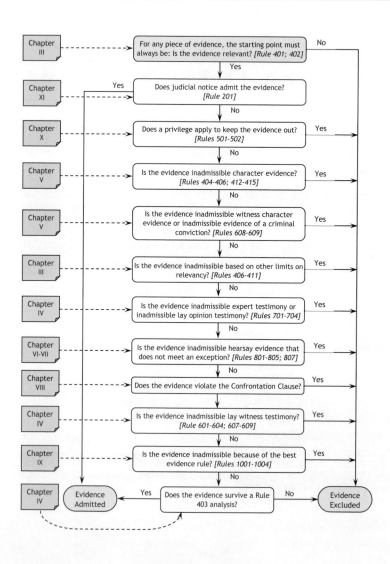

Federal Rules of Evidence

The following table reflects both the current Federal Rules of Evidence (in the right-hand column) which were effective December 1, 2011 *(including amendments through December 1, 2017)* and the former version of the rules (in the left-hand column), which were effective prior to the restyling project. Why would the former rules be included? Because many (if not most) of the reported cases, which interpret the rules, reflect the former language. This table enables you to compare the former language with the current language.

Article I: General Provisions

Former Rule	*Current Rule*
Rule 101. Scope	**Rule 101. Scope; Definitions**
These rules govern proceedings in the courts of the United States and before the United States bankruptcy	(a) **Scope.** These rules apply to proceedings in United States courts. The specific courts and proceedings

judges and United States magistrate judges, to the extent and with the exceptions stated in rule 1101.	to which the rules apply, along with exceptions, are set out in Rule 1101.
	
	(b) **Definitions.** In these rules:
	
	  (1) "civil case" means a civil action or proceeding;
	
	  (2) "criminal case" includes a criminal proceeding;
	
	  (3) "public office" includes a public agency;
	
	  (4) "record" includes a memorandum, report, or data compilation;
	
	  (5) a "rule prescribed by the Supreme Court" means a rule adopted by the Supreme Court under statutory authority; and
	
	  (6) a reference to any kind of written material or any other medium includes electronically stored information.

Former Rule	*Current Rule*
Rule 102. Purpose and Construction	**Rule 102. Purpose**
These rules shall be construed to secure fairness in administration, elimination of unjustifiable expense and delay, and promotion of growth and development of the law of evidence to the end that the truth may be ascertained and proceedings justly determined.	These rules should be construed so as to administer every proceeding fairly, eliminate unjustifiable expense and delay, and promote the development of evidence law, to the end of ascertaining the truth and securing a just determination.

Former Rule	*Current Rule*
Rule 103. Rulings of Evidence	**Rule 103. Rulings on Evidence**

(a) Effect of erroneous ruling. Error may not be predicated upon a ruling which admits or excludes evidence unless a substantial right of the party is affected, and
 	
  (1) Objection. In case the ruling is one admitting evidence, a timely objection or motion to strike appears of record, stating the specific ground of objection, if the specific ground was not apparent from the context; or
 	
  (2) Offer of proof. In case the ruling is one excluding evidence, the substance of the evidence was made known to the court by offer or was apparent from the context within which questions were asked.
 	
Once the court makes a definitive ruling on the record admitting or excluding evidence, either at or before trial, a party need not renew an objection or offer of proof to preserve a claim of error for appeal.
	(a) Preserving a Claim of Error. A party may claim error in a ruling to admit or exclude evidence only if the error affects a substantial right of the party and:
	
	  (1) if the ruling admits evidence, a party, on the record:
	
	    (A) timely objects or moves to strike; and
	
	    (B) states the specific ground, unless it was apparent from the context; or
	
	  (2) if the ruling excludes evidence, a party informs the court of its substance by an offer of proof, unless the substance was apparent from the context.
	
	(b) Not Needing to Renew an Objection or Offer of Proof. Once the court rules definitively on the record—either before or at trial—a party need not renew an objection or offer of proof to preserve a claim of error for appeal.

(b) Record of offer and ruling. The court may add any other or further statement which shows the character of the evidence, the form in which it was offered, the objection made, and the ruling thereon. It may direct the making of an offer in question and answer form.	**(c) Court's Statement About the Ruling; Directing an Offer of Proof.** The court may make any statement about the character or form of the evidence, the objection made, and the ruling. The court may direct that an offer of proof be made in question-and-answer form.

(c) Hearing of jury. In jury cases, proceedings shall be conducted, to the extent practicable, so as to prevent inadmissible evidence from being suggested to the jury by any means, such as making statements or offers of proof or asking questions in the hearing of the jury.	**(d) Preventing the Jury from Hearing Inadmissible Evidence.** To the extent practicable, the court must conduct a jury trial so that inadmissible evidence is not suggested to the jury by any means.
(d) Plain error. Nothing in this rule precludes taking notice of plain errors affecting substantial rights although they were not brought to the attention of the court.	**(e) Taking Notice of Plain Error.** A court may take notice of a plain error affecting a substantial right, even if the claim of error was not properly preserved.

Former Rule	*Current Rule*
Rule 104. Preliminary Questions	**Rule 104. Preliminary Questions**
(a) Questions of admissibility generally. Preliminary questions concerning the qualification of a person to be a witness, the existence of a privilege, or the admissibility of evidence shall be determined by the court, subject to the provisions of subdivision (b). In making its determination it is not bound by the rules of evidence except those with respect to privileges.	**(a) In General.** The court must decide any preliminary question about whether a witness is qualified, a privilege exists, or evidence is admissible. In so deciding, the court is not bound by evidence rules, except those on privilege.
(b) Relevancy conditioned on fact. When the relevancy of evidence depends upon the fulfillment of a condition of fact, the court shall admit it upon, or subject to, the introduction of evidence sufficient to support a finding of the fulfillment of the condition.	**(b) Relevance That Depends on a Fact.** When the relevance of evidence depends on whether a fact exists, proof must be introduced sufficient to support a finding that the fact does exist. The court may admit the proposed evidence on the condition that the proof be introduced later.
(c) Hearing of jury. Hearings on the admissibility of confessions shall in all cases be conducted out of the	**(c) Conducting a Hearing So That the Jury Cannot Hear It.** The court must conduct any hearing on a

hearing of the jury. Hearings on other preliminary matters shall be so conducted when the interests of justice require, or when an accused is a witness and so requests.	preliminary question so that the jury cannot hear it if: **(1)** the hearing involves the admissibility of a confession; **(2)** a defendant in a criminal case is a witness and so requests; or **(3)** justice so requires.
(d) Testimony by accused. The accused does not, by testifying upon a preliminary matter, become subject to cross-examination as to other issues in the case.	**(d) Cross-Examining a Defendant in a Criminal Case.** By testifying on a preliminary question, a defendant in a criminal case does not become subject to cross-examination on other issues in the case.
(e) Weight and credibility. This rule does not limit the right of a party to introduce before the jury evidence relevant to weight or credibility.	**(e) Evidence Relevant to Weight and Credibility.** This rule does not limit a party's right to introduce before the jury evidence that is relevant to the weight or credibility of other evidence.

Former Rule	*Current Rule*
Rule 105. Limited Admissibility	**Rule 105. Limited Evidence That Is Not Admissible Against Other Parties or for Other Purposes**
When evidence which is admissible as to one party or for one purpose but not admissible as to another party or for another purpose is admitted, the court, upon request, shall restrict the evidence to its proper scope and instruct the jury accordingly.	If the court admits evidence that is admissible against a party or for a purpose—but not against another party or for another purpose—the court, on timely request, must restrict the evidence to its proper scope and instruct the jury accordingly.

Former Rule	*Current Rule*
Rule 106. Remainder of or Related Writings or Recorded Statements	**Rule 106. Remainder of or Related Writings or Recorded Statements**
When a writing or recorded statement or part thereof is introduced by a party, an adverse party may require the introduction at that time of any other part or any other writing or recorded statement which ought in fairness to be considered contemporaneously with it.	If a party introduces all or part of a writing or recorded statement, an adverse party may require the introduction, at that time, of any other part—or any other writing or recorded statement—that in fairness ought to be considered at the same time.

Article II: Judicial Notice

Former Rule	*Current Rule*
Rule 201. Judicial Notice of Adjudicative Facts	**Rule 201. Judicial Notice of Adjudicative Facts**
(a) Scope of rule. This rule governs only judicial notice of adjudicative facts.	**(a) Scope.** This rule governs judicial notice of an adjudicative fact only, not a legislative fact.
(b) Kinds of facts. A judicially noticed fact must be one not subject to reasonable dispute in that it is either (1) generally known within the territorial jurisdiction of the trial court or (2) capable of accurate and ready determination by resort to sources whose accuracy cannot reasonably be questioned.	**(b) Kinds of Facts That May Be Judicially Noticed.** The court may judicially notice a fact that is not subject to reasonable dispute because it: (1) is generally known within the trial court's territorial jurisdiction; or (2) can be accurately and readily determined from sources whose accuracy cannot reasonably be questioned.
(c) When discretionary. A court may take judicial notice, whether requested or not. **(d) When mandatory.** A court shall take judicial notice if requested by a party and supplied with the necessary information.	**(c) Taking Notice.** The court: (1) may take judicial notice on its own; or (2) must take judicial notice if a party requests it and the court is supplied with the necessary information.
(e) Opportunity to be heard. A party is entitled upon timely request to an opportunity to be heard as to the propriety of taking judicial notice and the tenor of the matter noticed. In the absence of prior notification, the request may be made after judicial notice has been taken.	**(d) Timing.** The court may take judicial notice at any stage of the proceeding.

(f) Time of taking notice. Judicial notice may be taken at any stage of the proceeding.	**(e) Opportunity to Be Heard.** On timely request, a party is entitled to be heard on the propriety of taking judicial notice and the nature of the fact to be noticed. If the court takes judicial notice before notifying a party, the party, on request, is still entitled to be heard.
(g) Instructing jury. In a civil action or proceeding, the court shall instruct the jury to accept as conclusive any fact judicially noticed. In a criminal case, the court shall instruct the jury that it may, but is not required to, accept as conclusive any fact judicially noticed.	**(f) Instructing the Jury.** In a civil case, the court must instruct the jury to accept the noticed fact as conclusive. In a criminal case, the court must instruct the jury that it may or may not accept the noticed fact as conclusive.

Article III: Presumption in Civil Cases

Former Rule	*Current Rule*
Rule 301. Presumptions in General in Civil Actions and Proceedings	**Rule 301. Presumptions in Civil Cases Generally**
In all civil actions and proceedings not otherwise provided for by Act of Congress or by these rules, a presumption imposes on the party against whom it is directed the burden of going forward with evidence to rebut or meet the presumption, but does not shift to such party the burden of proof in the sense of the risk of nonpersuasion, which remains throughout the trial upon the party on whom it was originally cast.	In a civil case, unless a federal statute or these rules provide otherwise, the party against whom a presumption is directed has the burden of producing evidence to rebut the presumption. But this rule does not shift the burden of persuasion, which remains on the party who had it originally.

Former Rule	*Current Rule*
Rule 302. Applicability of State Law in Civil Actions and Proceedings	**Rule 302. Applying State Law to Presumptions in Civil Cases**
In civil actions and proceedings, the effect of a presumption respecting a fact which is an element of a claim or defense as to which State law supplies the rule of decision is determined in accordance with State law.	In a civil case, state law governs the effect of a presumption regarding a claim or defense for which state law supplies the rule of decision.

Article IV: Relevance and Its Limits

Former Rule	*Current Rule*
Rule 401. Definition of "Relevant Evidence"	**Rule 401. Test for Relevant Evidence**
"Relevant evidence" means evidence having any tendency to make the existence of any fact that is of consequence to the determination of the action more probable or less probable than it would be without the evidence.	Evidence is relevant if: **(a)** it has any tendency to make a fact more or less probable than it would be without the evidence; and **(b)** the fact is of consequence in determining the action.

Former Rule	*Current Rule*
Rule 402. Relevant Evidence Generally Admissible; Irrelevant Evidence Inadmissible	**Rule 402. General Admissibility of Relevant Evidence**
All relevant evidence is admissible, except as otherwise provided by the Constitution of the United States, by Act of Congress, by these rules, or by other rules prescribed by the Supreme Court pursuant to statutory authority. Evidence which is not relevant is not admissible.	Relevant evidence is admissible unless any of the following provides otherwise: • the United States Constitution; • a federal statute; • these rules; or • other rules prescribed by the Supreme Court. Relevant evidence is admissible unless any of the following provides otherwise:

Former Rule	*Current Rule*
Rule 403. Exclusion of Relevant Evidence on Grounds of Prejudice, Confusion, or Waste of Time	**Rule 403. Excluding Relevant Evidence for Prejudice, Confusion, Waste of Time, or Other Reasons**
Although relevant, evidence may be excluded if its probative value is substantially outweighed by the danger of unfair prejudice, confusion of the issues, or misleading the jury, or by considerations of undue delay, waste of time, or needless presentation of cumulative evidence.	The court may exclude relevant evidence if its probative value is substantially outweighed by a danger of one or more of the following: unfair prejudice, confusing the issues, misleading the jury, undue delay, wasting time, or needlessly presenting cumulative evidence.

Former Rule	*Current Rule*
Rule 404. Character Evidence Not Admissible to Prove Conduct; Exceptions; Other Crimes	**Rule 404. Character Evidence; Crimes or Other Acts**
(a) **Character evidence generally.** Evidence of a person's character or a trait of character is not admissible for the purpose of proving action in conformity therewith on a particular occasion, except: (1) **Character of accused.** In a criminal case, evidence of a pertinent trait of character offered by an accused, or by the prosecution to rebut the same, or if evidence of a trait of character of the alleged victim of the crime is offered by an accused and admitted under Rule 404(a)(2), evidence of the same trait of character of	(a) **Character Evidence.** (1) **Prohibited Uses.** Evidence of a person's character or character trait is not admissible to prove that on a particular occasion the person acted in accordance with the character or trait. (2) **Exceptions for a Defendant or Victim in a Criminal Case.** The following exceptions apply in a criminal case: (A) a defendant may offer evidence of the defendant's pertinent trait, and if the evidence is admitted, the

the accused offered by the prosecution;

(2) **Character of alleged victim.** In a criminal case, and subject to the limitations imposed by Rule 412, evidence of a pertinent trait of character of the alleged victim of the crime offered by an accused, or by the prosecution to rebut the same, or evidence of a character trait of peacefulness of the alleged victim offered by the prosecution in a homicide case to rebut evidence that the alleged victim was the first aggressor;

(3) **Character of witness.** Evidence of the character of a witness, as provided in Rules 607, 608, and 609.

prosecutor may offer evidence to rebut it;

(B) subject to the limitations in Rule 412, a defendant may offer evidence of an alleged victim's pertinent trait, and if the evidence is admitted, the prosecutor may:

    (i) offer evidence to rebut it; and

    (ii) offer evidence of the defendant's same trait; and

(C) in a homicide case, the prosecutor may offer evidence of the alleged victim's trait of peacefulness to rebut evidence that the victim was the first aggressor.

(3) **Exceptions for a Witness.** Evidence of a witness's character may be admitted under Rules 607, 608, and 609.

(b) **Other crimes, wrongs, or acts.** Evidence of other crimes, wrongs, or acts is not admissible to prove the character of a person in order to show action in conformity therewith. It may, however, be admissible for other purposes, such as proof of motive, opportunity, intent, preparation, plan, knowledge, identity, or absence of mistake or accident, provided that upon request by the accused, the prosecution in a criminal case shall provide reasonable notice in

(b) **Crimes, Wrongs, or Other Acts.**

(1) **Prohibited Uses.** Evidence of a crime, wrong, or other act is not admissible to prove a person's character in order to show that on a particular occasion the person acted in accordance with the character.

(2) **Permitted Uses; Notice in a Criminal Case.** This evidence may be admissible for another purpose, such as proving motive, opportunity,

advance of trial, or during trial if the court excuses pretrial notice on good cause shown, of the general nature of any such evidence it intends to introduce at trial.	intent, preparation, plan, knowledge, identity, absence of mistake, or lack of accident. On request by a defendant in a criminal case, the prosecutor must:
	(A) provide reasonable notice of the general nature of any such evidence that the prosecutor intends to offer at trial; and
	(B) do so before trial—or during trial if the court, for good cause, excuses lack of pretrial notice.

Former Rule	*Current Rule*
Rule 405. Methods of Proving Character	**Rule 405. Methods of Proving Character**
(a) Reputation or opinion. In all cases in which evidence of character or a trait of character of a person is admissible, proof may be made by testimony as to reputation or by testimony in the form of an opinion. On cross-examination, inquiry is allowable into relevant specific instances of conduct.	**(a) By Reputation or Opinion.** When evidence of a person's character or character trait is admissible, it may be proved by testimony about the person's reputation or by testimony in the form of an opinion. On cross-examination of the character witness, the court may allow an inquiry into relevant specific instances of the person's conduct.
(b) Specific instances of conduct. In cases in which character or a trait of character of a person is an essential element of a charge, claim, or defense, proof may also be made of specific instances of that person's conduct.	**(b) By Specific Instances of Conduct.** When a person's character or character trait is an essential element of a charge, claim, or defense, the character or trait may also be proved by relevant specific instances of the person's conduct.

Former Rule	*Current Rule*
Rule 406. Habit; Routine Practice	**Rule 406. Habit; Routine Practice**
Evidence of the habit of a person or of the routine practice of an organization, whether corroborated or not and regardless of the presence of eyewitnesses, is relevant to prove that the conduct of the person or organization on a particular occasion was in conformity with the habit or routine practice.	Evidence of a person's habit or an organization's routine practice may be admitted to prove that on a particular occasion the person or organization acted in accordance with the habit or routine practice. The court may admit this evidence regardless of whether it is corroborated or whether there was an eyewitness.

Former Rule	*Current Rule*
Rule 407. Subsequent Remedial Measures	**Rule 407. Subsequent Remedial Measures**
When, after an injury or harm allegedly caused by an event, measures are taken that, if taken previously, would have made the injury or harm less likely to occur, evidence of the subsequent measures is not admissible to prove negligence, culpable conduct, a defect in a product, a defect in a product's design, or a need for a warning or instruction. This rule does not require the exclusion of evidence of subsequent measures when offered for another purpose, such as proving ownership, control, or feasibility of precautionary measures, if controverted, or impeachment.	When measures are taken that would have made an earlier injury or harm less likely to occur, evidence of the subsequent measures is not admissible to prove: • negligence; • culpable conduct; • a defect in a product or its design; or • a need for a warning or instruction. But the court may admit this evidence for another purpose, such as impeachment or—if disputed—proving ownership, control, or the feasibility of precautionary measures.

Former Rule	Current Rule
Rule 408. Compromise and Offers to Compromise	**Rule 408. Compromise Offers and Negotiations**
(a) Prohibited uses. Evidence of the following is not admissible on behalf of any party, when offered to prove liability for, invalidity of, or amount of a claim that was disputed as to validity or amount, or to impeach through a prior inconsistent statement or contradiction: (1) furnishing or offering or promising to furnish—or accepting or offering or promising to accept—a valuable consideration in compromising or attempting to compromise the claim; and (2) conduct or statements made in compromise negotiations regarding the claim, except when offered in a criminal case and the negotiations related to a claim by a public office or agency in the exercise of regulatory, investigative, or enforcement authority.	**(a) Prohibited Uses.** Evidence of the following is not admissible—on behalf of any party—either to prove or disprove the validity or amount of a disputed claim or to impeach by a prior inconsistent statement or a contradiction: (1) furnishing, promising, or offering—or accepting, promising to accept, or offering to accept—a valuable consideration in compromising or attempting to compromise the claim; and (2) conduct or a statement made during compromise negotiations about the claim—except when offered in a criminal case and when the negotiations related to a claim by a public office in the exercise of its regulatory, investigative, or enforcement authority.
(b) Permitted uses. This rule does not require exclusion if the evidence is offered for purposes not prohibited by subdivision (a). Examples of permissible purposes include proving a witness's bias or prejudice; negating a contention of undue delay; and proving an effort to obstruct a criminal investigation or prosecution.	**(b) Exceptions.** The court may admit this evidence for another purpose, such as proving a witness's bias or prejudice, negating a contention of undue delay, or proving an effort to obstruct a criminal investigation or prosecution.

Former Rule	*Current Rule*
Rule 409. Payment of Medical and Similar Expenses	**Rule 409. Offers to Pay Medical and Similar Expenses**
Evidence of furnishing or offering or promising to pay medical, hospital, or similar expenses occasioned by an injury is not admissible to prove liability for the injury.	Evidence of furnishing, promising to pay, or offering to pay medical, hospital, or similar expenses resulting from an injury is not admissible to prove liability for the injury.

Former Rule	*Current Rule*
Rule 410. Inadmissibility of Pleas, Plea Discussions, and Related Statements	**Rule 410. Pleas, Plea Discussions, and Related Statements**
Except as otherwise provided in this rule, evidence of the following is not, in any civil or criminal proceeding, admissible against the defendant who made the plea or was a participant in the plea discussions: (1) a plea of guilty which was later withdrawn; (2) a plea of nolo contendere; (3) any statement made in the course of any proceedings under Rule 11 of the Federal Rules of Criminal Procedure or comparable state procedure regarding either of the foregoing pleas; or (4) any statement made in the course of plea discussions with an attorney for the prosecuting authority which do not result in a plea of guilty or which result in a	(a) **Prohibited Uses.** In a civil or criminal case, evidence of the following is not admissible against the defendant who made the plea or participated in the plea discussions: (1) a guilty plea that was later withdrawn; (2) a nolo contendere plea; (3) a statement made during a proceeding on either of those pleas under Federal Rule of Criminal Procedure 11 or a comparable state procedure; or (4) a statement made during plea discussions with an attorney for the prosecuting authority if the discussions did not result in a guilty plea or they resulted in a later-withdrawn guilty plea.

plea of guilty later withdrawn. However, such a statement is admissible (i) in any proceeding wherein another statement made in the course of the same plea or plea discussions has been introduced and the statement ought in fairness be considered contemporaneously with it, or (ii) in a criminal proceeding for perjury or false statement if the statement was made by the defendant under oath, on the record and in the presence of counsel.	**(b) Exceptions.** The court may admit a statement described in Rule 410(a)(3) or (4): **(1)** in any proceeding in which another statement made during the same plea or plea discussions has been introduced, if in fairness the statements ought to be considered together; or **(2)** in a criminal proceeding for perjury or false statement, if the defendant made the statement under oath, on the record, and with counsel present.

Former Rule	*Current Rule*
Rule 411. Liability Insurance	**Rule 411. Liability Insurance**
Evidence that a person was or was not insured against liability is not admissible upon the issue whether the person acted negligently or otherwise wrongfully. This rule does not require the exclusion of evidence of insurance against liability when offered for another purpose, such as proof of agency, ownership, or control, or bias or prejudice of a witness.	Evidence that a person was or was not insured against liability is not admissible to prove whether the person acted negligently or otherwise wrongfully. But the court may admit this evidence for another purpose, such as proving a witness's bias or prejudice or proving agency, ownership, or control.

Former Rule	*Current Rule*
Rule 412. Sex Offense Cases; Relevance of Alleged Victim's Past Sexual Behavior or Alleged Sexual Predisposition	**Rule 412. Sex-Offense Cases: The Victim's Sexual Behavior or Predisposition**
(a) Evidence Generally Inadmissible. The following evidence is not admissible in any civil or criminal proceeding involving	**(a) Prohibited Uses.** The following evidence is not admissible

alleged sexual misconduct except as provided in subdivisions (b) and (c):
 	
  (1) Evidence offered to prove that any alleged victim engaged in other sexual behavior.
 	
  (2) Evidence offered to prove any alleged victim's sexual predisposition.
	in a civil or criminal proceeding involving alleged sexual misconduct:
	
	  (1) evidence offered to prove that a victim engaged in other sexual behavior; or
	
	  (2) evidence offered to prove a victim's sexual predisposition.

(b)   **Exceptions.**
 	
  (1) In a criminal case, the following evidence is admissible, if otherwise admissible under these rules:
 	
    (A) evidence of specific instances of sexual behavior by the alleged victim offered to prove that a person other than the accused was the source of semen, injury or other physical evidence;
 	
    (B) evidence of specific instances of sexual behavior by the alleged victim with respect to the person accused of the sexual misconduct offered by the accused to prove consent or by the prosecution; and
 	
    (C) evidence the exclusion of which would violate the constitutional rights of the defendant.
 	
  (2) In a civil case, evidence offered to prove the sexual behavior or sexual
	(b) **Exceptions.**
	
	  (1) **Criminal Cases.** The court may admit the following evidence in a criminal case:
	
	    (A) evidence of specific instances of a victim's sexual behavior, if offered to prove that someone other than the defendant was the source of semen, injury, or other physical evidence;
	
	    (B) evidence of specific instances of a victim's sexual behavior with respect to the person accused of the sexual misconduct, if offered by the defendant to prove consent or if offered by the prosecutor; and
	
	    (C) evidence whose exclusion would violate the defendant's constitutional rights.
	
	  (2) **Civil Cases.** In a civil case, the court may admit evidence offered to prove a victim's sexual behavior or

predisposition of any alleged victim is admissible if it is otherwise admissible under these rules and its probative value substantially outweighs the danger of harm to any victim and of unfair prejudice to any party. Evidence of an alleged victim's reputation is admissible only if it has been placed in controversy by the alleged victim.

sexual predisposition if its probative value substantially outweighs the danger of harm to any victim and of unfair prejudice to any party. The court may admit evidence of a victim's reputation only if the victim has placed it in controversy.

(c) Procedure To Determine Admissibility.

(1) A party intending to offer evidence under subdivision (b) must—

(A) file a written motion at least 14 days before trial specifically describing the evidence and stating the purpose for which it is offered unless the court, for good cause requires a different time for filing or permits filing during trial; and

(B) serve the motion on all parties and notify the alleged victim or, when appropriate, the alleged victim's guardian or representative.

(2) Before admitting evidence under this rule the court must conduct a hearing in camera and afford the victim and parties a right to attend and

(c) Procedure to Determine Admissibility.

(1) **Motion.** If a party intends to offer evidence under Rule 412(b), the party must:

(A) file a motion that specifically describes the evidence and states the purpose for which it is to be offered;

(B) do so at least 14 days before trial unless the court, for good cause, sets a different time;

(C) serve the motion on all parties; and

(D) notify the victim or, when appropriate, the victim's guardian or representative.

(2) **Hearing.** Before admitting evidence under this rule, the court must conduct an in camera hearing and give the victim and parties a right to attend and be

be heard. The motion, related papers, and the record of the hearing must be sealed and remain under seal unless the court orders otherwise.	heard. Unless the court orders otherwise, the motion, related materials, and the record of the hearing must be and remain sealed.
	(d) Definition of "Victim." In this rule, "victim" includes an alleged victim.

Former Rule	*Current Rule*
Rule 413. Evidence of Similar Crimes in Sexual Assault Cases	**Rule 413. Similar Crimes in Sexual Assault Cases**
(a) In a criminal case in which the defendant is accused of an offense of sexual assault, evidence of the defendant's commission of another offense or offenses of sexual assault is admissible, and may be considered for its bearing on any matter to which it is relevant.	**(a) Permitted Uses.** In a criminal case in which a defendant is accused of a sexual assault, the court may admit evidence that the defendant committed any other sexual assault. The evidence may be considered on any matter to which it is relevant.
(b) In a case in which the Government intends to offer evidence under this rule, the attorney for the Government shall disclose the evidence to the defendant, including statements of witnesses or a summary of the substance of any testimony that is expected to be offered, at least fifteen days before the scheduled date of trial or at such later time as the court may allow for good cause.	**(b) Disclosure to the Defendant.** If the prosecutor intends to offer this evidence, the prosecutor must disclose it to the defendant, including witnesses' statements or a summary of the expected testimony. The prosecutor must do so at least 15 days before trial or at a later time that the court allows for good cause.
(c) This rule shall not be construed to limit the admission or consideration of evidence under any other rule.	**(c) Effect on Other Rules.** This rule does not limit the admission or consideration of evidence under any other rule.
(d) For purposes of this rule and Rule 415, "offense of sexual assault"	**(d) Definition of "Sexual Assault."** In this rule and Rule 415,

means a crime under Federal law or the law of a State (as defined in section 513 of title 18, United States Code) that involved—	"sexual assault" means a crime under federal law or under state law (as "state" is defined in 18 U.S.C. § 513) involving:
(1) any conduct proscribed by chapter 109A of title 18, United States Code;	(1) any conduct prohibited by 18 U.S.C. chapter 109A;
(2) contact, without consent, between any part of the defendant's body or an object and the genitals or anus of another person;	(2) contact, without consent, between any part of the defendant's body—or an object—and another person's genitals or anus;
(3) contact, without consent, between the genitals or anus of the defendant and any part of another person's body;	(3) contact, without consent, between the defendant's genitals or anus and any part of another person's body;
(4) deriving sexual pleasure or gratification from the infliction of death, bodily injury, or physical pain on another person; or	(4) deriving sexual pleasure or gratification from inflicting death, bodily injury, or physical pain on another person; or
(5) an attempt or conspiracy to engage in conduct described in paragraphs (1)-(4).	(5) an attempt or conspiracy to engage in conduct described in subparagraphs (1)-(4).

Former Rule	*Current Rule*
Rule 414. Evidence of Similar Crimes in Child Molestation Cases	**Rule 414. Similar Crimes in Child-Molestation Cases**
(a) In a criminal case in which the defendant is accused of an offense of child molestation, evidence of the defendant's commission of another offense or offenses of child molestation is admissible, and may be considered for its bearing on any matter to which it is relevant.	(a) **Permitted Uses.** In a criminal case in which a defendant is accused of child molestation, the court may admit evidence that the defendant committed any other child molestation. The evidence may be considered on any matter to which it is relevant.

(b) In a case in which the Government intends to offer evidence under this rule, the attorney for the Government shall disclose the evidence to the defendant, including statements of witnesses or a summary of the substance of any testimony that is expected to be offered, at least fifteen days before the scheduled date of trial or at such later time as the court may allow for good cause.	**(b)** **Disclosure to the Defendant.** If the prosecutor intends to offer this evidence, the prosecutor must disclose it to the defendant, including witnesses' statements or a summary of the expected testimony. The prosecutor must do so at least 15 days before trial or at a later time that the court allows for good cause.
(c) This rule shall not be construed to limit the admission or consideration of evidence under any other rule.	**(c)** **Effect on Other Rules.** This rule does not limit the admission or consideration of evidence under any other rule.
(d) For purposes of this rule and Rule 415, "child" means a person below the age of fourteen, and "offense of child molestation" means a crime under Federal law or the law of a State (as defined in section 513 of title 18, United States Code) that involved— (1) any conduct proscribed by chapter 109A of title 18, United States Code, that was committed in relation to a child; (2) any conduct proscribed by chapter 110 of title 18, United States Code; (3) contact between any part of the defendant's body or an object and the genitals or anus of a child; (4) contact between the genitals or anus of the	**(d)** Definition of "Child" and "Child Molestation." In this rule and Rule 415: (1) "child" means a person below the age of 14; and (2) "child molestation" means a crime under federal law or under state law (as "state" is defined in 18 U.S.C. § 513) involving: (A) any conduct prohibited by 18 U.S.C. chapter 109A and committed with a child; (B) any conduct prohibited by 18 U.S.C. chapter 110; (C) contact between any part of the defendant's body—or an object—and a child's genitals or anus;

defendant and any part of the body of a child;	**(D)** contact between the defendant's genitals or anus and any part of a child's body;
(5) deriving sexual pleasure or gratification from the infliction of death, bodily injury, or physical pain on a child; or	**(E)** deriving sexual pleasure or gratification from inflicting death, bodily injury, or physical pain on a child; or
(6) an attempt or conspiracy to engage in conduct described in paragraphs (1)-(5).	**(F)** an attempt or conspiracy to engage in conduct described in subparagraphs (A)-(E).

Former Rule	*Current Rule*
Rule 415. Evidence of Similar Acts in Civil Cases Concerning Sexual Assault or Child Molestation	**Rule 415. Similar Acts in Civil Cases Involving Sexual Assault or Child Molestation**
(a) In a civil case in which a claim for damages or other relief is predicated on a party's alleged commission of conduct constituting an offense of sexual assault or child molestation, evidence of that party's commission of another offense or offenses of sexual assault or child molestation is admissible and may be considered as provided in Rule 413 and Rule 414 of these rules.	**(a) Permitted Uses.** In a civil case involving a claim for relief based on a party's alleged sexual assault or child molestation, the court may admit evidence that the party committed any other sexual assault or child molestation. The evidence may be considered as provided in Rules 413 and 414.
(b) A party who intends to offer evidence under this Rule shall disclose the evidence to the party against whom it will be offered, including statements of witnesses or a summary of the substance of any testimony that is expected to be offered, at least fifteen days before the scheduled date of trial or at such	**(b) Disclosure to the Opponent.** If a party intends to offer this evidence, the party must disclose it to the party against whom it will be offered, including witnesses' statements or a summary of the expected testimony. The party must do so at least 15 days before trial or

later time as the court may allow for good cause.	at a later time that the court allows for good cause.
(c) This rule shall not be construed to limit the admission or consideration of evidence under any other rule.	**(c) Effect on Other Rules.** This rule does not limit the admission or consideration of evidence under any other rule.

Article V: Privileges

Former Rule	*Current Rule*
Rule 501. General Rule	**Rule 501. Privilege in General**
Except as otherwise required by the Constitution of the United States or provided by Act of Congress or in rules prescribed by the Supreme Court pursuant to statutory authority, the privilege of a witness, person, government, State, or political subdivision thereof shall be governed by the principles of the common law as they may be interpreted by the courts of the United States in the light of reason and experience. However, in civil actions and proceedings, with respect to an element of a claim or defense as to which State law supplies the rule of decision, the privilege of a witness, person, government, State, or political subdivision thereof shall be determined in accordance with State law.	The common law—as interpreted by United States courts in the light of reason and experience—governs a claim of privilege unless any of the following provides otherwise: • the United States Constitution; • a federal statute; or • rules prescribed by the Supreme Court But in a civil case, state law governs privilege regarding a claim or defense for which state law supplies the rule of decision.

Former Rule	*Current Rule*
Rule 502. Attorney-Client Privilege and Work Product; Limitations on Waiver	**Rule 502. Attorney-Client Privilege and Work Product; Limitations on Waiver**
The following provisions apply, in the circumstances set out, to disclosure of a communication or information covered by the attorney-client privilege or work-product protection.	The following provisions apply, in the circumstances set out, to disclosure of a communication or information covered by the attorney-client privilege or work-product protection.

(a) **Disclosure made in a Federal proceeding or to a Federal office or agency; scope of a waiver.** When the disclosure is made in a Federal proceeding or to a Federal office or agency and waives the attorney-client privilege or work-product protection, the waiver extends to an undisclosed communication or information in a Federal or State proceeding only if:

(1) the waiver is intentional;

(2) the disclosed and undisclosed communications or information concern the same subject matter; and

(3) they ought in fairness to be considered together.

(b) **Inadvertent disclosure.** When made in a Federal proceeding or to a Federal office or agency, the disclosure does not operate as a waiver in a Federal or State proceeding if:

(1) the disclosure is inadvertent;

(2) the holder of the privilege or protection took reasonable steps to prevent disclosure; and

(3) the holder promptly took reasonable steps to rectify the error, including (if applicable) following Federal Rule of Civil Procedure 26(b)(5)(B).

(c) **Disclosure made in a State proceeding.** When the disclosure is made in a State proceeding and is

(a) **Disclosure Made in a Federal Proceeding or to a Federal Office or Agency; Scope of a Waiver.** When the disclosure is made in a federal proceeding or to a federal office or agency and waives the attorney-client privilege or work-product protection, the waiver extends to an undisclosed communication or information in a federal or state proceeding only if:

(1) the waiver is intentional;

(2) the disclosed and undisclosed communications or information concern the same subject matter; and

(3) they ought in fairness to be considered together.

(b) **Inadvertent Disclosure.** When made in a federal proceeding or to a federal office or agency, the disclosure does not operate as a waiver in a federal or state proceeding if:

(1) the disclosure is inadvertent;

(2) the holder of the privilege or protection took reasonable steps to prevent disclosure; and

(3) the holder promptly took reasonable steps to rectify the error, including (if applicable) following Federal Rule of Civil Procedure 26(b)(5)(B).

(c) **Disclosure Made in a State Proceeding.** When the disclosure is made in a state proceeding and is not

not the subject of a State-court order concerning waiver, the disclosure does not operate as a waiver in a Federal proceeding if the disclosure:
 	
   (1) would not be a waiver under this rule if it had been made in a Federal proceeding; or
 	
   (2) is not a waiver under the law of the State where the disclosure occurred.
	the subject of a state-court order concerning waiver, the disclosure does not operate as a waiver in a federal proceeding if the disclosure:
	
	   (1) would not be a waiver under this rule if it had been made in a federal proceeding; or
	
	   (2) is not a waiver under the law of the state where the disclosure occurred.

(d) Controlling effect of a court order. A Federal court may order that the privilege or protection is not waived by disclosure connected with the litigation pending before the court—in which event the disclosure is also not a waiver in any other Federal or State proceeding.	**(d) Controlling Effect of a Court Order.** A federal court may order that the privilege or protection is not waived by disclosure connected with the litigation pending before the court—in which event the disclosure is also not a waiver in any other federal or state proceeding.
(e) Controlling effect of a party agreement. An agreement on the effect of disclosure in a Federal proceeding is binding only on the parties to the agreement, unless it is incorporated into a court order.	**(e) Controlling Effect of a Party Agreement.** An agreement on the effect of disclosure in a federal proceeding is binding only on the parties to the agreement, unless it is incorporated into a court order.
(f) Controlling effect of this rule. Notwithstanding Rules 101 and 1101, this rule applies to State proceedings and to Federal court-annexed and Federal court-mandated arbitration proceedings, in the circumstances set out in the rule. And notwithstanding Rule 501, this rule applies even if State law provides the rule of decision.	**(f) Controlling Effect of this Rule.** Notwithstanding Rules 101 and 1101, this rule applies to state proceedings and to federal court-annexed and federal court-mandated arbitration proceedings, in the circumstances set out in the rule. And notwithstanding Rule 501, this rule applies even if state law provides the rule of decision.

(g) Definitions. In this rule:

    (1) "attorney-client privilege" means the protection that applicable law provides for confidential attorney-client communications; and

    (2) "work-product protection" means the protection that applicable law provides for tangible material (or its intangible equivalent) prepared in anticipation of litigation or for trial.

(g) Definitions. In this rule:

    (1) "attorney-client privilege" means the protection that applicable law provides for confidential attorney-client communications; and

    (2) "work-product protection" means the protection that applicable law provides for tangible material (or its intangible equivalent) prepared in anticipation of litigation or for trial.

Article VI: Witnesses

Former Rule	*Current Rule*
Rule 601. General Rule of Competency	**Rule 601. Competency to Testify in General**
Every person is competent to be a witness except as otherwise provided in these rules. However, in civil actions and proceedings, with respect to an element of a claim or defense as to which State law supplies the rule of decision, the competency of a witness shall be determined in accordance with State law.	Every person is competent to be a witness unless these rules provide otherwise. But in a civil case, state law governs the witness's competency regarding a claim or defense for which state law supplies the rule of decision.

Former Rule	*Current Rule*
Rule 602. Lack of Personal Knowledge	**Rule 602. Need for Personal Knowledge**
A witness may not testify to a matter unless evidence is introduced sufficient to support a finding that the witness has personal knowledge of the matter. Evidence to prove personal knowledge may, but need not, consist of the witness' own testimony. This rule is subject to the provisions of rule 703, relating to opinion testimony by expert witnesses.	A witness may testify to a matter only if evidence is introduced sufficient to support a finding that the witness has personal knowledge of the matter. Evidence to prove personal knowledge may consist of the witness's own testimony. This rule does not apply to a witness's expert testimony under Rule 703.

Former Rule	*Current Rule*
Rule 603. Oath or Affirmation	**Rule 603. Oath or Affirmation to Testify Truthfully**
Before testifying, every witness shall be required to declare that the witness will testify truthfully, by oath or affirmation administered in a	Before testifying, a witness must give an oath or affirmation to testify truthfully. It must be in a form

| form calculated to awaken the witness' conscience and impress the witness' mind with the duty to do so. | designed to impress that duty on the witness's conscience. |

Former Rule	*Current Rule*
Rule 604. Interpreters	**Rule 604. Interpreter**
An interpreter is subject to the provisions of these rules relating to qualification as an expert and the administration of an oath or affirmation to make a true translation.	An interpreter must be qualified and must give an oath or affirmation to make a true translation.

Former Rule	*Current Rule*
Rule 605. Competency of Judge as Witness	**Rule 605. Judge's Competency as a Witness**
The judge presiding at the trial may not testify in that trial as a witness. No objection need be made in order to preserve the point.	The presiding judge may not testify as a witness at the trial. A party need not object to preserve the issue.

Former Rule	*Current Rule*
Rule 606. Competency of Juror as Witness	**Rule 606. Juror's Competency as a Witness**
(a) At the trial. A member of the jury may not testify as a witness before that jury in the trial of the case in which the juror is sitting. If the juror is called so to testify, the opposing party shall be afforded an opportunity to object out of the presence of the jury.	**(a) At the Trial.** A juror may not testify as a witness before the other jurors at the trial. If a juror is called to testify, the court must give a party an opportunity to object outside the jury's presence.
(b) Inquiry into validity of verdict or indictment. Upon an inquiry into the validity of a verdict or indictment, a juror may not testify as to any matter or statement occurring during the course of the	**(b) During an Inquiry into the Validity of a Verdict or Indictment.** **(1) Prohibited Testimony or Other Evidence.** During an inquiry into the validity of a verdict or indictment, a

jury's deliberations or to the effect of anything upon that or any other juror's mind or emotions as influencing the juror to assent to or dissent from the verdict or indictment or concerning the juror's mental processes in connection therewith. But a juror may testify about (1) whether extraneous prejudicial information was improperly brought to the jury's attention, (2) whether any outside influence was improperly brought to bear upon any juror, or (3) whether there was a mistake in entering the verdict onto the verdict form. A juror's affidavit or evidence of any statement by the juror may not be received on a matter about which the juror would be precluded from testifying.

juror may not testify about any statement made or incident that occurred during the jury's deliberations; the effect of anything on that juror's or another juror's vote; or any juror's mental processes concerning the verdict or indictment. The court may not receive a juror's affidavit or evidence of a juror's statement on these matters.

(2) **Exceptions.** A juror may testify about whether:

(A) extraneous prejudicial information was improperly brought to the jury's attention;

(B) an outside influence was improperly brought to bear on any juror; or

(C) a mistake was made in entering the verdict on the verdict form.

Former Rule	*Current Rule*
Rule 607. Who May Impeach	**Rule 607. Who May Impeach a Witness**
The credibility of a witness may be attacked by any party, including the party calling the witness.	Any party, including the party that called the witness, may attack the witness's credibility.

Former Rule	Current Rule
Rule 608. Evidence of Character and Conduct of Witness	**Rule 608. A Witness's Character for Truthfulness or Untruthfulness**
(a) Opinion and reputation evidence of character. The credibility of a witness may be attacked or supported by evidence in the form of opinion or reputation, but subject to these limitations: (1) the evidence may refer only to character for truthfulness or untruthfulness, and (2) evidence of truthful character is admissible only after the character of the witness for truthfulness has been attacked by opinion or reputation evidence or otherwise.	**(a) Reputation or Opinion Evidence.** A witness's credibility may be attacked or supported by testimony about the witness's reputation for having a character for truthfulness or untruthfulness, or by testimony in the form of an opinion about that character. But evidence of truthful character is admissible only after the witness's character for truthfulness has been attacked.
(b) Specific instances of conduct. Specific instances of the conduct of a witness, for the purpose of attacking or supporting the witness' character for truthfulness, other than conviction of crime as provided in rule 609, may not be proved by extrinsic evidence. They may, however, in the discretion of the court, if probative of truthfulness or untruthfulness, be inquired into on cross-examination of the witness (1) concerning the witness' character for truthfulness or untruthfulness, or (2) concerning the character for truthfulness or untruthfulness of another witness as to which character the witness being cross-examined has testified. The giving of testimony, whether by an accused or by any	**(b) Specific Instances of Conduct.** Except for a criminal conviction under Rule 609, extrinsic evidence is not admissible to prove specific instances of a witness's conduct in order to attack or support the witness's character for truthfulness. But the court may, on cross-examination, allow them to be inquired into if they are probative of the character for truthfulness or untruthfulness of: (1) the witness; or (2) another witness whose character the witness being cross-examined has testified about. By testifying on another matter, a witness does not waive any privilege against self-incrimination for

other witness, does not operate as a waiver of the accused's or the witness' privilege against self-incrimination when examined with respect to matters that relate only to character for truthfulness.	testimony that relates only to the witness's character for truthfulness.

Former Rule	*Current Rule*
Rule 609. Impeachment by Evidence of Conviction of Crime	**Rule 609. Impeachment by Evidence of a Criminal Conviction**
(a) General rule. For the purpose of attacking the character for truthfulness of a witness, (1) evidence that a witness other than an accused has been convicted of a crime shall be admitted, subject to Rule 403, if the crime was punishable by death or imprisonment in excess of one year under the law under which the witness was convicted, and evidence that an accused has been convicted of such a crime shall be admitted if the court determines that the probative value of admitting this evidence outweighs its prejudicial effect to the accused; and (2) evidence that any witness has been convicted of a crime shall be admitted regardless of the punishment, if it readily can be determined that establishing the elements of the crime required proof or admission of an act of	**(a) In General.** The following rules apply to attacking a witness's character for truthfulness by evidence of a criminal conviction: (1) for a crime that, in the convicting jurisdiction, was punishable by death or by imprisonment for more than one year, the evidence: (A) must be admitted, subject to Rule 403, in a civil case or in a criminal case in which the witness is not a defendant; and (B) must be admitted in a criminal case in which the witness is a defendant, if the probative value of the evidence outweighs its prejudicial effect to that defendant; and (2) for any crime regardless of the punishment, the evidence must be admitted if the court can readily determine that establishing the elements of the crime

dishonesty or false statement by the witness.	required proving—or the witness's admitting—a dishonest act or false statement.
(b) Time limit. Evidence of a conviction under this rule is not admissible if a period of more than ten years has elapsed since the date of the conviction or of the release of the witness from the confinement imposed for that conviction, whichever is the later date, unless the court determines, in the interests of justice, that the probative value of the conviction supported by specific facts and circumstances substantially outweighs its prejudicial effect. However, evidence of a conviction more than 10 years old as calculated herein, is not admissible unless the proponent gives to the adverse party sufficient advance written notice of intent to use such evidence to provide the adverse party with a fair opportunity to contest the use of such evidence.	**(b) Limit on Using the Evidence After 10 Years.** This subdivision (b) applies if more than 10 years have passed since the witness's conviction or release from confinement for it, whichever is later. Evidence of the conviction is admissible only if: (1) its probative value, supported by specific facts and circumstances, substantially outweighs its prejudicial effect; and (2) the proponent gives an adverse party reasonable written notice of the intent to use it so that the party has a fair opportunity to contest its use.
(c) Effect of pardon, annulment, or certificate of rehabilitation. Evidence of a conviction is not admissible under this rule if (1) the conviction has been the subject of a pardon, annulment, certificate of rehabilitation, or other equivalent procedure based on a finding of the rehabilitation of the person convicted, and that person has not been convicted of a subsequent crime that was punishable by death or imprisonment in excess of one	**(c) Effect of a Pardon, Annulment, or Certificate of Rehabilitation.** Evidence of a conviction is not admissible if: (1) the conviction has been the subject of a pardon, annulment, certificate of rehabilitation, or other equivalent procedure based on a finding that the person has been rehabilitated, and the person has not been convicted of a later crime

year, or (2) the conviction has been the subject of a pardon, annulment, or other equivalent procedure based on a finding of innocence.	punishable by death or by imprisonment for more than one year; or **(2)** the conviction has been the subject of a pardon, annulment, or other equivalent procedure based on a finding of innocence.
(d) Juvenile adjudications. Evidence of juvenile adjudications is generally not admissible under this rule. The court may, however, in a criminal case allow evidence of a juvenile adjudication of a witness other than the accused if conviction of the offense would be admissible to attack the credibility of an adult and the court is satisfied that admission in evidence is necessary for a fair determination of the issue of guilt or innocence.	**(d) Juvenile Adjudications.** Evidence of a juvenile adjudication is admissible under this rule only if: **(1)** it is offered in a criminal case; **(2)** the adjudication was of a witness other than the defendant; **(3)** an adult's conviction for that offense would be admissible to attack the adult's credibility; and **(4)** admitting the evidence is necessary to fairly determine guilt or innocence.
(e) Pendency of appeal. The pendency of an appeal therefrom does not render evidence of a conviction inadmissible. Evidence of the pendency of an appeal is admissible.	**(e) Pendency of an Appeal.** A conviction that satisfies this rule is admissible even if an appeal is pending. Evidence of the pendency is also admissible.

Former Rule	*Current Rule*
Rule 610. Religious Beliefs or Opinions	**Rule 610. Religious Beliefs or Opinions**
Evidence of the beliefs or opinions of a witness on matters of religion is not admissible for the purpose of showing that by reason of their	Evidence of a witness's religious beliefs or opinions is not admissible to attack or support the witness's credibility.

nature the witness' credibility is impaired or enhanced.	

Former Rule	*Current Rule*
Rule 611. Mode and Order of Interrogation and Presentation	**Rule 611. Mode and Order of Examining Witnesses and Presenting Evidence**
(a) Control by court. The court shall exercise reasonable control over the mode and order of interrogating witnesses and presenting evidence so as to (1) make the interrogation and presentation effective for the ascertainment of the truth, (2) avoid needless consumption of time, and (3) protect witnesses from harassment or undue embarrassment.	**(a) Control by the Court; Purposes.** The court should exercise reasonable control over the mode and order of examining witnesses and presenting evidence so as to: **(1)** make those procedures effective for determining the truth; **(2)** avoid wasting time; and **(3)** protect witnesses from harassment or undue embarrassment.
(b) Scope of cross-examination. Cross-examination should be limited to the subject matter of the direct examination and matters affecting the credibility of the witness. The court may, in the exercise of discretion, permit inquiry into additional matters as if on direct examination.	**(b) Scope of Cross-Examination.** Cross-examination should not go beyond the subject matter of the direct examination and matters affecting the witness's credibility. The court may allow inquiry into additional matters as if on direct examination.
(c) Leading questions. Leading questions should not be used on the direct examination of a witness except as may be necessary to develop the witness' testimony. Ordinarily leading questions should be permitted on cross-examination. When a party calls a hostile witness, an adverse party, or a witness identified with an adverse party,	**(c) Leading Questions.** Leading questions should not be used on direct examination except as necessary to develop the witness's testimony. Ordinarily, the court should allow leading questions: **(1)** on cross-examination; and **(2)** when a party calls a hostile witness, an adverse party,

| interrogation may be by leading questions. | or a witness identified with an adverse party. |

Former Rule	*Current Rule*
Rule 612. Writing Used To Refresh Memory	**Rule 612. Writing Used to Refresh a Witness's Memory**
Except as otherwise provided in criminal proceedings by section 3500 of title 18, United States Code, if a witness uses a writing to refresh memory for the purpose of testifying, either—	**(a) Scope.** This rule gives an adverse party certain options when a witness uses a writing to refresh memory:
(1) while testifying, or	**(1)** while testifying; or
(2) before testifying, if the court in its discretion determines it is necessary in the interests of justice,	**(2)** before testifying, if the court decides that justice requires the party to have those options.
an adverse party is entitled to have the writing produced at the hearing, to inspect it, to cross-examine the witness thereon, and to introduce in evidence those portions which relate to the testimony of the witness. If it is claimed that the writing contains matters not related to the subject matter of the testimony the court shall examine the writing in camera, excise any portions not so related, and order delivery of the remainder to the party entitled thereto. Any portion withheld over objections shall be preserved and made available to the appellate court in the event of an appeal. If a writing is not produced or delivered pursuant to order under this rule, the court shall make any order justice requires, except that in criminal cases when the prosecution elects not to comply, the order shall be one	**(b) Adverse Party's Options; Deleting Unrelated Matter.** Unless 18 U.S.C. § 3500 provides otherwise in a criminal case, an adverse party is entitled to have the writing produced at the hearing, to inspect it, to cross-examine the witness about it, and to introduce in evidence any portion that relates to the witness's testimony. If the producing party claims that the writing includes unrelated matter, the court must examine the writing in camera, delete any unrelated portion, and order that the rest be delivered to the adverse party. Any portion deleted over objection must be preserved for the record. **(c) Failure to Produce or Deliver the Writing.** If a writing is not produced or is not delivered as ordered, the court may issue any appropriate order. But if the prosecution does not comply in a

| striking the testimony or, if the court in its discretion determines that the interests of justice so require, declaring a mistrial. | criminal case, the court must strike the witness's testimony or—if justice so requires—declare a mistrial. |

Former Rule	*Current Rule*
Rule 613. Prior Statements of Witnesses	**Rule 613. Witness's Prior Statement**
(a) Examining witness concerning prior statement. In examining a witness concerning a prior statement made by the witness, whether written or not, the statement need not be shown nor its contents disclosed to the witness at that time, but on request the same shall be shown or disclosed to opposing counsel.	**(a) Showing or Disclosing the Statement During Examination.** When examining a witness about the witness's prior statement, a party need not show it or disclose its contents to the witness. But the party must, on request, show it or disclose its contents to an adverse party's attorney.
(b) Extrinsic evidence of prior inconsistent statement of witness. Extrinsic evidence of a prior inconsistent statement by a witness is not admissible unless the witness is afforded an opportunity to explain or deny the same and the opposite party is afforded an opportunity to interrogate the witness thereon, or the interests of justice otherwise require. This provision does not apply to admissions of a party-opponent as defined in rule 801(d)(2).	**(b) Extrinsic Evidence of a Prior Inconsistent Statement.** Extrinsic evidence of a witness's prior inconsistent statement is admissible only if the witness is given an opportunity to explain or deny the statement and an adverse party is given an opportunity to examine the witness about it, or if justice so requires. This subdivision (b) does not apply to an opposing party's statement under Rule 801(d)(2).

Former Rule	*Current Rule*
Rule 614. Calling and Interrogation of Witnesses by Court	**Rule 614. Court's Calling or Examining a Witness**
(a) Calling by court. The court may, on its own motion or at the	**(a) Calling.** The court may call a witness on its own or at a party's

suggestion of a party, call witnesses, and all parties are entitled to cross-examine witnesses thus called.	request. Each party is entitled to cross-examine the witness.
(b) Interrogation by court. The court may interrogate witnesses, whether called by itself or by a party.	**(b) Examining.** The court may examine a witness regardless of who calls the witness.
(c) Objections. Objections to the calling of witnesses by the court or to interrogation by it may be made at the time or at the next available opportunity when the jury is not present.	**(c) Objections.** A party may object to the court's calling or examining a witness either at that time or at the next opportunity when the jury is not present.

Former Rule	*Current Rule*
Rule 615. Exclusion of Witnesses	**Rule 615. Excluding Witnesses**
At the request of a party the court shall order witnesses excluded so that they cannot hear the testimony of other witnesses, and it may make the order of its own motion. This rule does not authorize exclusion of (1) a party who is a natural person, or (2) an officer or employee of a party which is not a natural person designated as its representative by its attorney, or (3) a person whose presence is shown by a party to be essential to the presentation of the party's cause, or (4) a person authorized by statute to be present.	At a party's request, the court must order witnesses excluded so that they cannot hear other witnesses' testimony. Or the court may do so on its own. But this rule does not authorize excluding: (a) a party who is a natural person; (b) an officer or employee of a party that is not a natural person, after being designated as the party's representative by its attorney; (c) a person whose presence a party shows to be essential to presenting the party's claim or defense; or (d) a person authorized by statute to be present.

Article VII: Opinions and Expert Testimony

Former Rule	Current Rule
Rule 701. Opinion Testimony by Lay Witnesses	**Rule 701. Opinion Testimony by Lay Witnesses**
If the witness is not testifying as an expert, the witness' testimony in the form of opinions or inferences is limited to those opinions or inferences which are (a) rationally based on the perception of the witness, and (b) helpful to a clear understanding of the witness' testimony or the determination of a fact in issue, and (c) not based on scientific, technical, or other specialized knowledge within the scope of Rule 702.	If a witness is not testifying as an expert, testimony in the form of an opinion is limited to one that is: (a) rationally based on the witness's perception; (b) helpful to clearly understanding the witness's testimony or to determining a fact in issue; and (c) not based on scientific, technical, or other specialized knowledge within the scope of Rule 702.

Former Rule	Current Rule
Rule 702. Testimony by Experts	**Rule 702. Testimony by Expert Witnesses**
If scientific, technical, or other specialized knowledge will assist the trier of fact to understand the evidence or to determine a fact in issue, a witness qualified as an expert by knowledge, skill, experience, training, or education, may testify thereto in the form of an opinion or otherwise, if (1) the testimony is based upon sufficient facts or data, (2) the testimony is the product of reliable principles and methods, and (3) the witness has applied the principles and methods reliably to the facts of the case.	A witness who is qualified as an expert by knowledge, skill, experience, training, or education may testify in the form of an opinion or otherwise if: (a) the expert's scientific, technical, or other specialized knowledge will help the trier of fact to understand the evidence or to determine a fact in issue; (b) the testimony is based on sufficient facts or data;

| | (c) the testimony is the product of reliable principles and methods; and |
| | (d) the expert has reliably applied the principles and methods to the facts of the case. |

Former Rule	*Current Rule*
Rule 703. Bases of Opinion Testimony by Experts	**Rule 703. Bases of an Expert's Opinion Testimony**
The facts or data in the particular case upon which an expert bases an opinion or inference may be those perceived by or made known to the expert at or before the hearing. If of a type reasonably relied upon by experts in the particular field in forming opinions or inferences upon the subject, the facts or data need not be admissible in evidence in order for the opinion or inference to be admitted. Facts or data that are otherwise inadmissible shall not be disclosed to the jury by the proponent of the opinion or inference unless the court determines that their probative value in assisting the jury to evaluate the expert's opinion substantially outweighs their prejudicial effect.	An expert may base an opinion on facts or data in the case that the expert has been made aware of or personally observed. If experts in the particular field would reasonably rely on those kinds of facts or data in forming an opinion on the subject, they need not be admissible for the opinion to be admitted. But if the facts or data would otherwise be inadmissible, the proponent of the opinion may disclose them to the jury only if their probative value in helping the jury evaluate the opinion substantially outweighs their prejudicial effect.

Former Rule	*Current Rule*
Rule 704. Opinion on Ultimate Issue	**Rule 704. Opinion on an Ultimate Issue**
(a) Except as provided in subdivision (b), testimony in the form of an opinion or inference otherwise admissible is not	**(a)** **In General—Not Automatically Objectionable.** An opinion is not objectionable just because it embraces an ultimate issue.

objectionable because it embraces an ultimate issue to be decided by the trier of fact.	
(b) No expert witness testifying with respect to the mental state or condition of a defendant in a criminal case may state an opinion or inference as to whether the defendant did or did not have the mental state or condition constituting an element of the crime charged or of a defense thereto. Such ultimate issues are matters for the trier of fact alone.	**(b)** **Exception.** In a criminal case, an expert witness must not state an opinion about whether the defendant did or did not have a mental state or condition that constitutes an element of the crime charged or of a defense. Those matters are for the trier of fact alone.

Former Rule	*Current Rule*
Rule 705. Disclosure of Facts or Data Underlying Expert Opinion	**Rule 705. Disclosing the Facts or Data Underlying an Expert's Opinion**
The expert may testify in terms of opinion or inference and give reasons therefor without first testifying to the underlying facts or data, unless the court requires otherwise. The expert may in any event be required to disclose the underlying facts or data on cross-examination.	Unless the court orders otherwise, an expert may state an opinion—and give the reasons for it—without first testifying to the underlying facts or data. But the expert may be required to disclose those facts or data on cross-examination.

Former Rule	*Current Rule*
Rule 706. Court Appointed Experts	**Rule 706. Court-Appointed Expert Witnesses**
(a) **Appointment.** The court may on its own motion or on the motion of any party enter an order to show cause why expert witnesses should not be appointed, and may request the parties to submit nominations. The court may appoint any expert witnesses agreed upon by the	**(a)** **Appointment Process.** On a party's motion or on its own, the court may order the parties to show cause why expert witnesses should not be appointed and may ask the parties to submit nominations. The court may appoint any expert that the parties agree on and any of its

parties, and may appoint expert witnesses of its own selection. An expert witness shall not be appointed by the court unless the witness consents to act. A witness so appointed shall be informed of the witness' duties by the court in writing, a copy of which shall be filed with the clerk, or at a conference in which the parties shall have opportunity to participate. A witness so appointed shall advise the parties of the witness' findings, if any; the witness' deposition may be taken by any party; and the witness may be called to testify by the court or any party. The witness shall be subject to cross-examination by each party, including a party calling the witness.

own choosing. But the court may only appoint someone who consents to act.

(b)   Expert's Role. The court must inform the expert of the expert's duties. The court may do so in writing and have a copy filed with the clerk or may do so orally at a conference in which the parties have an opportunity to participate. The expert:

(1)   must advise the parties of any findings the expert makes;

(2)   may be deposed by any party;

(3)   may be called to testify by the court or any party; and

(4)   may be cross-examined by any party, including the party that called the expert.

(b)   Compensation.   Expert witnesses so appointed are entitled to reasonable compensation in whatever sum the court may allow. The compensation thus fixed is payable from funds which may be provided by law in criminal cases and civil actions and proceedings involving just compensation under the fifth amendment. In other civil actions and proceedings the compensation shall be paid by the parties in such proportion and at such time as the court directs, and thereafter charged in like manner as other costs.

(c)   Compensation. The expert is entitled to a reasonable compensation, as set by the court. The compensation is payable as follows:

(1)   in a criminal case or in a civil case involving just compensation under the Fifth Amendment, from any funds that are provided by law; and

(2)   in any other civil case, by the parties in the proportion and at the time that the court directs—and the compensation is then charged like other costs.

| (c) **Disclosure of appointment.** In the exercise of its discretion, the court may authorize disclosure to the jury of the fact that the court appointed the expert witness. | (d) **Disclosing the Appointment to the Jury.** The court may authorize disclosure to the jury that the court appointed the expert. |
| (d) **Parties' experts of own selection.** Nothing in this rule limits the parties in calling expert witnesses of their own selection. | (e) **Parties' Choice of Their Own Experts.** This rule does not limit a party in calling its own experts. |

Article VIII: Hearsay

Former Rule	*Current Rule*
Rule 801. Definitions	**Rule 801. Definitions That Apply to This Article; Exclusions from Hearsay**
The following definitions apply under this article: **(a) Statement.** A "statement" is (1) an oral or written assertion or (2) nonverbal conduct of a person, if it is intended by the person as an assertion.	**(a) Statement.** "Statement" means a person's oral assertion, written assertion, or nonverbal conduct, if the person intended it as an assertion.
(b) Declarant. A "declarant" is a person who makes a statement.	**(b) Declarant.** "Declarant" means the person who made the statement.
(c) Hearsay. "Hearsay" is a statement, other than one made by the declarant while testifying at the trial or hearing, offered in evidence to prove the truth of the matter asserted.	**(c) Hearsay.** "Hearsay" means a statement that: **(1)** the declarant does not make while testifying at the current trial or hearing; and **(2)** a party offers in evidence to prove the truth of the matter asserted in the statement.
(d) Statements which are not hearsay. A statement is not hearsay if— **(1) Prior statement by witness.** The declarant testifies at the trial or hearing and is subject to cross-examination concerning the statement, and the statement is (A) inconsistent with the declarant's testimony, and was given under oath subject to the penalty of perjury at a trial, hearing, or other proceeding,	**(d) Statements That Are Not Hearsay.** A statement that meets the following conditions is not hearsay: **(1) A Declarant-Witness's Prior Statement.** The declarant testifies and is subject to cross-examination about a prior statement, and the statement: **(A)** is inconsistent with the declarant's testimony and was given under penalty of

or in a deposition, or (B) consistent with the declarant's testimony and is offered to rebut an express or implied charge against the declarant of recent fabrication or improper influence or motive, or (C) one of identification of a person made after perceiving the person; or	perjury at a trial, hearing, or other proceeding or in a deposition; **(B)** is consistent with the declarant's testimony and is offered: (i) to rebut an express or implied charge that the declarant recently fabricated it or acted from a recent improper influence or motive in so testifying; or (ii) to rehabilitate the declarant's credibility as a witness when attacked on another ground; or **(C)** identifies a person as someone the declarant perceived earlier.
(2) Admission by party-opponent. The statement is offered against a party and is (A) the party's own statement, in either an individual or a representative capacity or (B) a statement of which the party has manifested an adoption or belief in its truth, or (C) a statement by a person authorized by the party to make a statement concerning the subject, or (D) a statement by the party's agent or servant concerning a matter within the scope of the agency or employment, made during the existence of the relationship, or (E) a statement by a co-conspirator of a party during the course and in furtherance of the conspiracy. The contents of the statement shall be	**(2) An Opposing Party's Statement.** The statement is offered against an opposing party and: **(A)** was made by the party in an individual or representative capacity; **(B)** is one the party manifested that it adopted or believed to be true; **(C)** was made by a person whom the party authorized to make a statement on the subject; **(D)** was made by the party's agent or employee on a matter within the scope of that relationship and while it existed; or

considered but are not alone sufficient to establish the declarant's authority under subdivision (C), the agency or employment relationship and scope thereof under subdivision (D), or the existence of the conspiracy and the participation therein of the declarant and the party against whom the statement is offered under subdivision (E).	**(E)** was made by the party's co-conspirator during and in furtherance of the conspiracy. The statement must be considered but does not by itself establish the declarant's authority under (C); the existence or scope of the relationship under (D); or the existence of the conspiracy or participation in it under (E).

Former Rule	*Current Rule*
Rule 802. Hearsay Rule	**Rule 802. The Rule Against Hearsay**
Hearsay is not admissible except as provided by these rules or by other rules prescribed by the Supreme Court pursuant to statutory authority or by Act of Congress.	Hearsay is not admissible unless any of the following provides otherwise: • a federal statute; • these rules; or • other rules prescribed by the Supreme Court

Former Rule	*Current Rule*
Rule 803. Hearsay Exceptions; Availability of Declarant Immaterial	**Rule 803. Exceptions to the Rule Against Hearsay— Regardless of Whether the Declarant Is Available as a Witness**
The following are not excluded by the hearsay rule, even though the declarant is available as a witness: **(1) Present sense impression.** A statement describing or explaining an event or condition made while the declarant was perceiving the event or condition, or immediately thereafter.	The following are not excluded by the rule against hearsay, regardless of whether the declarant is available as a witness: **(1) Present Sense Impression.** A statement describing or explaining an event or condition, made while or immediately after the declarant perceived it.

(2) Excited utterance. A statement relating to a startling event or condition made while the declarant was under the stress of excitement caused by the event or condition.	**(2) Excited Utterance.** A statement relating to a startling event or condition, made while the declarant was under the stress of excitement that it caused.
(3) Then existing mental, emotional, or physical condition. A statement of the declarant's then existing state of mind, emotion, sensation, or physical condition (such as intent, plan, motive, design, mental feeling, pain, and bodily health), but not including a statement of memory or belief to prove the fact remembered or believed unless it relates to the execution, revocation, identification, or terms of declarant's will.	**(3) Then-Existing Mental, Emotional, or Physical Condition.** A statement of the declarant's then-existing state of mind (such as motive, intent, or plan) or emotional, sensory, or physical condition (such as mental feeling, pain, or bodily health), but not including a statement of memory or belief to prove the fact remembered or believed unless it relates to the validity or terms of the declarant's will.
(4) Statements for purposes of medical diagnosis or treatment. Statements made for purposes of medical diagnosis or treatment and describing medical history, or past or present symptoms, pain, or sensations, or the inception or general character of the cause or external source thereof insofar as reasonably pertinent to diagnosis or treatment.	**(4) Statement Made for Medical Diagnosis or Treatment.** A statement that: (A) is made for—and is reasonably pertinent to—medical diagnosis or treatment; and (B) describes medical history; past or present symptoms or sensations; their inception; or their general cause.
(5) Recorded recollection. A memorandum or record concerning a matter about which a witness once had knowledge but now has insufficient recollection to enable the witness to testify fully and accurately, shown to have been made or adopted by the witness	**(5) Recorded Recollection.** A record that: (A) is on a matter the witness once knew about but now cannot recall well enough to testify fully and accurately;

when the matter was fresh in the witness' memory and to reflect that knowledge correctly. If admitted, the memorandum or record may be read into evidence but may not itself be received as an exhibit unless offered by an adverse party.	**(B)** was made or adopted by the witness when the matter was fresh in the witness's memory; and **(C)** accurately reflects the witness's knowledge. If admitted, the record may be read into evidence but may be received as an exhibit only if offered by an adverse party.
(6) Records of regularly conducted activity. A memorandum, report, record, or data compilation, in any form, of acts, events, conditions, opinions, or diagnoses, made at or near the time by, or from information transmitted by, a person with knowledge, if kept in the course of a regularly conducted business activity, and if it was the regular practice of that business activity to make the memorandum, report, record or data compilation, all as shown by the testimony of the custodian or other qualified witness, or by certification that complies with Rule 902(11), Rule 902(12), or a statute permitting certification, unless the source of information or the method or circumstances of preparation indicate lack of trustworthiness. The term "business" as used in this paragraph includes business, institution, association, profession, occupation, and calling of every kind, whether or not conducted for profit.	**(6) Records of a Regularly Conducted Activity.** A record of an act, event, condition, opinion, or diagnosis if: **(A)** the record was made at or near the time by—or from information transmitted by—someone with knowledge; **(B)** the record was kept in the course of a regularly conducted activity of a business, organization, occupation, or calling, whether or not for profit; **(C)** making the record was a regular practice of that activity; **(D)** all these conditions are shown by the testimony of the custodian or another qualified witness, or by a certification that complies with Rule 902(11) or (12) or with a statute permitting certification; and **(E)** the opponent does not show that the source of information or the method or circumstances of

	preparation indicate a lack of trustworthiness.
(7) Absence of entry in records kept in accordance with the provisions of paragraph (6). Evidence that a matter is not included in the memoranda reports, records, or data compilations, in any form, kept in accordance with the provisions of paragraph (6), to prove the nonoccurrence or nonexistence of the matter, if the matter was of a kind of which a memorandum, report, record, or data compilation was regularly made and preserved, unless the sources of information or other circumstances indicate lack of trustworthiness.	**(7) Absence of a Record of a Regularly Conducted Activity.** Evidence that a matter is not included in a record described in paragraph (6) if: (A) the evidence is admitted to prove that the matter did not occur or exist; (B) a record was regularly kept for a matter of that kind; and (C) the opponent does not show that the possible source of the information no other circumstances indicate a lack of trustworthiness.

(8) Public records and reports. Records, reports, statements, or data compilations, in any form, of public offices or agencies, setting forth (A) the activities of the office or agency, or (B) matters observed pursuant to duty imposed by law as to which matters there was a duty to report, excluding, however, in criminal cases matters observed by police officers and other law enforcement personnel, or (C) in civil actions and proceedings and against the Government in criminal cases, factual findings resulting from an investigation made pursuant to authority granted by law, unless the sources of information or other circumstances indicate lack of trustworthiness.	**(8) Public Records.** A record or statement of a public office if:
	
	 (A) it sets out:
	
	    (i) the office's activities;
	
	    (ii) a matter observed while under a legal duty to report, but not including, in a criminal case, a matter observed by law-enforcement personnel; or
	
	    (iii) in a civil case or against the government in a criminal case, factual findings from a legally authorized investigation; and
	
	 (B) neither the source of information nor other circumstances indicate a lack of trustworthiness.

(9) Records of vital statistics. Records or data compilations, in any form, of births, fetal deaths, deaths, or marriages, if the report thereof was made to a public office pursuant to requirements of law.	**(9) Public Records of Vital Statistics.** A record of a birth, death, or marriage, if reported to a public office in accordance with a legal duty.
(10) Absence of public record or entry. To prove the absence of a record, report, statement, or data compilation, in any form, or the nonoccurrence or nonexistence of a matter of which a record, report, statement, or data compilation, in any form, was regularly made and preserved by a public office or agency, evidence in the form of a certification in accordance with rule 902, or testimony, that diligent search failed to disclose the record, report, statement, or data compilation, or entry.	**(10) Absence of a Public Record.** Testimony—or a certification under Rule 902—that a diligent search failed to disclose a public record or statement if: **(A)** the testimony or certification is admitted to prove that: **(i)** the record or statement does not exist; or **(ii)** a matter did not occur or exist, if a public office regularly kept a record or statement for a matter of that kind; and **(B)** in a criminal case, a prosecutor who intends to offer a certification provides written notice of that intent at least 14 days before trial, and the defendant does not object in writing within 7 days of receiving the notice or the objection.
(11) Records of religious organizations. Statements of births, marriages, divorces, deaths, legitimacy, ancestry, relationship by blood or marriage, or other similar facts of personal or family history, contained in a regularly kept record of a religious organization.	**(11) Records of Religious Organizations Concerning Personal or Family History.** A statement of birth, legitimacy, ancestry, marriage, divorce, death, relationship by blood or marriage, or similar facts of personal or family

	history, contained in a regularly kept record of a religious organization.
(12) Marriage, baptismal, and similar certificates. Statements of fact contained in a certificate that the maker performed a marriage or other ceremony or administered a sacrament, made by a clergyman, public official, or other person authorized by the rules or practices of a religious organization or by law to perform the act certified, and purporting to have been issued at the time of the act or within a reasonable time thereafter.	**(12) Certificates of Marriage, Baptism, and Similar Ceremonies.** A statement of fact contained in a certificate: (A) made by a person who is authorized by a religious organization or by law to perform the act certified; (B) attesting that the person performed a marriage or similar ceremony or administered a sacrament; and (C) purporting to have been issued at the time of the act or within a reasonable time after it.
(13) Family records. Statements of fact concerning personal or family history contained in family Bibles, genealogies, charts, engravings on rings, inscriptions on family portraits, engravings on urns, crypts, or tombstones, or the like.	**(13) Family Records.** A statement of fact about personal or family history contained in a family record, such as a Bible, genealogy, chart, engraving on a ring, inscription on a portrait, or engraving on an urn or burial marker.
(14) Records of documents affecting an interest in property. The record of a document purporting to establish or affect an interest in property, as proof of the content of the original recorded document and its execution and delivery by each person by whom it purports to have been executed, if the record is a record of a public office and an applicable statute authorizes the recording of documents of that kind in that office.	**(14) Records of Documents That Affect an Interest in Property.** The record of a document that purports to establish or affect an interest in property if: (A) the record is admitted to prove the content of the original recorded document, along with its signing and its delivery by each person who purports to have signed it;

	(B) the record is kept in a public office; and
	(C) a statute authorizes recording documents of that kind in that office.
(15) Statements in documents affecting an interest in property. A statement contained in a document purporting to establish or affect an interest in property if the matter stated was relevant to the purpose of the document, unless dealings with the property since the document was made have been inconsistent with the truth of the statement or the purport of the document.	**(15) Statements in Documents That Affect an Interest in Property.** A statement contained in a document that purports to establish or affect an interest in property if the matter stated was relevant to the document's purpose—unless later dealings with the property are inconsistent with the truth of the statement or the purport of the document.
(16) Statements in ancient documents. Statements in a document in existence twenty years or more the authenticity of which is established.	*[Effective 12/1/17]* **(16) Statements in Ancient Documents.** A statement in a document that was prepared before January 1, 1998, and whose authenticity is established.
(17) Market reports, commercial publications. Market quotations, tabulations, lists, directories, or other published compilations, generally used and relied upon by the public or by persons in particular occupations.	**(17) Market Reports and Similar Commercial Publications.** Market quotations, lists, directories, or other compilations that are generally relied on by the public or by persons in particular occupations.
(18) Learned treatises. To the extent called to the attention of an expert witness upon cross-examination or relied upon by the expert witness in direct examination, statements contained in published treatises, periodicals, or pamphlets on a subject of history, medicine, or other science or art,	**(18) Statements in Learned Treatises, Periodicals, or Pamphlets.** A statement contained in a treatise, periodical, or pamphlet if: **(A)** the statement is called to the attention of an expert witness on cross-examination or relied on by

established as a reliable authority by the testimony or admission of the witness or by other expert testimony or by judicial notice. If admitted, the statements may be read into evidence but may not be received as exhibits.	the expert on direct examination; and **(B)** the publication is established as a reliable authority by the expert's admission or testimony, by another expert's testimony, or by judicial notice. If admitted, the statement may be read into evidence but not received as an exhibit.
(19) Reputation concerning personal or family history. Reputation among members of a person's family by blood, adoption, or marriage, or among a person's associates, or in the community, concerning a person's birth, adoption, marriage, divorce, death, legitimacy, relationship by blood, adoption, or marriage, ancestry, or other similar fact of personal or family history.	**(19) Reputation Concerning Personal or Family History.** A reputation among a person's family by blood, adoption, or marriage—or among a person's associates or in the community—concerning the person's birth, adoption, legitimacy, ancestry, marriage, divorce, death, relationship by blood, adoption, or marriage, or similar facts of personal or family history.
(20) Reputation concerning boundaries or general history. Reputation in a community, arising before the controversy, as to boundaries of or customs affecting lands in the community, and reputation as to events of general history important to the community or State or nation in which located.	**(20) Reputation Concerning Boundaries or General History.** A reputation in a community—arising before the controversy—concerning boundaries of land in the community or customs that affect the land, or concerning general historical events important to that community, state, or nation.
(21) Reputation as to character. Reputation of a person's character among associates or in the community.	**(21) Reputation Concerning Character.** A reputation among a person's associates or in the community concerning the person's character.

(22) Judgment of previous conviction. Evidence of a final judgment, entered after a trial or upon a plea of guilty (but not upon a plea of nolo contendere), adjudging a person guilty of a crime punishable by death or imprisonment in excess of one year, to prove any fact essential to sustain the judgment, but not including, when offered by the Government in a criminal prosecution for purposes other than impeachment, judgments against persons other than the accused. The pendency of an appeal may be shown but does not affect admissibility.	**(22) Judgment of a Previous Conviction.** Evidence of a final judgment of conviction if: (A) the judgment was entered after a trial or guilty plea, but not a nolo contendere plea; (B) the conviction was for a crime punishable by death or by imprisonment for more than a year; (C) the evidence is admitted to prove any fact essential to the judgment; and (D) when offered by the prosecutor in a criminal case for a purpose other than impeachment, the judgment was against the defendant. The pendency of an appeal may be shown but does not affect admissibility.
(23) Judgment as to personal, family, or general history, or boundaries. Judgments as proof of matters of personal, family or general history, or boundaries, essential to the judgment, if the same would be provable by evidence of reputation.	**(23) Judgments Involving Personal, Family, or General History, or a Boundary.** A judgment that is admitted to prove a matter of personal, family, or general history, or boundaries, if the matter: (A) was essential to the judgment; and (B) could be proved by evidence of reputation.
(24) [Other exceptions.] [Transferred to Rule 807]	**(24) [Other Exceptions.]** [Transferred to Rule 807.]

Former Rule	*Current Rule*
Rule 804. Hearsay Exceptions; Declarant Unavailable	**Rule 804. Exceptions to the Rule Against Hearsay—When the Declarant Is Unavailable as a Witness**
(a) Definition of unavailability. "Unavailability as a witness" includes situations in which the declarant—	**(a) Criteria for Being Unavailable.** A declarant is considered to be unavailable as a witness if the declarant:
(1) is exempted by ruling of the court on the ground of privilege from testifying concerning the subject matter of the declarant's statement; or	**(1)** is exempted from testifying about the subject matter of the declarant's statement because the court rules that a privilege applies;
(2) persists in refusing to testify concerning the subject matter of the declarant's statement despite an order of the court to do so; or	**(2)** refuses to testify about the subject matter despite a court order to do so;
(3) testifies to a lack of memory of the subject matter of the declarant's statement; or	**(3)** testifies to not remembering the subject matter;
(4) is unable to be present or to testify at the hearing because of death or then existing physical or mental illness or infirmity; or	**(4)** cannot be present or testify at the trial or hearing because of death or a then-existing infirmity, physical illness, or mental illness; or
(5) is absent from the hearing and the proponent of a statement has been unable to procure the declarant's attendance (or in the case of a hearsay exception under subdivision (b)(2), (3), or (4), the declarant's attendance or testimony)	**(5)** is absent from the trial or hearing and the statement's proponent has not been able, by process or other reasonable means, to procure:
	(A) the declarant's attendance, in the case of a hearsay exception under Rule 804(b)(1) or (6); or
	(B) the declarant's attendance or testimony, in the case of

by process or other reasonable means. A declarant is not unavailable as a witness if exemption, refusal, claim of lack of memory, inability, or absence is due to the procurement or wrongdoing of the proponent of a statement for the purpose of preventing the witness from attending or testifying.	a hearsay exception under Rule 804(b)(2), (3), or (4). But this subdivision (a) does not apply if the statement's proponent procured or wrongfully caused the declarant's unavailability as a witness in order to prevent the declarant from attending or testifying.

(b) Hearsay exceptions. The following are not excluded by the hearsay rule if the declarant is unavailable as a witness:
 	
   (1) Former testimony. Testimony given as a witness at another hearing of the same or a different proceeding, or in a deposition taken in compliance with law in the course of the same or another proceeding, if the party against whom the testimony is now offered, or, in a civil action or proceeding, a predecessor in interest, had an opportunity and similar motive to develop the testimony by direct, cross, or redirect examination.
	(b) The Exceptions. The following are not excluded by the rule against hearsay if the declarant is unavailable as a witness:
	
	   (1) Former Testimony. Testimony that:
	
	     (A) was given as a witness at a trial, hearing, or lawful deposition, whether given during the current proceeding or a different one; and
	
	     (B) is now offered against a party who had—or, in a civil case, whose predecessor in interest had—an opportunity and similar motive to develop it by direct, cross-, or redirect examination.

(2) Statement under belief of impending death. In a prosecution for homicide or in a civil action or proceeding, a statement made by a declarant while believing that the declarant's death was imminent, concerning the cause or	**(2) Statement Under the Belief of Imminent Death.** In a prosecution for homicide or in a civil case, a statement that the declarant, while believing the declarant's death to be imminent, made about its cause or circumstances.

circumstances of what the declarant believed to be impending death.	
(3) Statement against interest. A statement that:	**(3) Statement Against Interest.** A statement that:
(A) a reasonable person in the declarant's position would have made only if the person believed it to be true because, when made, it was so contrary to the declarant's proprietary or pecuniary interest or had so great a tendency to invalidate the declarant's claim against someone else or to expose the declarant to civil or criminal liability; and	**(A)** a reasonable person in the declarant's position would have made only if the person believed it to be true because, when made, it was so contrary to the declarant's proprietary or pecuniary interest or had so great a tendency to invalidate the declarant's claim against someone else or to expose the declarant to civil or criminal liability; and
(B) is supported by corroborating circumstances that clearly indicate its trustworthiness, if it is offered in a criminal case as one that tends to expose the declarant to criminal liability.	**(B)** is supported by corroborating circumstances that clearly indicate its trustworthiness, if it is offered in a criminal case as one that tends to expose the declarant to criminal liability.
(4) Statement of personal or family history.	**(4) Statement of Personal or Family History.** A statement about:
(A) A statement concerning the declarant's own birth, adoption, marriage, divorce, legitimacy, relationship by blood, adoption, or marriage, ancestry, or other similar fact of personal or family history, even though declarant had no means of acquiring personal	**(A)** the declarant's own birth, adoption, legitimacy, ancestry, marriage, divorce, relationship by blood, adoption, or marriage, or similar facts of personal or family history, even though the declarant had no way of acquiring personal knowledge about that fact; or

knowledge of the matter stated; or **(B)** a statement concerning the foregoing matters, and death also, of another person, if the declarant was related to the other by blood, adoption, or marriage or was so intimately associated with the other's family as to be likely to have accurate information concerning the matter declared.	**(B)** another person concerning any of these facts, as well as death, if the declarant was related to the person by blood, adoption, or marriage or was so intimately associated with the person's family that the declarant's information is likely to be accurate.
(5) **[Other exceptions.]** [Transferred to Rule 807]	**(5)** **[Other Exceptions.]** [Transferred to Rule 807.]
(6) **Forfeiture by wrongdoing.** A statement offered against a party that has engaged or acquiesced in wrongdoing that was intended to, and did, procure the unavailability of the declarant as a witness.	**(6)** **Statement Offered Against a Party That Wrongfully Caused the Declarant's Unavailability.** A statement offered against a party that wrongfully caused—or acquiesced in wrongfully causing—the declarant's unavailability as a witness, and did so intending that result.

Former Rule	*Current Rule*
Rule 805. Hearsay Within Hearsay	**Rule 805. Hearsay Within Hearsay**
Hearsay included within hearsay is not excluded under the hearsay rule if each part of the combined statements conforms with an exception to the hearsay rule provided in these rules.	Hearsay within hearsay is not excluded by the rule against hearsay if each part of the combined statements conforms with an exception to the rule.

Former Rule	*Current Rule*
Rule 806. Attacking and Supporting Credibility of Declarant	**Rule 806. Attacking and Supporting the Declarant's Credibility**
When a hearsay statement, or a statement defined in Rule 801(d)(2)(C), (D), or (E), has been admitted in evidence, the credibility of the declarant may be attacked, and if attacked may be supported, by any evidence which would be admissible for those purposes if declarant had testified as a witness. Evidence of a statement or conduct by the declarant at any time, inconsistent with the declarant's hearsay statement, is not subject to any requirement that the declarant may have been afforded an opportunity to deny or explain. If the party against whom a hearsay statement has been admitted calls the declarant as a witness, the party is entitled to examine the declarant on the statement as if under cross-examination.	When a hearsay statement—or a statement described in Rule 801(d)(2)(C), (D), or (E)—has been admitted in evidence, the declarant's credibility may be attacked, and then supported, by any evidence that would be admissible for those purposes if the declarant had testified as a witness. The court may admit evidence of the declarant's inconsistent statement or conduct, regardless of when it occurred or whether the declarant had an opportunity to explain or deny it. If the party against whom the statement was admitted calls the declarant as a witness, the party may examine the declarant on the statement as if on cross-examination.

Former Rule	*Current Rule*
Rule 807. Residual Exception	**Rule 807. Residual Exception**
A statement not specifically covered by Rule 803 or 804 but having equivalent circumstantial guarantees of trustworthiness, is not excluded by the hearsay rule, if the court determines that (A) the statement is offered as evidence of a material fact; (B) the statement is more probative on the point for which it is offered than any other	(a) **In General.** Under the following circumstances, a hearsay statement is not excluded by the rule against hearsay even if the statement is not specifically covered by a hearsay exception in Rule 803 or 804: (1) the statement has equivalent circumstantial guarantees of trustworthiness;

evidence which the proponent can procure through reasonable efforts; and (C) the general purposes of these rules and the interests of justice will best be served by admission of the statement into evidence. However, a statement may not be admitted under this exception unless the proponent of it makes known to the adverse party sufficiently in advance of the trial or hearing to provide the adverse party with a fair opportunity to prepare to meet it, the proponent's intention to offer the statement and the particulars of it, including the name and address of the declarant.

(2) it is offered as evidence of a material fact;

(3) it is more probative on the point for which it is offered than any other evidence that the proponent can obtain through reasonable efforts; and

(4) admitting it will best serve the purposes of these rules and the interests of justice.

(b) Notice. The statement is admissible only if, before the trial or hearing, the proponent gives an adverse party reasonable notice of the intent to offer the statement and its particulars, including the declarant's name and address, so that the party has a fair opportunity to meet it.

Article IX: Authentication and Identification

Former Rule	*Current Rule*
Rule 901. Requirement of Authentication or Identification	**Rule 901. Authenticating or Identifying Evidence**
(a) General provision. The requirement of authentication or identification as a condition precedent to admissibility is satisfied by evidence sufficient to support a finding that the matter in question is what its proponent claims.	**(a) In General.** To satisfy the requirement of authenticating or identifying an item of evidence, the proponent must produce evidence sufficient to support a finding that the item is what the proponent claims it is.
(b) Illustrations. By way of illustration only, and not by way of limitation, the following are examples of authentication or identification conforming with the requirements of this rule:	**(b) Examples.** The following are examples only—not a complete list—of evidence that satisfies the requirement:
(1) Testimony of witness with knowledge. Testimony that a matter is what it is claimed to be.	**(1) Testimony of a Witness with Knowledge.** Testimony that an item is what it is claimed to be.
(2) Nonexpert opinion on handwriting. Nonexpert opinion as to the genuineness of handwriting, based upon familiarity not acquired for purposes of the litigation.	**(2) Nonexpert Opinion About Handwriting.** A nonexpert's opinion that handwriting is genuine, based on a familiarity with it that was not acquired for the current litigation.
(3) Comparison by trier or expert witness. Comparison by the trier of fact or by expert witnesses with specimens which have been authenticated.	**(3) Comparison by an Expert Witness or the Trier of Fact.** A comparison with an authenticated specimen by an expert witness or the trier of fact.
(4) Distinctive characteristics and the like. Appearance,	**(4) Distinctive Characteristics and the Like.** The

contents, substance, internal patterns, or other distinctive characteristics, taken in conjunction with circumstances.	appearance, contents, substance, internal patterns, or other distinctive characteristics of the item, taken together with all the circumstances.
(5) Voice identification. Identification of a voice, whether heard firsthand or through mechanical or electronic transmission or recording, by opinion based upon hearing the voice at any time under circumstances connecting it with the alleged speaker.	**(5) Opinion About a Voice.** An opinion identifying a person's voice—whether heard firsthand or through mechanical or electronic transmission or recording—based on hearing the voice at any time under circumstances that connect it with the alleged speaker.
(6) Telephone conversations. Telephone conversations, by evidence that a call was made to the number assigned at the time by the telephone company to a particular person or business, if (A) in the case of a person, circumstances, including self-identification, show the person answering to be the one called, or (B) in the case of a business, the call was made to a place of business and the conversation related to business reasonably transacted over the telephone.	**(6) Evidence About a Telephone Conversation.** For a telephone conversation, evidence that a call was made to the number assigned at the time to: **(A)** a particular person, if circumstances, including self-identification, show that the person answering was the one called; or **(B)** a particular business, if the call was made to a business and the call related to business reasonably transacted over the telephone.
(7) Public records or reports. Evidence that a writing authorized by law to be recorded or filed and in fact	**(7) Evidence About Public Records.** Evidence that: **(A)** a document was recorded or filed in a

recorded or filed in a public office, or a purported public record, report, statement, or data compilation, in any form, is from the public office where items of this nature are kept.	public office as authorized by law; or **(B)** a purported public record or statement is from the office where items of this kind are kept.
(8) Ancient documents or data compilation. Evidence that a document or data compilation, in any form, (A) is in such condition as to create no suspicion concerning its authenticity, (B) was in a place where it, if authentic, would likely be, and (C) has been in existence 20 years or more at the time it is offered.	**(8) Evidence About Ancient Documents or Data Compilations.** For a document or data compilation, evidence that it: **(A)** is in a condition that creates no suspicion about its authenticity; **(B)** was in a place where, if authentic, it would likely be; and **(C)** is at least 20 years old when offered.
(9) Process or system. Evidence describing a process or system used to produce a result and showing that the process or system produces an accurate result.	**(9) Evidence About a Process or System.** Evidence describing a process or system and showing that it produces an accurate result.
(10) Methods provided by statute or rule. Any method of authentication or identification provided by Act of Congress or by other rules prescribed by the Supreme Court pursuant to statutory authority.	**(10) Methods Provided by Statute or Rule.** Any method of authentication or identification allowed by a federal statute or a rule prescribed by the Supreme Court.

Former Rule	Current Rule
Rule 902. Self-authentication	**Rule 902. Evidence That Is Self-Authenticating** *[Scheduled to be amended December 1, 2017]*
Extrinsic evidence of authenticity as a condition precedent to admissibility is not required with respect to the following:	The following items of evidence are self-authenticating; they require no extrinsic evidence of authenticity in order to be admitted:
(1) Domestic public documents under seal. A document bearing a seal purporting to be that of the United States, or of any State, district, Commonwealth, territory, or insular possession thereof, or the Panama Canal Zone, or the Trust Territory of the Pacific Islands, or of a political subdivision, department, officer, or agency thereof, and a signature purporting to be an attestation or execution.	**(1) Domestic Public Documents That Are Sealed and Signed.** A document that bears: (A) a seal purporting to be that of the United States; any state, district, commonwealth, territory, or insular possession of the United States; the former Panama Canal Zone; the Trust Territory of the Pacific Islands; a political subdivision of any of these entities; or a department, agency, or officer of any entity named above; and (B) a signature purporting to be an execution or attestation.
(2) Domestic public documents not under seal. A document purporting to bear the signature in the official capacity of an officer or employee of any entity included in paragraph (1) hereof, having no seal, if a public officer having a seal and having official duties in the district or political subdivision of the officer or employee certifies under seal that the signer has the official capacity and that the signature is genuine.	**(2) Domestic Public Documents That Are Not Sealed but Are Signed and Certified.** A document that bears no seal if: (A) it bears the signature of an officer or employee of an entity named in Rule 902(1)(A); and (B) another public officer who has a seal and official duties within that same entity certifies under seal—or its

	equivalent—that the signer has the official capacity and that the signature is genuine.
(3) Foreign public documents. A document purporting to be executed or attested in an official capacity by a person authorized by the laws of a foreign country to make the execution or attestation, and accompanied by a final certification as to the genuineness of the signature and official position (A) of the executing or attesting person, or (B) of any foreign official whose certificate of genuineness of signature and official position relates to the execution or attestation or is in a chain of certificates of genuineness of signature and official position relating to the execution or attestation. A final certification may be made by a secretary of an embassy or legation, consul general, consul, vice consul, or consular agent of the United States, or a diplomatic or consular official of the foreign country assigned or accredited to the United States. If reasonable opportunity has been given to all parties to investigate the authenticity and accuracy of official documents, the court may, for good cause shown, order that they be treated as presumptively authentic without final certification or permit them to be evidenced by an attested summary with or without final certification.	**(3) Foreign Public Documents.** A document that purports to be signed or attested by a person who is authorized by a foreign country's law to do so. The document must be accompanied by a final certification that certifies the genuineness of the signature and official position of the signer or attester—or of any foreign official whose certificate of genuineness relates to the signature or attestation or is in a chain of certificates of genuineness relating to the signature or attestation. The certification may be made by a secretary of a United States embassy or legation; by a consul general, vice consul, or consular agent of the United States; or by a diplomatic or consular official of the foreign country assigned or accredited to the United States. If all parties have been given a reasonable opportunity to investigate the document's authenticity and accuracy, the court may, for good cause, either: (A) order that it be treated as presumptively authentic without final certification; or (B) allow it to be evidenced by an attested summary with or without final certification.

(4) Certified copies of public records. A copy of an official record or report or entry therein, or of a document authorized by law to be recorded or filed and actually recorded or filed in a public office, including data compilations in any form, certified as correct by the custodian or other person authorized to make the certification, by certificate complying with paragraph (1), (2), or (3) of this rule or complying with any Act of Congress or rule prescribed by the Supreme Court pursuant to statutory authority.	**(4) Certified Copies of Public Records.** A copy of an official record—or a copy of a document that was recorded or filed in a public office as authorized by law—if the copy is certified as correct by: (A) the custodian or another person authorized to make the certification; or (B) a certificate that complies with Rule 902(1), (2), or (3), a federal statute, or a rule prescribed by the Supreme Court.
(5) Official publications. Books, pamphlets, or other publications purporting to be issued by public authority.	**(5) Official Publications.** A book, pamphlet, or other publication purporting to be issued by a public authority.
(6) Newspapers and periodicals. Printed materials purporting to be newspapers or periodicals.	**(6) Newspapers and Periodicals.** Printed material purporting to be a newspaper or periodical.
(7) Trade inscriptions and the like. Inscriptions, signs, tags, or labels purporting to have been affixed in the course of business and indicating ownership, control, or origin.	**(7) Trade Inscriptions and the Like.** An inscription, sign, tag, or label purporting to have been affixed in the course of business and indicating origin, ownership, or control.
(8) Acknowledged documents. Documents accompanied by a certificate of acknowledgment executed in the manner provided by law by a notary public or other officer authorized by law to take acknowledgments.	**(8) Acknowledged Documents.** A document accompanied by a certificate of acknowledgment that is lawfully executed by a notary public or another officer who is authorized to take acknowledgments.
(9) Commercial paper and related documents. Commercial paper, signatures thereon, and	**(9) Commercial Paper and Related Documents.** Commercial paper, a signature on it, and related

documents relating thereto to the extent provided by general commercial law.	documents, to the extent allowed by general commercial law.
(10) Presumptions under Acts of Congress. Any signature, document, or other matter declared by Act of Congress to be presumptively or prima facie genuine or authentic.	**(10) Presumptions Under a Federal Statute.** A signature, document, or anything else that a federal statute declares to be presumptively or prima facie genuine or authentic.

(11) Certified domestic records of regularly conducted activity. The original or a duplicate of a domestic record of regularly conducted activity that would be admissible under Rule 803(6) if accompanied by a written declaration of its custodian or other qualified person, in a manner complying with any Act of Congress or rule prescribed by the Supreme Court pursuant to statutory authority, certifying that the record—
 	
   (A)   was made at or near the time of the occurrence of the matters set forth by, or from information transmitted by, a person with knowledge of those matters;
 	
   (B)   was kept in the course of the regularly conducted activity; and
 	
   (C)   was made by the regularly conducted activity as a regular practice.
 	
 A party intending to offer a record into evidence under this paragraph must provide written notice of that intention to all adverse parties, and must make the record and
	(11) Certified Domestic Records of a Regularly Conducted Activity. The original or a copy of a domestic record that meets the requirements of Rule 803(6)(A)-(C), as shown by a certification of the custodian or another qualified person that complies with a federal statute or a rule prescribed by the Supreme Court. Before the trial or hearing, the proponent must give an adverse party reasonable written notice of the intent to offer the record—and must make the record and certification available for inspection—so that the party has a fair opportunity to challenge them.

declaration available for inspection sufficiently in advance of their offer into evidence to provide an adverse party with a fair opportunity to challenge them.	

(12) Certified foreign records of regularly conducted activity. In a civil case, the original or a duplicate of a foreign record of regularly conducted activity that would be admissible under Rule 803(6) if accompanied by a written declaration by its custodian or other qualified person certifying that the record—
 	
    (A) was made at or near the time of the occurrence of the matters set forth by, or from information transmitted by, a person with knowledge of those matters;
 	
    (B) was kept in the course of the regularly conducted activity; and
 	
    (C) was made by the regularly conducted activity as a regular practice.
 	
 The declaration must be signed in a manner that, if falsely made, would subject the maker to criminal penalty under the laws of the country where the declaration is signed. A party intending to offer a record into evidence under this paragraph must provide written notice of that intention to all adverse parties, and must make the record and declaration available for inspection sufficiently in advance of
	(12) Certified Foreign Records of a Regularly Conducted Activity. In a civil case, the original or a copy of a foreign record that meets the requirements of Rule 902(11), modified as follows: the certification, rather than complying with a federal statute or Supreme Court rule, must be signed in a manner that, if falsely made, would subject the maker to a criminal penalty in the country where the certification is signed. The proponent must also meet the notice requirements of Rule 902(11).

their offer into evidence to provide an adverse party with a fair opportunity to challenge them.	
	[Effective 12/1/17] **(13) Certified Records Generated by an Electronic Process or System.** A record generated by an electronic process or system that produces an accurate result, as shown by a certification by a qualified person that complies with the certification requirements of Rule 902(11) or Rule 902(12). The proponent must meet the notice requirements of Rule 902(11).
	[Effective 12/1/17] **(14) Certified Data Coped From an Electronic Device, Storage Media or File.** Data copied from an electronic device, storage media, or electronic file, if authenticated by a process of digital identification, as shown by a certification by a qualified person that complies with the certification requirements of Rule 902(11) or Rule 902(12). The proponent must meet the notice requirements of Rule 902(11).

Former Rule	*Current Rule*
Rule 903. Subscribing Witness' Testimony Unnecessary	**Rule 903. Subscribing Witness's Testimony**
The testimony of a subscribing witness is not necessary to authenticate a writing unless required by the laws of the jurisdiction whose laws govern the validity of the writing.	A subscribing witness's testimony is necessary to authenticate a writing only if required by the law of the jurisdiction that governs its validity.

Article X: Contents of Writings, Recordings, and Photographs

Former Rule	*Current Rule*
Rule 1001. Definitions	**Rule 1001. Definitions That Apply to This Article**
For purposes of this article the following definitions are applicable: **(1) Writings and recordings.** "Writings" and "recordings" consist of letters, words, or numbers, or their equivalent, set down by handwriting, typewriting, printing, photostating, photographing, magnetic impulse, mechanical or electronic recording, or other form of data compilation. **(2) Photographs.** "Photographs" include still photographs, X-ray films, video tapes, and motion pictures. **(3) Original.** An "original" of a writing or recording is the writing or recording itself or any counterpart intended to have the same effect by a person executing or issuing it. An "original" of a photograph includes the negative or any print therefrom. If data are stored in a computer or similar device, any printout or other output readable by sight, shown to reflect the data accurately, is an "original". **(4) Duplicate.** A "duplicate" is a counterpart produced by the same impression as the original, or from the same matrix, or by means of photography, including enlargements and miniatures, or by	In this article: **(a)** A "writing" consists of letters, words, numbers, or their equivalent set down in any form. **(b)** A "recording" consists of letters, words, numbers, or their equivalent recorded in any manner. **(c)** A "photograph" means a photographic image or its equivalent stored in any form. **(d)** An "original" of a writing or recording means the writing or recording itself or any counterpart intended to have the same effect by the person who executed or issued it. For electronically stored information, "original" means any printout—or other output readable by sight—if it accurately reflects the information. An "original" of a photograph includes the negative or a print from it. **(e)** A "duplicate" means a counterpart produced by a mechanical, photographic, chemical, electronic, or other equivalent process or technique that accurately reproduces the original.

mechanical or electronic re-recording, or by chemical reproduction, or by other equivalent techniques which accurately reproduces the original.

Former Rule   Current Rule

Rule 1002. Requirement of Original	Rule 1002. Requirement of the Original
To prove the content of a writing, recording, or photograph, the original writing, recording, or photograph is required, except as otherwise provided in these rules or by Act of Congress.	An original writing, recording, or photograph is required in order to prove its content unless these rules or a federal statute provides otherwise.

Former Rule   Current Rule

Rule 1003. Admissibility of Duplicates	Rule 1003. Admissibility of Duplicates
A duplicate is admissible to the same extent as an original unless (1) a genuine question is raised as to the authenticity of the original or (2) in the circumstances it would be unfair to admit the duplicate in lieu of the original.	A duplicate is admissible to the same extent as the original unless a genuine question is raised about the original's authenticity or the circumstances make it unfair to admit the duplicate.

Former Rule   Current Rule

Rule 1004. Admissibility of Other Evidence of Contents	Rule 1004. Admissibility of Other Evidence of Contents
The original is not required, and other evidence of the contents of a writing, recording, or photograph is admissible if— **(1) Originals lost or destroyed.** All originals are lost or have been destroyed, unless the proponent lost or destroyed them in bad faith; or	An original is not required and other evidence of the content of a writing, recording, or photograph is admissible if: (a) all the originals are lost or destroyed, and not by the proponent acting in bad faith;

(2) Original not obtainable. No original can be obtained by any available judicial process or procedure; or **(3) Original in possession of opponent.** At a time when an original was under the control of the party against whom offered, that party was put on notice, by the pleadings or otherwise, that the contents would be a subject of proof at the hearing, and that party does not produce the original at the hearing; or **(4) Collateral matters.** The writing, recording, or photograph is not closely related to a controlling issue.	**(b)** an original cannot be obtained by any available judicial process; **(c)** the party against whom the original would be offered had control of the original; was at that time put on notice, by pleadings or otherwise, that the original would be a subject of proof at the trial or hearing; and fails to produce it at the trial or hearing; or **(d)** the writing, recording, or photograph is not closely related to a controlling issue.

Former Rule	*Current Rule*
Rule 1005. Public Records	**Rule 1005. Copies of Public Records to Prove Content**
The contents of an official record, or of a document authorized to be recorded or filed and actually recorded or filed, including data compilations in any form, if otherwise admissible, may be proved by copy, certified as correct in accordance with rule 902 or testified to be correct by a witness who has compared it with the original. If a copy which complies with the foregoing cannot be obtained by the exercise of reasonable diligence, then other evidence of the contents may be given.	The proponent may use a copy to prove the content of an official record—or of a document that was recorded or filed in a public office as authorized by law—if these conditions are met: the record or document is otherwise admissible; and the copy is certified as correct in accordance with Rule 902(4) or is testified to be correct by a witness who has compared it with the original. If no such copy can be obtained by reasonable diligence, then the proponent may use other evidence to prove the content.

Former Rule	*Current Rule*
Rule 1006. Summaries	**Rule 1006. Summaries to Prove Content**
The contents of voluminous writings, recordings, or photographs which cannot conveniently be examined in court may be presented in the form of a chart, summary, or calculation. The originals, or duplicates, shall be made available for examination or copying, or both, by other parties at reasonable time and place. The court may order that they be produced in court.	The proponent may use a summary, chart, or calculation to prove the content of voluminous writings, recordings, or photographs that cannot be conveniently examined in court. The proponent must make the originals or duplicates available for examination or copying, or both, by other parties at a reasonable time and place. And the court may order the proponent to produce them in court.

Former Rule	*Current Rule*
Rule 1007. Testimony or Written Admission of Party	**Rule 1007. Testimony or Statement of a Party to Prove Content**
Contents of writings, recordings, or photographs may be proved by the testimony or deposition of the party against whom offered or by that party's written admission, without accounting for the nonproduction of the original.	The proponent may prove the content of a writing, recording, or photograph by the testimony, deposition, or written statement of the party against whom the evidence is offered. The proponent need not account for the original

Former Rule	*Current Rule*
Rule 1008. Functions of Court and Jury	**Rule 1008. Functions of the Court and Jury**
When the admissibility of other evidence of contents of writings, recordings, or photographs under these rules depends upon the fulfillment of a condition of fact, the question whether the condition has been fulfilled is ordinarily for the	Ordinarily, the court determines whether the proponent has fulfilled the factual conditions for admitting other evidence of the content of a writing, recording, or photograph under Rule 1004 or 1005. But in a jury trial, the jury determines—in

court to determine in accordance with the provisions of rule 104. However, when an issue is raised (a) whether the asserted writing ever existed, or (b) whether another writing, recording, or photograph produced at the trial is the original, or (c) whether other evidence of contents correctly reflects the contents, the issue is for the trier of fact to determine as in the case of other issues of fact.

accordance with Rule 104(b)—any issue about whether:

(a) an asserted writing, recording, or photograph ever existed;

(b) another one produced at the trial or hearing is the original; or

(c) other evidence of content accurately reflects the content.

Article XI: Miscellaneous Rules

Former Rule	*Current Rule*
Rule 1101. Applicability of Rules	**Rule 1101. Applicability of Rules**
(a) Courts and judges. These rules apply to the United States district courts, the District Court of Guam, the District Court of the Virgin Islands, the District Court for the Northern Mariana Islands, the United States courts of appeals, the United States Claims Court, and to United States bankruptcy judges and United States magistrate judges, in the actions, cases, and proceedings and to the extent hereinafter set forth. The terms "judge" and "court" in these rules include United States bankruptcy judges and United States magistrate judges.	**(a) To Courts and Judges.** These rules apply to proceedings before: • United States district courts; • United States bankruptcy and magistrate judges; • United States courts of appeals; • the United States Court of Federal Claims; and • the district courts of Guam, the Virgin Islands, and the Northern Mariana Islands.
(b) Proceedings generally. These rules apply generally to civil actions and proceedings, including admiralty and maritime cases, to criminal cases and proceedings, to contempt proceedings except those in which the court may act summarily, and to proceedings and cases under title 11, United States Code.	**(b) To Cases and Proceedings.** These rules apply in: • civil cases and proceedings, including bankruptcy, admiralty, and maritime cases; • criminal cases and proceedings; and • contempt proceedings, except those in which the court may act summarily.
(c) Rule of privilege. The rule with respect to privileges applies at all stages of all actions, cases, and proceedings.	**(c) Rules on Privilege.** The rules on privilege apply to all stages of a case or proceeding.
(d) Rules inapplicable. The rules (other than with respect to	**(d) Exceptions.** These rules—except for those on privilege—do not apply to the following:

privileges) do not apply in the following situations:

(1) **Preliminary questions of fact.** The determination of questions of fact preliminary to admissibility of evidence when the issue is to be determined by the court under rule 104.

(2) **Grand jury.** Proceedings before grand juries.

(3) **Miscellaneous proceedings.** Proceedings for extradition or rendition; preliminary examinations in criminal cases; sentencing, or granting or revoking probation; issuance of warrants for arrest, criminal summonses, and search warrants; and proceedings with respect to release on bail or otherwise.

(1) the court's determination, under Rule 104(a), on a preliminary question of fact governing admissibility;

(2) grand-jury proceedings; and

(3) miscellaneous proceedings such as:

- extradition or rendition;
- issuing an arrest warrant, criminal summons, or search warrant;
- a preliminary examination in a criminal case;
- sentencing;
- granting or revoking probation or supervised release; and
- considering whether to release on bail or otherwise.

(e) Rules applicable in part. In the following proceedings these rules apply to the extent that matters of evidence are not provided for in the statutes which govern procedure therein or in other rules prescribed by the Supreme Court pursuant to statutory authority: the trial of misdemeanors and other petty offenses before United States magistrate judges; review of agency actions when the facts are subject to trial de novo under section 706(2)(F) of title 5, United States Code; review of orders of the Secretary of Agriculture under section 2 of the

(e) **Other Statutes and Rules.** A federal statute or a rule prescribed by the Supreme Court may provide for admitting or excluding evidence independently from these rules.

Act entitled "An Act to authorize association of producers of agricultural products" approved February 18, 1922 (7 U.S.C. 292), and under sections 6 and 7(c) of the Perishable Agricultural Commodities Act, 1930 (7 U.S.C. 499f, 499g(c)); naturalization and revocation of naturalization under sections 310-318 of the Immigration and Nationality Act (8 U.S.C. 1421-1429); prize proceedings in admiralty under sections 7651-7681 of title 10, United States Code; review of orders of the Secretary of the Interior under section 2 of the Act entitled "An Act authorizing associations of producers of aquatic products" approved June 25, 1934 (15 U.S.C. 522); review of orders of petroleum control boards under section 5 of the Act entitled "An Act to regulate interstate and foreign commerce in petroleum and its products by prohibiting the shipment in such commerce of petroleum and its products produced in violation of State law, and for other purposes", approved February 22, 1935 (15 U.S.C. 715d); actions for fines, penalties, or forfeitures under part V of title IV of the Tariff Act of 1930 (19 U.S.C. 1581-1624), or under the Anti-Smuggling Act (19 U.S.C. 1701-1711); criminal libel for condemnation, exclusion of imports, or other proceedings under the Federal Food, Drug, and Cosmetic Act (21 U.S.C. 301-392); disputes between seamen under sections 4079, 4080, and 4081 of the Revised Statutes (22 U.S.C. 256-258); habeas corpus under sections 2241-2254 of title 28, United States Code; motions to vacate, set aside or correct sentence under section 2255 of title 28, United States Code; actions for penalties for refusal to transport destitute seamen under section 4578 of the Revised Statutes (46 U.S.C. 679); actions against the United States under the Act entitled "An Act authorizing suits against the United States in admiralty for damage caused by and salvage service rendered to public vessels belonging to the United States, and for other purposes", approved March 3, 1925 (46 U.S.C. 781-790), as implemented by section 7730 of title 10, United States Code.

Former Rule	*Current Rule*
Rule 1102. Amendments	**Rule 1102. Amendments**
Amendments to the Federal Rules of Evidence may be made as provided in section 2072 of title 28 of the United States Code.	These rules may be amended as provided in 28 U.S.C. § 2072.

Former Rule	*Current Rule*
Rule 1103. Title	**Rule 1103. Title**
These rules may be known and cited as the Federal Rules of Evidence.	These rules may be cited as the Federal Rules of Evidence.